Dogs —

A PLUME BOOK

DOGAGE®

DONDI S. DAHLGAARD is an emergency-care veterinarian at South-Paws Veterinary Referral Center in Washington, D.C. RealAge, Inc., is a leading media company for consumer health care information whose previous book projects include the bestseller *RealAge: Are You as Young as You Can Be?*

Take the DogAge Test and Give Your Best Friend a Longer, Healthier Life!

- Add over a year to your dog's life by keeping him slim.
- Your dog could live six months longer if you give her teeth-cleaning chews or biscuits.
- Exercise with your dog fifteen minutes, three times a day, and add six months to his life.
- Spend three more months with your dog by giving him medications as prescribed by your veterinarian.
- Add over a year to your dog's life by training him to respond to your commands.

Dondi S. Dahlgaard, DVM

DogAge®

*How to Keep Your Dog
Youthful and Healthy*

℗

A PLUME BOOK

PLUME
Published by Penguin Group
Penguin Group (USA) Inc., 375 Hudson Street, New York, New York 10014, U.S.A.
Penguin Group (Canada), 90 Eglinton Avenue East, Suite 700, Toronto, Ontario,
Canada M4P 2Y3 (a division of Pearson Penguin Canada Inc.)
Penguin Books Ltd., 80 Strand, London WC2R 0RL, England
Penguin Ireland, 25 St. Stephen's Green, Dublin 2, Ireland (a division of Penguin Books Ltd.)
Penguin Group (Australia), 250 Camberwell Road, Camberwell, Victoria 3124,
Australia (a division of Pearson Australia Group Pty. Ltd.)
Penguin Books India Pvt. Ltd., 11 Community Centre, Panchsheel Park,
New Delhi – 110 017, India
Penguin Books (NZ), cnr Airborne and Rosedale Roads, Albany, Auckland 1310, New Zealand
(a division of Pearson New Zealand Ltd.)
Penguin Books (South Africa) (Pty.) Ltd., 24 Sturdee Avenue, Rosebank,
Johannesburg 2196, South Africa

Penguin Books Ltd., Registered Offices: 80 Strand, London WC2R 0RL, England

Published by Plume, a member of Penguin Group (USA) Inc. Previously published in a
Dutton edition.

First Plume Printing, February 2006
1 3 5 7 9 10 8 6 4 2

Copyright © RealAge, Inc., 2005
All rights reserved
Ⓟ REGISTERED TRADEMARK—MARCA REGISTRADA

CIP data is available.
ISBN 0-525-94867-8 (hc.)
ISBN 0-452-28713-8 (pbk.)

Printed in the United States of America
Original hardcover design by Francesca Belanger

PUBLISHER'S NOTE
The scanning, uploading, and distribution of this book via the Internet or via any other means
without the permission of the publisher is illegal and punishable by law. Please purchase only
authorized electronic editions, and do not participate in or encourage electronic piracy of copy-
righted materials. Your support of the author's rights is appreciated.

BOOKS ARE AVAILABLE AT QUANTITY DISCOUNTS WHEN USED TO PROMOTE PRODUCTS OR SERVICES. FOR
INFORMATION PLEASE WRITE TO PREMIUM MARKETING DIVISION, PENGUIN GROUP (USA) INC., 375 HUDSON
STREET, NEW YORK, NEW YORK 10014.

This book is dedicated to my mom, for fostering my love of animals by indulging me in every one that I brought home. To my dad, for encouraging me to pursue my dream of becoming a veterinarian. And to all of my canine patients who have taught me that miracles do happen.

Contents

Acknowledgments

Above all, I would like to thank my canine patients, for lending me their stories and the inspiration to bring *DogAge* into the world. I hope this book helps them and all my future patients live safer, longer, healthier lives. I am also very grateful for all the people who helped make this book a reality: Charles Silver of RealAge, for bringing me this opportunity; Laurie Chittenden, my talented editor, and her assistant, Erika Kahn; the staff of SouthPaws Veterinary Center, for their help and guidance on content; Nestlé Purina PetCare, for all their ongoing canine health research and for their permission to use their obesity chart and dog food labels in the book; Paul Chutkow, for his invaluable help; the content team at RealAge, including Shelly Bowen and Susan Baldwin, for helping organize and fine-tune the content, and Andrea Paulus and Julius Willis, for their DogAge design contributions; and the production team at RealAge, who so brilliantly made the DogAge test an online, interactive experience at DogAge.com. Also, tremendous thanks to Candice Fuhrman, for bringing us all together and keeping us on track. Finally, I'd like to thank my beautiful dogs, Hannah, Georgia, and Chili Beyoncé, for their love and support every step of the way.

CHAPTER ONE

Introducing DogAge

ONE DAY a man drove up to our clinic in a complete panic. Annie, his beloved golden retriever, was sprawled in the backseat of his car, unconscious and obviously near death. She was sedated, had an endotracheal tube (breathing tube) placed so that she could breathe, and was barely hanging on. The man was frantic; he had no idea what to do. Nor did his regular veterinarian. When the man arrived at our hospital, he was in a desperate state.

"I need to talk to a surgeon!" he shouted at the receptionist. "Right away!"

The man refused to bring Annie in from the car. He also refused to sign the necessary consent form that would allow us to examine and treat his dog. No one else was going to put a finger on his dog until he met with a surgeon face-to-face. Our receptionist saw his agitation and immediately called me in the ICU.

"Dr. Dahlgaard," she said, "I have a gentleman here who is very upset. He says he will not bring his dog in until he speaks with a doctor. Can you come up?"

As I entered the waiting room, the man blurted out his story. Annie was in great overall health, he explained, but four days earlier she had developed a mysterious cough. Right away he took her to her vet, who diagnosed the problem as common kennel cough. The vet prescribed antibiotics and a cough suppressant. Overnight, though, Annie's cough got much worse, and she was having trouble breathing. By nightfall, she was gasping for breath. Fearing the worst, the man rushed Annie to an emergency clinic. The diagnosis was not good: the doctor said that Annie's larynx was paralyzed; she would need surgery first thing in the morning. A few short hours later, with Annie fighting for her life, her owner rushed Annie back to her regular vet, pleading: "Please, *do* something!"

Now an entire team of vets was called in to examine Annie, and they came up with another diagnosis. Annie's larynx was fine, they decided, but she was suffering from a collapsed trachea; her breathing passage was blocked. As a stop-gap measure, they sedated her and inserted a breathing tube down her throat, to get some oxygen flowing into her system. But the vets said there was only one solution: emergency surgery. And that, finally, led Annie to me.

At our clinic in northern Virginia we specialize in emergency animal care, and we have twenty-seven veterinarians on staff. I run the intensive-care unit, and we have five other staff doctors who help me handle the emergency cases. We have a very busy practice—we do surgeries every weekday, and many vets in the area, like Annie's, send us their most difficult cases. Annie's owner did not know us at all, so he arrived at our door confused and downright angry. And I understood why. For four days, he had been frantically trying to find care for his dog, but she just kept getting worse despite all of the attempts to treat her. After receiving so much conflicting advice, Annie's owner was left frantic and confused. Just put yourself in his shoes: your dog is dying and no one can seem to figure out what is going on. I'd be frantic, too!

After relaying his story, the man finally allowed me to take a look at Annie. Poor girl: she lay sedated and motionless in the backseat. Her owner showed me her X-rays, and I could see that the soft tissues surrounding the trachea were, indeed, ten times denser than normal. This was putting pressure on her trachea, to the point where it was almost totally closed. The airway opening was now down to less than one centimeter. We had to move—*fast!*

Still, this made no sense to me. It is usually smaller dogs that suffer collapsed tracheas, not golden retrievers. Also, Annie was only three years old; I doubted it was a tumor that was causing her problem. And if she did have some sort of tumor, I doubted it could grow so large in the space of just four days. Fortunately I had a hunch, and I put it directly to Annie's owner: "Do you put out rat poison?"

The man was taken aback. "Yes . . . but not where she can get at it. Listen, my dog needs a surgeon!"

"Sir," I told him, "I need to run a blood test—urgently. I'm concerned that Annie is bleeding into her chest." Reluctantly, Annie's owner agreed, and within three or four minutes we had run a Prothrombin/Partial Thromboplastin test, which measures how effectively the dog's blood is able to clot. We quickly had the results: Annie's blood was unable to clot at all. It was indeed blood that was pouring into the soft tissues surrounding her trachea, and it was blood that was putting pressure on her airway. My hunch had been right: rat poisoning.

We immediately rushed Annie into the ICU and treated her with vitamin K and transfusions of fresh frozen plasma, a blood component that contains vital clotting factors. For the next three days we kept her anesthetized in the ICU with a breathing tube in place. By day three Annie was breathing normally without the tube, and by day four she was able to eat normally. Then we sent her home with her pal. Today I am happy to report that Annie has made a full recovery.

I tell Annie's story to make this point loud and clear: Annie's near-death experience should never have happened in the first place. Annie's owner had experience with dogs, and he loved her to pieces, but he simply did not know some basic elements of accident prevention and good dog care. For instance, rat poison is manufactured to taste good to rats, but dogs find it irresistible as well. If Annie's owner had known that, he would never have set it out in the first place. That sweet, sweet dog almost died, and a little prior knowledge could have spared Annie that entire ordeal. With dogs, as with people, I strongly believe in the old adage that "an ounce of prevention is worth a pound of cure," and I guarantee you that Annie's owner now believes in it, too.

Sadly, Annie's is not an isolated case. We are a dog-loving nation: there are about 65 million dogs in America, and about 40 million families and single people have at least one dog in the house. And get this: each year we Americans spend about $35 *billion* on our dogs, cats, and other pets. Those are amazing numbers. But the painful truth is this: very few of our 40 million dog owners have a clear understanding of what they need to do to keep their dogs healthy and safe. How bad is the problem? Very: accidents—most of them avoidable—kill millions of dogs each year; only cancer takes a higher toll. And most of those dogs could have been spared—if only their owners had been better informed about proper dog safety and care.

Accidents are not the only problem. Each year, some 200,000 dogs come down with preventable diseases such as heartworm and Lyme disease, which ends up being fatal to many of those dogs. Again, most of them could be saved—if their owners knew more about disease prevention. Now let me tell you a real shocker: in the United States, between 8 million and 12 million dogs end up in shelters each year, with no families to adopt them. And each year millions of those dogs are put to death. *Millions!* That just breaks my heart. The cold, hard truth is this: we as a nation need to do a much better job of educating dog owners about how to take care of their pets. We need to drive home the message that owning a dog is one of life's greatest joys—but it is also a serious responsibility. Take it lightly and your dog may wind up sick—or dead.

Now, why did I write this book? The answer should be obvious: I want to teach you and every other dog owner everything you need to know about keeping your dog healthy, safe, and happy. Whether you own a frisky little Jack Russell terrier or a big, lumbering bullmastiff, I want you to understand, in depth, your dog's temperament and behavior, his health-care needs, his physical and emotional needs, and more. I will tell you everything you need to know about your dog's nutrition, training, exercise, and grooming, and what you need to do to protect your dog against accidents, disease, fleas, ticks, heartworm—even testy cats and bigger dogs. I will also show you how to find and work with a qualified veterinarian to make sure that your dog gets the best medical care possible, and I will show you, in specific detail, how to keep your dog safe at home, in the yard, in the car or truck, in the kennel, and even when he rides on airplanes. In sum, this is it: a complete, informative, easy-to-read owners' manual for dog lovers.

I bring to this book a lifetime of working with dogs and other animals, and I bring to it my many years of experience as an emergency-care veterinarian. I also bring to the book something else: a full-scale partnership with the masterminds behind two new, innovative learning tools: the DogAge Test and the popular dog-care Web site, DogAge.com. The folks at DogAge have developed fascinating ways to educate dog owners, and I'd like to take a moment to explain why I joined forces with them and what we hope to accomplish by working together.

The story begins back in the summer of 2003. I was spending most of my waking hours caring for sick and injured animals and teaching their owners about accident prevention and proper animal care. Then one day I was approached by the team at www.RealAge.com, which had developed a new, interactive learning system called RealAge®, a pioneering way to teach people how to lead longer, healthier lives. I didn't know much about the RealAge system, but its creators set before me an enticing idea. The RealAge system was designed for human care. Would I help them develop a similar system for dog care?

I found their idea appealing, but I didn't jump in right away. First, I wanted to learn everything I could about the RealAge system and how it worked. I did some serious study and came away impressed. Very impressed. The RealAge system has a noble purpose: it is designed to teach people how to examine their lives and their daily habits, and then to make positive changes that will help them lead longer, healthier, more fulfilling lives. The system, I discovered, is simple and easy to use. It relies on two sets of tools: RealAge books and the RealAge.com Web site. Using either one, the first step is to take what is called the RealAge Test. No, you don't have to have your blood drawn or run on a treadmill. All you have to do is answer a questionnaire that asks you for your chronological age, your gender, height, weight, blood pressure, resting heart rate, cholesterol levels, and the like. It also asks you about your personal health history, your parents' health history, what medications you take, and how you eat, drink, exercise, and relax.

From your answers to these questions, the RealAge Test calculates your "real age," meaning your actual biological age. If you take good care of yourself, your biological age probably will be younger than your calendar age. If you take poor care of yourself, your RealAge will indicate that—uh-oh—your biological age is actually *older* than what the calendar and your birthdays say it is. That means that you might not live as long as you hope to—unless you make serious changes in the way you live and the way you manage your health.

Now here is the truly ingenious part: the RealAge system actually informs you about and guides you toward specific, positive changes you can make to improve your health and to add additional years to your life. If you are overweight, RealAge explains how that cuts down your life expectancy—and shows you exactly what you can do to slim down. If you drink alcohol to excess, smoke cigarettes, or fail to get proper exercise, the RealAge system will explain to you the consequences—and show you the consequences in the months and years that are being peeled away from your life expectancy. Then the RealAge system goes a step further: it tells you that if you quit smoking, your RealAge will get younger and you will live longer. Lose weight and you will be even younger. Eat a more balanced diet and you'll be even younger! Through this process, the RealAge system helps you develop a comprehensive, lifelong wellness program just for you. And here's the best news: if you follow that program carefully, you can live many years longer. I took the RealAge Test and thought, "Wow, what a marvelous tool!"

As I studied the RealAge system, I saw how perfectly it coincided with my own personal mission as a veterinarian. In my work, I put the highest priority, of course, on treating sick or injured animals. But I also spend a great deal of my time teaching. Most of the pet owners who come to me are caring, good-hearted people, and they will do anything they can to take good care of their animals. Unfortunately, sometimes their good intentions are not enough; they need sound, reliable information and advice about how to care for their pets. I do my best to teach them about the accident that happened or about the particular disease that has laid their dog low—and how it could have been prevented in the first place. Inevitably, they say to me, "Oh, Dr. Dondi, if only we had known that beforehand!" This, I knew, was where a DogAge system could be a godsend. It could teach dog owners valuable things that they needed to know, and it could do so in a lively, interactive way. By using the DogAge system, dog owners would become much better informed and much more proactive in the health and care of their animals. That was already wonderful. At the same time, too, maybe we could do something else: maybe we could actually prevent millions of terrible accidents and illnesses from occurring in the first place. What a service that would be!

Once I saw the full potential of a partnership, of course I decided to join forces with the DogAge team. We worked hard to develop and polish the DogAge Test, which you will find in the next chapter, and we worked hard to make the DogAge Web site, www.DogAge.com, a lively, engaging, and informative learning site. And now comes this book. I designed and wrote it to bring my knowledge and experience together in a comprehensive guide to proper dog care. I also designed it to work in tandem with the DogAge Test. If the test indicates, for instance, that you should improve your dog's diet and better manage his weight, I will explain exactly how to do that, in Chapter Six. If the DogAge Test indicates that you need to be much more careful regarding your dog's safety, I will show you exactly how to do that, in Chapter Eight. And if the DogAge Test shows that you need to pay better attention to your dog's medical care, I will show you how to do that, too, in Chapters Three and Five.

As you will see, one theme unfurls itself across the entire book: prevention is the golden key to helping your dog lead a longer, healthier, safer life. In chapter after chapter I will show you what you can do to prevent accidents and diseases. Every week I see an Annie or some other dog who has been struck by an accident or illness that could have been prevented. I want to make sure this doesn't happen to your dog. In the following chapters, I will cover every element of proper wellness: nutrition, weight management, good exercise, dog safety, and much, much more. In the end, these different elements come together to form a cohesive package: Dr. Dondi's DogAge Wellness Program. It is my firm conviction that if you carefully follow my program, your dog will lead a longer, healthier, safer life—and you will have many more happy years together.

One more thing: as you will quickly see, this book is a true labor of love. I have had dogs all my life, and I now have three: Hannah, Georgia, and little Chili Beyoncé. They are my heart and soul. Having them in my life brings me true joy. We spend much time together and share a deep and loving bond. They don't seem to care what I'm wearing or look like, whether I'm funny or smart or insecure. If my shoes don't match my belt or if I'm having a bad hair day, it's all the same to them. When I'm down I can always count on them to stand by me and listen to whatever I have to say, offering an encouraging nudge and undivided attention coupled with unconditional love. I spoil them, but I wouldn't have it any other way.

In my experience, dogs really are "man's best friend," but they are even more than that. In ways that we barely understand, our dogs actually *take care of us*. They become members of our family, they make us smile and laugh, and they keep us active as we grow older. In fact, scientific studies have shown that dogs can help us reduce stress, lower our blood pressure, ward off depression, and even help us rebound from a heart attack or other serious illness. Now, on four legs or two, you can't find a better friend than that!

Dogs are also marvelous teachers. They help us teach our children and grandchildren about life and death, caring and unconditional love, about personal responsibility, and about how we should treat all of nature's creatures. Most of you know about "seeing-eye dogs," those amazing animals who are specially trained to help the blind carry on with their daily lives. Well, I believe that almost all dogs are "seeing-eye dogs." They can see and smell and sense things that we humans miss entirely. Sometimes, too, dogs can size up people and situations far quicker and far more accurately than we can. It's true: our dogs take wonderful care of us. In return, it is our obligation—and our joy!—to take the best possible care of them. I dedicate this book to that noble purpose.

CHAPTER TWO

The DogAge Test

I LEARNED THE HARD WAY. Some kids, even when they're very small, know that when they grow up they want to be a police officer, a firefighter, or a teacher. I knew, right from the beginning, that I wanted to be a veterinarian. I loved animals. My mom was great at indulging my interest (I think she enjoyed my pets as much as I did), and she allowed me to have all kinds of creatures. We had a pet bunny named Mr. McIntyre and a Dalmatian named Patch, and at one time or another we had cats and guinea pigs, birds and snakes, and we had several families of mice as well. As a child, I did not learn how to take care of my animals by reading a book; I learned by *doing*.

When I became a teenager, my training began in earnest. I joined the Future Farmers of America (FFA), an organization geared toward teaching young people like me. In the FFA, I began learning about large animals: cows, horses, sheep, and goats. Even pigs. Again, this wasn't book-learning; this was hands-on, roll-up-your-sleeves, boots-in-the-mud learning. And I just loved it.

When I was a senior in vet school, I finally got my first puppy, "Georgia." I bought her out of a box at a gas station for twenty-five dollars. I had never had a puppy before, but I was sure that I could handle it because, of course, I was a veterinary student. Well, let me tell you, it was probably more of a learning experience for me than it was for my new puppy. The next year taught me more about the difficulties of housebreaking, socialization, obedience training, and dog behavior than four years of veterinary school ever could. I can remember cleaning up one accident on the floor as Georgia squatted next to me making another one. Many times I thought, "What have I done?" Through trials and tribulations, though, Georgia and I grew into a team. A family. She became my best friend, and has been that for the past eleven years. She is definitely the best twenty-five dollars I've ever spent.

Though raising Georgia was one of the biggest joys of my life, it wasn't easy, because I had no guide. I had to learn the hard way. I sure wish I had had the DogAge Test then. This is a marvelous tool. Thanks to the test, you don't need to learn the hard way. You don't need to join Future Farmers of America, and you don't need to go on to years and years of veterinary school and training, as I did. Instead, the DogAge Test will provide you with your pet's DogAge in people years and will begin teaching you everything you need to know about caring for your dog.

I took the test for Georgia, who is eleven calendar years. If you use the traditional method of multiplying by seven, she'd be seventy-seven in people years. But her DogAge is only 51.8; that's more than twenty DogAge years *younger* than other dogs of the same breed. That's great! Basically, Georgia's DogAge means that if she were a person, she would be as strong and healthy as a fifty-one-year-old.

As you take the test, you will gain invaluable insights into your dog and how well you are taking care of him. You will also see what you can do better in several different areas: your dog's health, nutrition, exercise, training, safety, and medical care. Taking the test will lay the foundation for you. From there, I will show you exactly how to build a lifelong prevention and wellness program for your dog, to help him lead a longer, healthier, and happier life. Ready to start?

The DogAge Test

You can take the DogAge Test in two ways: 1) on paper, using the questionnaire included in this chapter, or 2) online at www.DogAge.com. Both tests' questions are the same, and although the online version will do the calculation for you, the print version in this book is a great visual reminder of all the dog health areas that you should focus on. I encourage you to flag these pages and write on them, so that when you revisit the test in three months, you can see how much you and your dog have improved.

The DogAge Test is divided into five sections, each one covering one essential aspect of your dog's health and wellness: General Health and Prevention, Medical History, Food and Nutrition, Exercise Habits, and Safety. Within each of these sections, you will answer a series of easy questions. The answers are multiple-choice; just circle your answer. Then, to the right of each answer, you will find a number with a plus or minus sign, such as (+1) or (−2). Circle that, as well. At the end of each section, you will be asked to add up the pluses and minuses and record your total. And when you finish all five sections, you'll just add up the section totals to tabulate your final score. Easy, right?

Now, before you take the test, I need to explain one more thing. Before you start answering the questions, the DogAge Test will ask you for two simple bits of information: how big is your dog, and what is his chronological age? Then, using an easy-to-read table, you will find what we call your dog's "base age." Hold onto that. At the end of the test, you will use that base age to calculate your dog's "DogAge," meaning whether he is biologically older or younger than his calendar years, and by how much. "DogAge" is represented in people years. Also at the end of the test, I will help you interpret the results and determine where you can do better in helping your dog stay young, active, and healthy. And I'll give you a list of handy DogAge tips that you can use for guidance. Okay? Let's go!

Step 1: Determine the size of your dog

Toy/mini (fits in a small basket or purse)
Small (good as a lap dog)
Medium (generally knee-height)
Large (could take you for a walk)
Giant (seems like a small pony)

Step 2: Find your dog's *base* age (average age in people years) using your dog's size and chronological age:

	Toy	Small	Medium	Large	Giant
1–6 months	3.24	3.24	3.24	3.24	3.24
7–12 months	8.52	8.52	8.52	8.52	8.52
13–17 months	13.36	13.36	13.36	13.36	13.36
18–30 months	16	16	16	16	16
3 years	16.5	17.1	17.7	19.3	20.8
4 years	22	22.8	23.7	25.6	27.7
5 years	27.5	28.5	29.6	32.1	34.6
6 years	33	34.2	35.5	38.5	41.5
7 years	38.5	39.9	41.4	44.9	48.5
8 years	44	45.6	47.4	51.3	55.4

	Toy	Small	Medium	Large	Giant
9 years	49.5	51.3	53.3	57.7	62.3
10 years	55	57	59.2	64.2	69.3
11 years	60.5	62.7	65.2	70.6	71.3
12 years	66	68.4	71.1	73.6	73.6
13 years	71.5	74.14	75.9	75.9	75.9
14 years	78.2	78.2	78.2	78.2	78.2
15 years	80.5	80.5	80.5	80.5	80.5
16 years	82.8	82.8	82.8	82.8	82.8
17 years	85.1	85.1	85.1	85.1	85.1
18 years	87.4	87.4	87.4	87.4	87.4

Step 3: Take the DogAge test:

The DogAge Test   **Points**
Section 1: General Health and Prevention

1. What is your dog's gender? Circle one.
    a. Male and neutered
                                    a. (−2)
    b. Female and spayed   b. (−2)
    c. Male and NOT neutered   c. (+1)
    d. Female and NOT spayed   d. (+1)

2. What is your dog's breed? Circle one.
    a. Mixed breed   a. (−1)
    b. Purebred   b. (+1)
    c. I don't know   c. (0)

3. Which description best fits your dog? Circle one.
    a. Slim with a noticeable waist; I can feel ribs   a. (−2)
    b. Husky; I can barely feel ribs   b. (+1)
    c. Very thin; I can see ribs   c. (+1)

d. Round or thick all over; I cannot feel ribs   d. (+4)

e. Bony; I can see ribs and backbone   e. (+4)

4. Does anyone in the household smoke indoors? Circle one.

   a. No   a. (−2)

   b. Yes   b. (+1)

5. Do any of the following describe your dog's oral hygiene?
   Circle as many as apply, and add points for each choice.

   a. Perfectly white teeth   a. (−2)

   b. Really bad breath   b. (+1)

   c. Discolored teeth   c. (+1)

   d. Sensitive teeth (difficulty chewing hard food)   d. (+1)

   e. Bleeding gums   e. (+2)

   f. Tooth loss (only for dogs over one year old)   f. (+3)

6. How often do you take your dog to the veterinarian for a
   regular checkup? Circle one.

   a. Twice or more per year   a. (−3)

   b. Once per year   b. (−2)

   c. Never   c. (+1)

Add up all your positive (+) points and then subtract all your
negative (−) points. Write the total in the box.

Section 1 Total:

Section 2: *Medical History*   *Points*

1. Which vaccinations or preventive therapies has your dog
   had? (Add points for each choice)
   - a. A multicomponent (adenovirus, coronavirus,
     distemper, parainfluenza, parvovirus, rabies)   a. (−2)
   - b. Bordetellosis (kennel cough) and/or
     Borrelia burgdorferi (Lyme disease)   b. (−2)
   - c. Other   c. (−2)
   - d. Heartworm and/or flea-and-tick   d. (−2)
   - e. I'm not sure if my dog has had a vaccination   e. (+1)
   - f. None   f. (+4)

2. Does your dog have any of the following conditions or
   symptoms? Circle up to five choices.
   - a. None   a. (−4)
   - b. Allergies, food and/or skin   b. (+1)
   - c. Ear mites and/or fleas and ticks   c. (+1)
   - d. Skin problems or infection   d. (+1)
   - e. Respiratory infection and/or
     breathing problems   e. (+1)
   - f. Hearing problems and/or eyesight or
     eye problems   f. (+1)
   - g. Anxiety due to separation   g. (+1)
   - h. Bladder control problems (not related to
     lack of training), or urinary infection or
     urinary tract problems   h. (+1)
   - i. Lameness, joint pain, osteoarthritis,
     or canine hip dysplasia   i. (+1)
   - j. Heartworm, intestinal worms (tapeworms,
     hookworms, roundworms), or ringworm   j. (+2)

k. Cognitive Dysfunction Syndrome
   (Canine Alzheimer's)   k. (+2)
l. Diabetes   l. (+3)
m. Heart, spinal, and/or kidney disease   m. (+3)
n. Epilepsy   n. (+3)
o. High blood pressure, autoimmune disease,
   and/or cancer   o. (+4)

Add up all your positive (+) points and then subtract all your negative (−) points. Write the total in the box.

Section 2 Total:

Section 3: Food and Nutrition   *Points*

1. Does your dog eat any of the following foods? Circle up to three choices.
   a. Breed-specific dog food   a. (−2)
   b. Dog food recommended by your
      veterinarian for a specific condition   b. (−2)
   c. Dog food that's only available at a pet
      or specialty store   c. (−2)
   d. Puppy food (if under one year old)   d. (−2)
   e. Senior dog food   e. (−2)
   f. Weight-control dog food   f. (−2)
   g. Another pet's food
      (including another dog's food)   g. (+1)
   h. Cat food   h. (+1)
   i. Puppy food (if over one year old)   i. (+1)
   j. Treats   j. (+1)

k. People food   k. (+1)

l. Dry dog food   l. (+1)

m. Wet (canned) dog food   m. (0)

2. What kind of people food does your dog eat? Circle up to three choices.

   a. Vegetables   a. (−2)

   b. Fruits   b. (−2)

   c. Cooked red-meat bones   c. (−2)

   d. Sweets   d. (+1)

   e. Raw red meat or bones   e. (+1)

   f. Cooked poultry bones   f. (+1)

   g. Anything and everything   g. (+2)

   h. None   h. (0)

3. How do you usually determine how much to feed your dog at mealtime? Circle up to two choices.

   a. I follow the instructions on the dog food label a. (−2)

   b. I follow the advice of the veterinarian b. (−2)

   c. I use a measuring cup or scoop and feed the same amount every day c. (−2)

   d. I fill up the bowl to the top at each mealtime d. (+1)

   e. I keep the bowl filled all the time e. (+1)

   f. My dog lets me know how much to provide f. (+2)

4. When does your dog eat? Circle one.

   a. Food is provided 3–4 times a day (puppy) a. (−2)

   b. Food is provided once or twice a day (adult dog) b. (−2)

   c. Food is available all the time c. (+4)

d. Whenever I eat   d. (+4)

e. Whenever my dog asks for food   e. (+4)

Add up all your positive (+) points and then subtract all your negative (−) points. Write the total in the box.

Section 3 Total:

Section 4: Exercise Habits   *Points*

1. How would you describe your dog's overall activity level? Circle one.

    a. Hyperactive, always on the move   a. (−3)

    b. Very active   b. (−2)

    c. Not very active   c. (+1)

    d. Very slow paced   d. (+1)

    e. Downright lazy   e. (+2)

2. How often does your dog become active for at least fifteen minutes at a time? Circle one.

    a. More than three times a day   a. (−3)

    b. 1–3 times a day   b. (−2)

    c. Less than once a week   c. (+1)

    d. Never   d. (+2)

3. Does your dog do the following activities? (Only check the activities your dog does OFTEN.) Circle up to two choices.

    a. Play at the park   a. (−2)

    b. Play catch   b. (−2)

    c. Play with toys   c. (−2)

    d. Run around the yard or room   d. (−2)

e. Swim	e. (−2)
f. Take walks	f. (−2)
g. Play outside unsupervised	g. (+1)
h. Run away from me	h. (+1)
i. Chase cars	i. (+1)
j. Chase children	j. (+1)

Add up all your positive (+) points and then subtract all your negative (−) points. Write the total in the box.

Section 4 Total:

Section 5: Safety   *Points*

1. When you go for a drive, where does your dog sit most often? Circle one.

a. In a dog carrier	a. (−3)
b. In the back seat	b. (−2)
c. In the back of a hatchback, station wagon, or sport utility vehicle	c. (−2)
d. My dog never rides in a vehicle	d. (−2)
e. On my lap	e. (+1)
f. In the passenger seat	f. (+1)
g. Wherever he/she wants	g. (+1)
h. In the open back of a pickup truck (tied or untied)	h. (+2)

2. When you take your dog for a walk, do you use a leash, harness, or gentle leader? Circle one.

a. Yes	a. (−2)
b. No	b. (+1)
c. We don't go for walks	c. (+2)

3. Is there a fence around your dog's yard or play space? Circle one.

    a. Yes   a. (−2)

    b. No, but I use a secure dog run   b. (−2)

    c. No, but I always clip the dog's collar to a length of leash secured to something in the yard   c. (−2)

    d. No   d. (+1)

4. When your dog meets someone new or a new dog, what does your dog do *first*? Circle one.

    a. Sits politely   a. (−2)

    b. Sniffs in a friendly way   b. (−2)

    c. Wags tail   c. (−2)

    d. Barks   d. (+1)

    e. Growls   e. (+1)

    f. Attacks   f. (+2)

5. What has your dog been trained to do *very well* most of the time? Circle up to three choices.

    a. Recognize his/her name   a. (−2)

    b. Come when called   b. (−2)

    c. Sit   c. (−2)

    d. Lie down   d. (−2)

    e. Walk politely on a leash   e. (−2)

    f. Go to a certain place, such as a dog crate   f. (−2)

    g. Stay   g. (−2)

    h. Heel   h. (−2)

    i. Respond to commands even with distractions   i. (−2)

    j. Do tricks, such as fetch and roll over   j. (−2)

    k. None   k. (+2)

6. Does your dog have any behavior problems? Circle up to five choices.

a. None. My dog is well-behaved	a. (−3)
b. Aggression toward other dogs or people	b. (+1)
c. Inappropriate or excessive barking, begging, biting, or whining	c. (+1)
d. Compulsively repeats one activity, such as pacing, licking, circling, or fly-biting	d. (+1)
e. Destructive to house or my things, and yard	e. (+1)
f. Eating stool (feces) (own or other pet's)	f. (+1)
g. Escaping the yard, running into the street	g. (+1)
h. Relieving bowels or bladder indoors	h. (+1)
i. Uncomfortable or doesn't behave around children	i. (+1)

Add up all your positive (+) points and then subtract all your negative (−) points. Write the total in the box.

Section 5 Total:

Step 4: Calculate your dog's DogAge:

1. Add up the total points from Sections 1–5 of the DogAge Test. Have your dog's base age (page 14) ready.

   The result: _____ (Total points)

2. Multiply _____ (Total points) × 0.0035 = _____ (DogAge Points)

3. Multiply your dog's base age (see page 14) _____ × _____ (DogAge points). The difference is: _____

4. Add (or subtract if negative) _____ (that difference) + _____ (base age) to get the final result:

Your pet's DogAge* is _____

Interpreting the Results

The first step is simple: is your pet's DogAge lower than his base age? If so, that's great. It means that what you are doing is helping to keep your dog younger and healthier than the average dog of that size and calendar age. Or is your pet's DogAge *higher* than his base age? That means trouble: your dog will probably not live as long as most dogs of his size—unless you make significant changes in his routine and health care. More on those in a moment.

Whichever the result is, go back through each section and see where you and your dog scored well and where you did not. Let's start at the beginning, in the section titled General Health and Prevention. If you circled "yes" when asked if your dog has been spayed or neutered, your score on that question was a −2. That's good. It means that you reduced your dog's biological age by a significant amount right there. Why? Because as I explain at length in Chapter Eleven, spaying and neutering actually helps protect your dog against several potential diseases and other problems. If, on the other hand, you circled not spayed or neutered, you get a +1 score, and that means that by a small margin you are increasing your dog's biological age, meaning that he will probably not live quite as long as he otherwise would.

---

*DogAge is your dog's biological age in people years.

Another important element in Section One is the way your dog looks in terms of weight and huskiness. If you answered "Slim with a noticeable waist; I can feel ribs," that's good: you score a −2. If, on the other hand, you answered, "Round or thick all over; I cannot feel ribs," that's bad and you score a +4. The same is true if you answered, "Bony; I can see ribs and backbone"—it's a +4. And those +4 scores mean that your dog is way too heavy or way too skinny, and his health and longevity are suffering as a result. It also means that if you want to extend your dog's life, you had better put him on a much better diet.

By now I'm sure you are getting the hang of how this test works: where your answer results in a negative (−) score, your dog is doing well. Where your answer results in a positive (+) score your dog is not doing well, and it is in that precise area that you need to make changes for the better. Now, right here, I suggest you go back through the test and make a list of each of those areas where you need to make positive changes. Keep that list at your side as you read the rest of this book. I give you extensive, reliable information about how to implement those necessary changes.

Here, though, is a good thumbnail overview of what your test scores mean—and some suggestions about what you can do to help your dog live a longer, healthier life. Obviously, I go into greater detail and explanation during the course of the book. But this primer, developed by the DogAge team, is a good place to start.

Section One: General Health and Prevention

Improving your dog's overall health, including weight, hygiene, and neutering or spaying, can help your dog live a longer, healthier life.

- Recent studies show that controlling your dog's weight may help make his DogAge up to 20% younger. Weight control also helps ward off conditions such as osteoarthritis and joint pain.
- Neutering or spaying your dog has many beneficial health effects: lower risk for certain cancers; decreased risk of illness; and reduced risk of behavioral problems, especially in males, that can lead to accidental death or euthanasia.
- Pay attention to dental care: tooth and gum disease can cause your dog great discomfort and expose him to serious infections.

Section Two: Medical History

It is essential to take your dog to a licensed veterinarian for regular examinations and vaccinations.

- Veterinarians believe that vaccinations have saved the lives of millions of dogs. There are two types of vaccination programs: core and non-core. Core vaccinations protect against diseases that are serious and sometimes fatal. Non-core vaccinations are for dogs that might be at a specific risk for infection due to their lifestyle habits or surrounding environment. Both protect against diseases and illnesses that can lead to death. Some are recommended for all dogs, and some are recommended based on the area in which you live or play.
- Prevention is also the best way to protect your dog against fleas, ticks, and heartworm. These are more than canine nuisances; they can be dangerous to your dog's health—and to yours.

Section Three: Food and Nutrition

Good eating habits help make your dog younger. Different dogs have different nutritional needs. Deciding which type of food and how much food is best for your dog can be confusing. Use the following steps to help shape your dog's menu—and his physique!

* Food Quantity: recent studies indicate that managing your dog's weight can lead to a longer, healthier life. Follow dog food package instructions. Using a measuring scoop or cup is the best way to control food quantity and reduce the risk of obesity. Also, don't forget that treats count as food, too. So keep these to a minimum if your dog is overweight.
* Dog Food and Nutrition: obesity can predispose your dog to diabetes, arthritis, and breathing problems. You can keep your dog lean by feeding him or her a well-balanced, quantity-controlled diet. The age and size of your dog determines the number of times he or she should eat each day.

Section Four: Exercise Habits

Numerous studies show that exercise can help prevent disease, keep your dog slim, and prevent boredom. Exercise can also strengthen your bond with your dog and encourage good behavior.

* Dogs of all breeds and ages need daily exercise to keep them young and active. Generally I recommend fifteen minutes of exercise three times a day. Caution: some activities, such as

Frisbee® or riding a bicycle with a dog on a leash running alongside, can be dangerous.

- Some dogs require walks around the block while others require hours of running and playing to match their activity levels. Even senior dogs enjoy being outdoors after a day in the house.
- Beware of heatstroke. Always carry water for your dog, especially in summer, and avoid prolonged activity in extreme temperatures.

Section Five: Safety

Keeping your dog safe helps avoid unnecessary accidents. Training your dog to behave well is vital: it can keep your dog safe, and your family safe as well.

- In public, keep your dog on a leash at all times. Leashes come in many different styles and lengths. Short leashes are recommended for busy and congested streets so you can keep your dog close to your side. Longer leashes can be used at parks or beaches.
- The way your dog acts when meeting new people or dogs can indicate if he has behavioral issues. Inappropriate aggression (constant barking, jumping, and biting) or inappropriate submissiveness (shaking, hiding, and backing/running away) can denote a problem. Behavioral issues are often reasons that people give up their dogs to shelters.

If you follow the above suggestions, what will the result be for your dog? Using primary research and a careful, elaborated metric, the DogAge team has come up with a formula that can give you a very good idea. They calculated the benefits listed in the following table by using as an example a four-calendar-year-old, large-breed dog (base DogAge 25.6). Other factors, such as canine diseases and other health problems, and the effect of one benefit on another, are not factored in to their summaries. Still, this table will give you good ideas about how to keep your dog trim and healthy.

To have a younger DogAge, your dog should:	DogAge benefits
1. Keep a slim figure, with a noticeable waist.	1.8 years younger
2. Chew on teeth-cleaning chews or biscuits and have his/her teeth brushed three times per week.	6 months younger
3. Avoid people food as much as possible.	6 months younger
4. Get his/her vaccinations and visit the veterinarian for regular checkups.	6 months younger
5. Take his/her medications as prescribed by the veterinarian, if applicable.	3 months younger
6. Eat only the amount of dog food necessary to maintain an ideal body condition, measured with a standardized measuring cup, and monitor body condition regularly.	1.8 years younger
7. Exercise or play actively at least three times per day for at least fifteen minutes each time.	6 months younger

To have a younger DogAge, your dog should:	DogAge benefits
8. Be trained to respond to your commands most of the time.	1.3 years younger
9. Be safe in the yard, on walks, and on trips through the use of protective barriers and gear such as fences, leashes, and dog carriers.	6 months younger
10. Be happy!	6 months younger

Source: www.DogAge.com Benefits are calculated based on a 4-calendar-year-old, mid-sized dog (base DogAge is 25.6). Other factors, such as dog diseases and other dog health problems, and the effect of one benefit on another, are not considered.

Now, dear reader, you have a pretty clear idea about how you and your dog are doing—and where you can work harder. So now it is time to go much, much deeper. I'm going to tell you everything you need to know.

CHAPTER THREE

Your Dog's Body: What You Need to Know

I LOVE WHAT I DO. I love working with animals, I love treating dogs and cats who are sick or injured, and I love teaching pet owners what they need to know about taking proper care of their animals. At times I have been able to follow a dog through several life stages and give counsel and advice to his owners throughout his life. But you know what? When it comes to the health of your dog, your vet is not the most important person in your dog's life. That role belongs to you.

As a first step, I am going to show you what you need to know about your dog's body and how to spot any signs of trouble in the making. There is a simple tool for doing this: a monthly physical exam that you can do at home. The exam is easy to do, it's quick, and it is vital to the long-term health and longevity of your dog. There are also two very specific benefits of doing a monthly exam. First, it will allow your dog to become accustomed to being handled, and that will make it easier when you take him to the vet. Second, you might spot a problem that needs urgent medical attention. Always remember: early detection can save your dog's life. So I urge you to set aside a little time each month to do the exam.

As a first-time or new dog owner, you may ask yourself, "There is so much to know about my dog's health. Where do I begin?" My answer is this: learn to be observant. In the course of your daily routine, pay close attention to your dog's normal habits and behavior. Notice when he likes to play, how and what he likes to eat, when he likes to sleep, and when he seems most alert and happy. By observing his habits and watching for any changes in his behavior, you will get to know your dog better, and you may spot clues about his underlying health and well-being. For instance, if your dog suddenly refuses to eat his regular food, that could be a sign of an underlying medical problem. Sure, you may think that he is just bored with his same old food, but watch out: if you offer your dog a new brand of food it might just mask the problem—and delay a necessary trip to the vet. So watch for even subtle changes in appetite. Also watch for unusual weight gain or loss, any bouts of lethargy, increased thirst or urination, extended periods of diarrhea, and the like. If you see such symptoms, get the dog to the vet. No matter what, being observant every day will make the monthly exam even more productive.

Starting the exam. When I do a routine physical exam at my clinic, I start by visiting with the dog to help him feel relaxed and comfortable. Then I start at the nose and work toward the tail. I look at the dog head-on, to make sure that everything looks symmetrical: the eyelids, the sides of the mouth, and the musculature of the back and hips. I also check to see if the dog stands comfortably on all fours. Chapter Four contains a chart of the most common illnesses that pass through my clinic.

The eyes. Carefully examine your dog's eyes every month. I first check the pupils to see if they are the same size, then I check the whites of the eyes. If you have a dog who is dark in color, the whites of the eyes may have some brown pigmentation. If you gently pull back the upper eyelid, though, you should see a white area. The white part of the eye is called the *sclera*. (In dogs and cats, the structure of the eyes is different from ours. When you look at a person you see the whites of their eyes; that's because our eyes are not fully encased in our eyelids. In most dogs, the eyes are fully encased in their eyelids, so the part of their eyes that you see is actually only the iris and the pupil.) If you pull back the lid and find that the white part is pink in color, or that it has a lot of blood vessels or is irritated, that might suggest conjunctivitis. Usually, though, conjunctivitis is accompanied by squinting or tearing. It is normal to see a few blood vessels in the white of the eye. But if you see a lot of them, or if you find swelling of the tissues under the eyelid, take your dog to the vet. A sclera that appears yellow or orange may be a sign of serious illness that requires immediate medical attention.

The nose. I always give the nose a quick check, to make sure the color hasn't changed. Ulcers, rough spots, or peeling can all be signs of a problem. Then I check the nostrils for symmetry and any unusual growths or discharge. Right here let me discuss a common misconception about a dog's nose. Many people say that if a dog's nose is cold and wet, it means he's healthy; if it's dry, it means he has a fever. I do not put much credence in that. Medically speaking, the temperature and relative moisture of the nose are more a reflection of the outside temperature and humidity than of the dog's internal medical condition. So I urge you: do not rely on the nose as an indicator of how your dog is feeling.

Your dog's temperature. Our bodies, when healthy, usually register 98.6 on a Fahrenheit thermometer. Your dog's normal body temperature tends to run somewhat higher, between 100 and 102.5 degrees Fahrenheit. So if you touch a non-haired portion of your dog, such as the underside of the ears or the tummy, it will naturally feel warmer to you. My clients often say to me, "Dr. Dondi, I think my dog has a fever; his ears feel warm to me." Most of the time, that's because the owner is suddenly paying attention to what the dog feels like, and they naturally do feel warmer to the touch. To avoid that, practice getting a feel for what your dog's temperature feels like when he's well. Feel under the ear, put your hand on his tummy on a regular basis. That will help you gauge subtle changes in your dog's temperature. Remember: feeling the underside of the ears or the tummy is a much better indicator than feeling the nose.

When should you take your dog's temperature? I do not make this a part of the monthly exam. It is not pleasant for you or the dog, and it's not important to do it every month. If you go to a vet once or twice a year for a routine physical exam, your vet should take a basal body temperature and record it in the medical record. Now, what if your dog gets sick? Then monitor your dog's temperature during that period. This is easy: you can use the same type of thermometers that you use for humans. Ear thermometers give you an approximate reading, but they tend to be less accurate than rectal thermometers. That said, if you are going to use a rectal thermometer, be very careful. Use cooking oil or Vaseline as a lubricant, as you would with a baby. Most dogs don't like to have their temperatures taken in this manner, so be careful: even the sweetest dog might snap or bite.

The ears. If your dog has floppy ears, lift up the flap and inspect the *pinna*, the cartilage-rich area that flaps over and protects the ear canal. Hair loss around the edges of the pinna can indicate such problems as ringworm, fly strike, or sarcoptic mange. Now inspect the ear canal. To do so, you do not need to put anything into the canal, just take a cursory look and make sure it looks the same as the last time. Check for black or brown discharge. A little bit is normal, but an excessive amount can suggest infection. Look for redness or swelling of the ear canal, which can also suggest a problem. A foul smell to the ears or the presence of discharge on the underside of the pinna may suggest a problem. So might excessive head shaking or scratching of the ears.

The mouth. To check your pooch's mouth, gently lift the lips and check the teeth for discoloration or the presence of tartar. The gums should be the color of bubble gum; that's normal. Some dogs, though, like chows and rottweillers, have darker gums. In that case, pay more attention to the color of the tongue. (Chows tend to have black tongues so it can be difficult to assess the color of their gums and tongue as an indication of health status.) With all dogs, you want to examine the gum line to make sure there are no abnormal growths there. Most dogs won't tolerate your looking under the tongue, so it may be difficult to get a good look. By opening the dog's mouth, you can see if the tongue is raised higher on one side than the other, which might suggest a problem. Always check the rest of the mouth, too, for any abnormalities.

What is normal wear and tear on a dog's teeth? Most dogs show little wearing down of their teeth unless they chew on rocks or other hard surfaces. Separation anxiety or boredom can sometimes cause these behaviors, but for the most part, normal dog food and rawhide chews do not cause significant flattening of the teeth. Most dogs, though not all, do develop some degree of dental tartar. (See Chapter Eleven for detailed information about dental care.) Many large-breed dogs, though, are just not prone to tartar. Georgia, my boxer mix, is ten and she doesn't have an ounce of tartar on her teeth. Hannah, my rottweiler, tends to accumulate a little tartar on her canine teeth, but her back teeth are fine. Neither of my big dogs has required a professional dental cleaning. Many small dogs, such as Yorkshire terriers, poodles, shelties, and dachshunds, tend to develop significant dental tartar, as well as gum disease. For this reason, I am trying to get Chili used to having her teeth rubbed, and I feed her hard dog food that she has to chew on. Owners of small or toy breed dogs should clean their dogs' teeth at home, by regular brushing. Teeth-cleaning bones and chews can also be effective. But also ask your vet about professional dental cleaning. This is not just a cosmetic issue; it's a health issue. Dogs with significant dental tartar and gum disease may have trouble eating. Some dental disease can also lead to serious infections.

The neck and shoulders. At the base of the jawline, check the salivary glands and the submandibular lymph nodes. In thin dogs, if you work at it, you should be able to discern these as a circular, semi-firm area, but you should detect nothing that is prominent or painful around the base of the jaw. To check the base of the jawline, use your thumb and index finger and apply gentle pressure to the skin to feel for any lumps or other problems. Do that around the circumference of the neck. Then move to the shoulders to continue a complete check of the lymph nodes. Check in front of the shoulder blades for the prescapular nodes, then check behind the elbows against the side of the chest for the axillary lymph nodes. Next, go up underneath the thigh in the flank region where the thigh meets the abdomen: this is where the inguinal lymph nodes are located. At the back of the knees above the hock, which is like the elbow of the rear leg, is where you find the popliteal lymph nodes. All of these lymph nodes should basically be imperceptible to the touch. If you do feel firm, round structures in these areas, it is abnormal and you should take your pet to the vet immediately.

The coat and skin. To examine the coat and skin, use your fingertips, a brush, or a comb to push the hair in the reverse direction from the direction that it grows and examine the skin underneath. The back is a good area to do that. Check the color of the skin, to make sure that it does not look red or inflamed. Also check for the presence of black, crusty material, which might suggest that the dog has fleas. Then pass your hand over the entire dog, feeling for any new lumps or bumps. Notice, too, if there is any focus of sensitivity or discomfort. Most dogs don't like to have their feet touched, but if one foot appears to be more sensitive than another, that might suggest a problem.

Lumps and bumps. If you find a lump, don't panic. There are all kinds of things that cause lumps. Some of them are problematic and some of them aren't. Some will turn out to be enlarged lymph nodes. Others will be sebaceous adenomas, which are growths that look like warts. Some bumps result from fatty tumors underneath the skin. These are lipomas and are common in aging dogs, especially if they are overweight, but they occur in thin dogs as well. Keep this in mind: just because a lump isn't painful to your dog, that doesn't mean you should ignore it. My advice is this: if you discover a new lump, bump, or growth, always have your vet evaluate it. He may recommend a quick test called a *fine-needle aspirate*, where he places a small needle in the abnormal tissue and draws out some cells to examine under the microscope. This may yield some information as to what kind of lump it really is, and whether it might cause a problem. Let me say it again: it's better to catch something early, before it has time to develop into something more serious.

Should all lumps and bumps be seen on an urgent basis? If during your monthly exam you find a new lump on your dog, I urge you to call and make an appointment with your veterinarian as soon as it's convenient for you. It doesn't necessarily have to be the same day unless your dog is acting sick or all of his lymph nodes are enlarged. If you get in to see the vet within two weeks, that should be sufficient.

The feet. It is always good to get your dog used to having his feet examined—it will help the vet should your dog develop a limp. To examine the feet, feel carefully between the toe pads. Make sure the toes are symmetrical, and that there are no unusual growths or sensitivities. Do that on all four feet. Thorns or injuries to the skin can be very difficult to find. I use my fingertips because they tend to work much better than my eyes where the fur is heavy. If you use gentle pressure and just rustle your fingertips through the fur, if there's a scab or something sticking in the paw, you will feel it with your fingertips before you can see it. You can also identify a focus of discomfort while moving from one toe to the next. Move through the entire foot in that manner, using very light pressure. If you identify an area of sensitivity, take a close look. Paw checks are easiest if you have the dog lie down comfortably.

The genitals, rear, and tail. First lift up the tail to make sure that everything looks in proper order, whether the dog is male or female. As I will discuss in a later chapter, I recommend neutering male dogs, but if they're intact, check the testicles for any lumps, growths, or asymmetries. With female dogs, feel the underside for any lumps in the mammary glands. Breast cancer does occur in dogs, just as in people. Then check the tail for anything unusual. The rear and tail areas are also good spots to check for flea infestation.

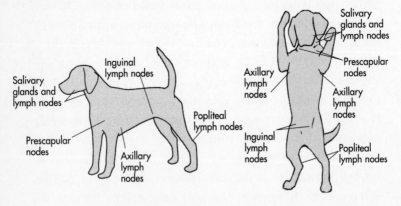

Provided by RealAge, creators of DogAge, © RealAge, Inc.

Weight. As you learned from the DogAge Test, maintaining a good weight is absolutely vital to your dog's health and longevity. Keeping your dog slim, with a tucked-up waist, may increase his longevity by as much as 1.8 DogAge years. You can also tell a lot about your dog's general health from his weight, so I recommend a weigh-in as part of your dog's monthly physical exam—unless your dog is huge. If you have a scale that is conducive to this procedure, stand on it, weigh yourself, and then pick up the dog. Take the combined weight, subtract your weight, and that gives you the weight of your dog. If you do have a huge dog, do not try a monthly weigh-in; you or your dog might get hurt. Instead, have your vet weigh your dog every time you go to the clinic.

Keep an accurate record of your dog's weight. You can follow your dog's weight by looking at his medical record at the vet's office, or you can chart it at home. On a month-to-month basis, your dog's weight is probably not going to change much, unless you have changed his diet or unless you have a roommate or family member who might be feeding him treats. I will discuss proper nutrition and weight management at length in Chapter Six, DogAge Nutrition.

Body mass. To assess your dog's physical mass, stand over him and check to see if his waist tucks in behind the rib cage. It should if he is at his proper weight. The hip bones should be palpable beneath muscle tissue and should not be prominent or impossible to find. You should be able to push in lightly with your fingers on the rib cage and discern the edges of the ribs. If you have to exert a lot of pressure to find the ribs, or go through a lot of fatty tissue, your dog is probably too heavy. Remember, this can be a serious health risk.

The pulse. While it is not essential, it can be beneficial for you to know your dog's resting pulse rate when he's healthy. To find the pulse, locate the femoral artery by using gentle pressure on the inside of the thigh, where it meets the body up in the groin area. Try feeling around, holding your fingers in one position and moving them back and forth. Eventually you will feel the thump of the femoral artery. Count how many pulses occur in fifteen seconds, then multiply by four. This will give you your dog's normal pulse rate. Large-breed dogs can have a resting pulse rate ranging from 60 to 100, and small breed dogs from 80 to 120, depending on how much exercise they get. If your dog's pulse seems faster or slower than usual, and your dog is not acting like himself, it may warrant a visit to the vet.

The resting respiratory rate. There is one more thing for you to check on a monthly basis: your dog's resting respiratory rate. I think this is important for owners to know, and it's easy to do. When your dog is sleeping, count how many times his chest moves up in fifteen seconds, then multiply that by four. This will give you a resting respiratory rate. Don't do this after a walk: the rate will vary and be higher than it will be at rest. In any case, changes in the resting respiratory rate can be very significant and worth checking with a vet.

Panting. During the monthly exam, check to see if your dog is panting in an unusual manner. Excessive panting can be a sign of a lot of different things. First, it is a normal way for a dog to expel heat. After a walk, a lot of dogs will pant for a good half an hour to an hour when they come back home. Panting can also suggest discomfort, fear, or stress. Some dogs who have seizures will have a pre-ictal period during which they know a seizure is coming, and they'll pant during that. There are also some disease processes that can cause panting, as I will explain in a later chapter. For our purposes here, remember that most panting you see is caused by warm or hot weather or your dog's activity level, but if your dog won't stop panting or cannot get comfortable, take him to the vet.

When to rush to the vet. The monthly exam is an excellent way to monitor your dog's health, and it may turn up problems that require immediate medical attention. Take a look at Chapter Four for a chart of the most common canine conditions. As with the case of Annie the golden retriever, any time your dog has serious trouble breathing or has an increased respiratory rate, get him to the vet right away. Act quickly, too, if your dog's gums look pale, ashen, white, yellow, or orange. This can indicate serious problems. Also, if the whites of the eyes are yellow or orange, get to the vet right away. Other symptoms that require immediate professional attention include excessive vomiting, bleeding, ongoing diarrhea, increased thirst or urination, lethargy, and lack of appetite. In Chapter Nine, I discuss how specific breeds have distinct predispositions to various diseases and infirmities. In each of these cases, though, the essential first step is to understand your dog's body when he is well and happy, so that you can pick up the first signs of illness early on.

Call the vet immediately if:

Your dog cannot stop vomiting or having diarrhea.

Your dog is profoundly lethargic or unresponsive.

Your dog is vomiting unproductively and cannot get comfortable.

Your dog has a seizure.

Your dog collapses and cannot get up.

Your dog is straining to urinate and producing nothing.

Your dog has not eaten for more than one day and this is unusual behavior.

Your dog ingests any sort of toxin or medication not prescribed for him.

Your dog is bitten by another dog or other animal.

Your dog is hit by a car.
Your dog has a fever higher than 103.5 Fahrenheit.
Your dog is having difficulty breathing.
Your dog's gums and tongue are pale, gray, or bluish in color.
Your dog has any abnormal bleeding.
Your dog has been limping for more than three days.
Your dog will not open an eye or eyes.
The whites of your dog's eyes appear yellow or orange.

I have a pit bull patient named Harry, whose owner's monthly physical exam saved him much pain and suffering. Now Harry is a handsome devil and is as charming as he is good-looking. Everyone in the hospital swoons when he arrives, and he thrives on the attention. He and his owner spend a lot of time together, because he goes to work with her every day in their antique store. Harry's mom is a very diligent and devoted owner, and checks him over at least monthly. Knowing his breed's predisposition to mast-cell tumors, she watches his skin carefully. When she noticed a tiny (smaller than a pea!) bump appear over his shoulder, she brought him right in. A fine-needle aspirate confirmed that this bump indeed was a mast-cell tumor. A large section of skin surrounding the bump was surgically removed with it, because the nature of this tumor is to send out tiny tentacles into the skin, thus spreading the cancer. When the biopsy came back, we rejoiced. The surgery had been successful at removing the entire tumor, including a few baby tentacles!! Because of Harry's mom's vigilance and rapid intervention, Harry was spared further radical surgery and danger to his life. So take a lesson from Harry's mom: do your dog's monthly physical exam. It might save his life!

CHAPTER FOUR

Common Problems and Diseases

No matter how careful and diligent you are with your dog, some dogs will get sick. Most often, it's not your fault. It could be genetics or an accident. In any case, when your dog is behaving oddly, appears ill, or has any of the symptoms explained in the previous chapter, the only thing to do is to take him to the veterinarian for help. I know how nerve-racking it is to sit in the veterinarian's waiting room or at home waiting for an explanation about why your dog isn't feeling well. When the diagnosis comes, it can be even more anxiety-provoking when you're not sure what your veterinarian means. To help you understand common dog health conditions and diseases, I have compiled a concise guide to the most common canine diseases, along with brief explanations of each. The guide will help you understand the severity of the problem and decide what you should do in response.

Now, let me be crystal clear: the purpose of this guide is *not* to lead you to a definitive medical diagnosis or treatment; only a qualified, licensed veterinarian can do that. Instead, the guide is designed to help you understand what is ailing your dog. If you haven't been to a vet yet, and you have any doubts or worries about your dog's condition, I encourage you to call your veterinarian or go to an emergency-care clinic in a timely fashion. It could save your dog's life.

MUCOUS MEMBRANES

Anemia Dehydration Oxygen- deprivation	Check the gums. In dogs that don't have pigmentation in these areas, the gums should be the color of pink bubble gum. If the gums look pale or ashen, it may indicate **anemia or oxygen deprivation**. The tongue should be pink too, unless your dog has naturally dark gums and tongue, like in chow chows. Normally, the gums should also be very slick and slippery. If they are dry to the touch—you should actually stick your finger in and touch them—it may indicate **dehydration**. If your dog is acting sick and the gums are dry or pale, see a vet right away.

**Immune-
   mediated
   disease**
	The areas where the skin meets the lips, nose, vulva, anus, and footpads are called mucocutaneous junctions. If you see ulcers or erosions at these areas, they may indicate an **immune-mediated disease** process or other problems.

NOSE, EYES, AND EARS

Nose conditions: *Inflammation* *Nasal tumors*	Unusual growths or one-sided nasal discharge can be signs of **nasal tumors**. Yellow discharge or clear, thick mucus can be signs of **upper-respiratory infections** or **sinusitis**. Inhaled seeds or grass can also

Sinusitis *Upper-respiratory infections*	lodge in the nose and cause irritation and discharge.

Eye conditions: *Cataracts* *Conjunctivitis* *Ectopic cilia* *Entropion* *Eyelid lacerations* *Glaucoma* *Globe proptosis* *KCS, or kerato-conjunctiv-itis sicca* *Tumors* *Ulcers* *Uveitis*	Pinkness or redness in the whites of the eyes can be associated with **conjunctivitis**, which can be allergic or bacterial. Excessive tearing or squinting can be a sign of an abrasion or ulcer on the cornea. If left untreated, they can lead to serious problems. **Entropion** is a condition in which the eyelids roll inward and the eyelashes rub the cornea, causing constant irritation. A thick yellow discharge or dull look to the surface of the eye can be a sign of **KCS, or keratoconjunctivitis sicca**, a condition in which the dog doesn't produce enough tears. It can be treated with drops that stimulate tear production. **Ectopic cilia** are eyelashes that grow on the inside of the eyelid. This is treated by either freezing or lasering those areas so that the lashes don't grow back. **Proptosis** is a condition in which the globe of the eye protrudes out of the socket farther than it should. It can be caused by trauma, infection, or tumors, and is usually addressed surgically. **Eyelid lacerations** of any sort should be taken seriously. Such lacerations must be put back together by the vet very carefully, because if the eyelid

Eye conditions	heals in a skewed position or if there's an area where the eyelashes contact the cornea, it can cause very serious chronic problems.
	A bluish, hazy appearance to the eye may be a sign of **uveitis**, an inflammation of the eye. This condition can be associated with tick-borne diseases, immune-mediated disease, and some cancers. **Cataracts** appear as a blue or white discoloration of the pupil. Glaucoma can cause bulging of the eye, pain, or squinting, and/or dilation or enlargement of the pupil.

Ear conditions: *Infection* *Tumors*	Irritation, discharge, or a foul odor emanating from an ear can all be signs of an ear infection. If an ear infection fails to respond to therapy or becomes recurrent, your dog may need to be evaluated for a resistant bacteria or other problem like hypothyroidism, allergies to pollen or food, a foreign body in the ear, or a tumor. Deep examination of the ear, cultures, and skin testing can help to discern the problem.

INTEGUMENT (SKIN)

Skin infections	**Skin infections** are common in both short- and long-haired dogs. Signs of these include itchiness; red bumps or blisters; hair loss; red, thickened skin; and/or scabs. Hives can indicate an **allergic reaction.**

Skin infestations: *Fleas* *Ticks* *Mites* *Mange* *Demodectic mange* *Sarcoptic mange*	Signs of fleas include itchiness, hair loss, and black dirtlike debris on the skin. The actual fleas and "flea dirt" are most commonly found around the neck and tail. If you brush the hair backward, you'll likely see the parasites themselves moving around or the black debris they leave behind. **Ticks** are small teardrop-shaped insects that can be found embedded in the skin most commonly around the ears and neck, but actually can exist anywhere on the dog. **Mange** is a general term that refers to a skin condition associated with one of two mites. **Demodectic mange** is caused by the *Demodex canis* mite, which is transmitted from the mother to her puppies during nursing. These mites are present in very small numbers in the skin of all dogs, and usually don't cause any problems. When they exist in greater than normal numbers, signs can include thickened and or hairless skin on any part of the body, but commonly on the head and face. Treatment consists of topical ointments (Goodwinol), oral Ivermectin, or oral Milbemycin. This type of mange is not contagious to other dogs and humans. **Sarcoptic mange** is associated with the mite Sarcoptes scabiei and can occur

Skin infestations:	in dogs of any age. It causes severe itching and hair loss on the ears, legs, and underside. Treatment consists of Lyme Sulfur dips and/or treatment with Ivermectin. This type of mange is contagious to other dogs and humans, and is spread through direct contact or through items such as blankets, combs, and brushes.
Skin problems: *Mis-cellaneous*	Pinpoint red spots or large areas of bruising can be signs of problems in the blood such as low platelets, platelet dysfunction, or clotting problems. A yellow tint to the skin can indicate high levels of bilirubin in the bloodstream, which can occur with liver disease or red-blood-cell breakdown.
Skin cancers *Squamous-cell carcinoma* *Malignant melanoma* *Cutaneous lymphoma* *Mast-cell tumors*	**Common skin cancers** include **squamous-cell carcinoma, melanoma, and mast-cell tumors.** We also see **cutaneous lymphoma,** which can appear as raised bumps, ulcers, or crusts that fail to heal.

CARDIOVASCULAR SYSTEM (HEART AND ARTERIES)

Heart problems	Signs for any of the following heart conditions consist of exercise intolerance, persistent cough, respiratory difficulty, collapse, weight loss, and lack of appetite:
Congestive heart failture	**Congestive heart failure** occurs when the heart is unable to do its job pumping blood out to the body, and fluid builds up in the lungs. This condition usually results from leaky heart valves. It is treated initially with oxygen support, diuretics, and sometimes vasodilators. A cardiac ultrasound can help tell whether there are other medications that can be given to help the heart do its job more effectively.
Dilated cardiomyopathy	
Arrhythmias	
Sick sinus syndrome	
Pericardial effusion	

Signs for any of the following heart conditions consist of exercise intolerance, persistent cough, respiratory difficulty, collapse, weight loss, and lack of appetite:

Congestive heart failure occurs when the heart is unable to do its job pumping blood out to the body, and fluid builds up in the lungs. This condition usually results from leaky heart valves. It is treated initially with oxygen support, diuretics, and sometimes vasodilators. A cardiac ultrasound can help tell whether there are other medications that can be given to help the heart do its job more effectively.

Dilated cardiomyopathy tends to be an inherited condition in which the heart muscle is flabby and thin, and the heart is much larger than normal. This condition can lead to arrhythmias and congestive heart failure.

An **arrhythmia** is an abnormal heartbeat. Arrhythmias can occur because of electrolyte abnormalities or abnormalities in the heart muscle or electrical conduction system in the heart. Tendencies toward some arrhythmias like sick sinus syndrome can be inherited.

Pericardial effusion is a condition in which fluid builds up in the sac that surrounds the heart. Pressure from this fluid compresses the heart, and keeps it from being able to do its job. This can

	result from the presence of a tumor on the heart, infection, inflammatory or immune-mediated disease, or clotting problems. Initially, treatment involves removing the fluid from the sac to relieve the pressure on the heart. After this, the underlying cause must be identified before further treatment can be recommended.

PULMONARY SYSTEM (BREATHING)

Kennel cough	Kennel cough is an upper-respiratory infection caused by the bacteria *Bordatella bronchiseptica*. It causes a dry, hacking cough but can lead to pneumonia. It is typically treated with cough suppressants and antibiotics.
Airway problems *Tracheal collapse* *Hypoplastic trachea*	Tracheal collapse usually occurs in toy or small-breed dogs. The tracheal rings are weak, and the trachea collapses when the dog breathes in. The result is a dry, "honking" cough. Treatment consists of weight loss if the dog is overweight, cough suppressants, bronchodilators, antihistamines, and sometimes short courses of corticosteroids. In some severe cases, tracheal stints or braces can be surgically placed to help keep the trachea from collapsing. Hypoplastic trachea is a condition in which the trachea is smaller and more narrow than it should be. Signs include a

Airway problems *Chronic Obstructive Pulmonary Disease*	chronic cough and respiratory difficulty in a young puppy. The condition is typically diagnosed using X-rays. We see it most commonly in bulldogs but it can occur in any breed. Unfortunately, there is no cure for this problem. Some dogs can be treated with the same medications that are used to treat a collapsing trachea, but those severely affected usually succumb to the condition. **Chronic Obstructive Pulmonary Disease** (COPD) is characterized by a hardening and narrowing of the airways, and is caused either by an allergic disease or an immune-mediated disease. Dogs who live with smokers can develop COPD.
Lung cancer	The most common **lung tumors** that we see are carcinomas. The grade and lymph node involvement determine the severity and treatability of the tumor. We also find metastases, or spread of other tumors that grow in other parts of the body, most commonly in the lungs. Some lung tumors cause coughing or weight loss but many cause no symptoms at all. Most can be diagnosed with an X-ray, and all are serious.
Asthma	Asthma is very unusual in dogs.
Lung problems	**Pleural effusion** is a fluid accumulation in the chest surrounding the lungs, between the lung itself and the chest wall. The

Lung problems *Pleural effusion* *Pulmonary thrombo-embolism*	result is compression of the lungs, which causes coughing and/or respiratory difficulty. This condition can be caused by tumors, heart failure, infections, and immune-mediated disease, and can be diagnosed with an X-ray. It's a serious condition.
	A **pulmonary thromboembolism** is a blood clot that lodges in a blood vessel that feeds the lungs. This is a serious condition and is usually terminal. Unfortunately, most dogs with this condition don't live no matter what we do. This condition usually occurs as a result of an underlying disease such as Cushing's disease, cancer, diabetes, some severe inflammatory condition, or an immune-mediated disease.

ENDOCRINE SYSTEM

Cushing's Disease	**Cushing's Disease** is characterized by adrenal glands that produce too much cortisol. This results from either a tumor in the adrenal gland itself or a tumor in the pituitary gland of the brain. Signs include a dry or sparse coat, increased thirst and urination, thin skin, and a pot-bellied appearance. It can be treated with medications and sometimes surgery.
Addison's Disease	**Addison's Disease** is actually the opposite condition to Cushing's disease. With this disease, the adrenal glands don't produce

	enough cortisol. It is commonly seen in young standard poodles and West Highland white terriers but can occur in any breed at any age. Signs include vomiting, diarrhea, decreased appetite or weight loss, and in severe cases collapse. Dogs with this condition will frequently have electrolyte abnormalities (specifically low sodium and high potassium) on bloodwork, but not always. Dogs who are treated and monitored appropriately can live absolutely normal lives.
Diabetes	Signs of diabetes are the same in dogs as they are in people. These include increased thirst and urination and weight loss in the face of a normal or increased appetite early on. If left untreated, the dog may become lethargic and lose his appetite altogether. Diagnosis is made by evaluating blood sugar levels and sugar levels in the urine in addition to the above-mentioned clinical signs. Treatment consists of insulin injections given one to two times daily depending on the individual dog's requirements.

GASTROINTESTINAL (GI) SYSTEM (DIGESTION)

Viruses *Parvovirus* *Coronavirus*	**Parvovirus** is a virus that occurs in young puppies, and causes protracted vomiting, diarrhea, lethargy, low white-blood-cell counts, and inappetence (no appetite). It is

	a very serious illness, and puppies should be hospitalized for supportive care to give them the best chance of surviving.
Coronavirus	**Coronavirus** is a more-benign illness that causes self-limiting diarrhea in puppies.
Gastric dilatation-volvulus	**Gastric dilatation-volvulus** (GDV) is a condition in which the stomach bloats and twists on its axis, but not necessarily in this order. The symptoms of GDV are unproductive vomiting, swollen stomach, visible discomfort, and collapse. This condition occurs more often in large-breed dogs, and is a surgical emergency.
Inflammatory bowel disease	**Inflammatory bowel disease** (IBD) can cause vomiting, diarrhea, weight loss, and inappetence. It is diagnosed via biopsies obtained either surgically or with endoscopy. Treatment consists of medication and changing to a diet with a novel protein and carbohydrate source.
GI cancer	We see a lot of different types of cancer in the gastrointestinal tract. They can affect the esophagus, stomach, small intestine, large intestine, and colon. Signs consist of persistent vomiting, diarrhea, weight loss, and inappetence. Diagnosis is made via biopsies obtained surgically or with endoscopy. Treatment depends on the type of cancer, where it is, and if it has spread.

Megaesoph-agus	**Megaesophagus** is a condition in which the esophagus is dilated and flaccid, and doesn't contract as it normally should. As a result, any food or water that the dog consumes accumulates in the esophagus, along with the saliva that is normally produced and swallowed.
	Signs include regurgitation and weight loss. The condition can be associated with an esophagitis, Addison's disease, myasthenia gravis, or hypothyroidism. It can also occur without an underlying cause.
	In some instances, owners have success managing this condition by hand-feeding afflicted dogs in an upright position and then keeping them upright for another twenty minutes after they eat. They can also experiment, by trial and error, with different foods and feeding methods—dry food hand-fed, meatballs, or canned food. Some dogs even do well with dog food milk shakes!
Ulcer	**Ulcers** can be associated with IBD, liver disease, kidney disease, Cushing's Disease, or medications given for arthritis. Signs consist of vomiting digested blood, which resembles coffee grounds, and passing digested blood in the stools, called melena. This makes the feces appear black and tarry. Treatment consists of medications to decrease acid secretion (Pepcid, Zantac, and Prilosec) and patch bleeding ulcers (Sucralfate).

Hemorrhagic gastro-enteritis	**Hemorrhagic gastroenteritis** (HGE) is characterized by vomiting and bloody diarrhea. It can be caused by any number of things, including diet change, viruses, and bacteria, and it results in the dog having very concentrated blood or a packed-cell volume that is much higher than normal. This is a condition that must be taken very seriously—it can be fatal if not treated appropriately. Treatment consists of hospitalization for IV fluid support and antibiotics as well as medication to help with nausea. While in the hospital, dogs are usually given no food or water orally for 24 hours after the last episode of vomiting, then started back on small amounts of water and a bland diet.
Intestinal parasites	**Intestinal parasites** are probably the most common condition that we see causing gastrointestinal problems. Common intestinal parasites include roundworms, hookworms, whip worms, coccidia, and giardia. Signs include vomiting, diarrhea, and weight loss. We treat these with anthelmintics, which are drugs that kill worms, or with antibiotics. Here's good news: most heartworm preventatives now include medication that kills intestinal parasites as well.

MUSCULOSKELETAL SYSTEM

Obesity	**Obesity** is probably the most common musculoskeletal problem we see. Most people don't even think of obesity as a disease, but they should. After all, dogs who are obese live shorter lives than dogs who are their appropriate weight. They also live more difficult lives, because they have a greater tendency toward arthritis and a harder time getting around. See the diagram in Chapter Six to help you determine if your dog is overweight.
Bone problems *Broken bones*	Most broken bones or fractures cause severe pain and lameness. These are treated with splints or surgery depending on the location and severity of the fracture.
Bone cancer	The most common type of tumor that we see occur in bones is osteosarcoma, but other types do occur. Typically, treatment consists of surgical removal of the limb, followed by chemotherapy. Dogs who have no evidence of metastasis and receive this treatment can live up to a year or more. There are also some new alternative treatments being developed, including "Limb Sparing" and stereotactic radio surgery.
Intervertebral disc disease	**Intervertebral disc disease** (IVDD) is a shift in the cartilage disc (which sometimes becomes calcified or hardened)

	so that it pushes on the spinal cord. Signs range from pain to incoordination or limb weakness to complete paralysis. Treatment can include cage confinement and medications to control pain and inflammation in mild cases to surgery in more severely affected dogs.
ACL tears	Tears in the **anterior cruciate ligament** (ACL) are extremely common sports injuries, and some may have an immune-mediated component to them. Signs include persistent rear limb lameness that can range from mild to severe. We used to treat torn ACLs by creating an artificial ligament with nylon suture materials. More recently, surgeons have begun to use a relatively new procedure called a TPLO, or Tibial Plateau Leveling Ostectomy. Here, the angle of the knee joint is actually changed by cutting the tibia, redirecting its position, and securing it with a metal plate. This has been especially effective in treating large dogs. The long-term outcome is better, because recovery time is shorter, and there is less resultant arthritis.
Arthritis and joint pain	**Arthritis** in dogs can result in persistent lameness, difficulty rising, and trouble with steps or slippery surfaces. Acupuncture can be very helpful in treating arthritis by reducing inflammation, and can help make dogs more comfortable. There are also some benign preparations that can be effective,

	namely glucosamine with chondroitin sulfate, and Cosequin, which can help to increase the viscosity of the joint fluid. Anti-inflammatory drugs like Rimadyl, aspirin, and prednisone can help decrease pain and improve mobility. Ask your veterinarian about potential side effects such as GI ulceration, liver damage, and kidney damage.

LYMPHATICS/LYMPH NODES

Lymphadeno-pathy (lymph node enlarge-ment)	Lymph node enlargement is something that you can easily identify at home. Enlargement of one or many lymph nodes can indicate tick-borne disease, immune-mediated disease, infection, or cancer. Typically, a veterinarian performs a fine-needle aspirate to help discern what the cause of the lymph node enlargement is so that therapy can be implemented. Blood tests may also be required.

URINARY TRACT

Bladder problems *Infections and cancer Bladder stones*	**Bladder infections** occur more commonly in females than in males, but they can occur in both. Signs include blood in the urine and/or straining to urinate. Bladder infections are treated with antibiotics. Chemotherapy is often tried,

but we tend to have only limited success with it.

Bladder stones are fairly common in many breeds, and very common in Dalmatians. The causes include metabolic factors, liver problems, and bacterial infections. Most bladder stones need to be removed surgically. However, there are diets that are tailored to affect the pH of the urine and help dissolve the stones. There can be a problem here, though: when the dissolving bladder stones shrink small enough to leave the bladder, they go into the urethra and can become stuck there. If this is not corrected quickly, it can cause kidney failure and bladder rupture. Diagnosis of some stones may be made using X-rays but some stones that don't show up must be diagnosed using ultrasound or a contrast study of X-rays.

Bladder tumors can occur in male or female dogs. Signs are similar to those that occur with bladder stones. Treatment of bladder tumors consists of a combination of surgery and chemotherapy depending on the location and type of tumor.

Prostate problems *Prostate Infections*	**Prostate infections** can occur in un-neutered male dogs. Signs are similar to a urinary-tract infection but may also include straining to defecate if the prostate is very large. A urine culture and sensitivity should be done to help pick an appropriate

Prostatic hyperplasia *Prostatic cancer*	antibiotic, which should be given for 6–8 weeks. The dog should also be neutered to decrease the chance of recurrence. **Prostatic hyperplasia and cysts** can also cause enlargement of the prostate, and can lead to signs including difficult urination and defecation. X-rays and ultrasound can aid in diagnosis. Treatment usually consists of neutering the dog and surgical removal of cysts. **Prostatic cancer** is typically the only prostate problem that we see in neutered male dogs. It also occurs in male dogs who have not been neutered. Signs are the same as those listed above, and diagnosis is usually made using ultrasound and needle or surgical biopsy. Unfortunately, we don't have a lot of treatment options for this problem. Piroxicam is a medication that can be used to try to shrink the prostate to improve urination and defecation, and stool softeners can help if constipation ensues. A tube can be surgically placed into the bladder (cystostomy tube) to facilitate emptying of the bladder if the tumor in the prostate closes off the urethra.
Kidneys *Kidney infections* *Kidney failure*	**Kidney infections** have similar signs as urinary-tract infections, but may also include signs such as abdominal pain, lethargy, decreased appetite, and sometimes elevated kidney values on bloodwork. Treatment usually consists of long-term antibiotic treatment (6–8 weeks), which is

Kidneys
Kidney
tumors
	tailored to the results from a urine culture. IV fluids may also be recommended.
	
	  Kidney failure can occur in any age dog and in any breed. Signs include increased thirst and urination, weight loss, and decreased appetite. Diagnosis is made using blood-work and a urinalysis. Treatment consists of IV fluid therapy, which can be somewhat effective in small dogs but is not typically very effective in large dogs. We usually keep dogs in the hospital on IV fluids until their kidney values normalize or plateau. Then, if the dogs are feeling well enough to eat and drink without vomiting, they are sent home, and their owners are taught how to give fluids under the skin for as long as the dogs feel good.
	
	  Kidney tumors can occur in any dog. They can cause blood in the urine, weight loss, abdominal pain, vomiting, or no signs at all. An enlarged kidney can be identified using X-rays and ultrasound but diagnosis typically must be made surgically with a biopsy. Treatment and prognosis depend on the type of tumor found.

NERVOUS SYSTEM

Seizures	**Seizures** can be caused by many things, including organ failure, toxin exposure, low blood sugar, inflammatory disease, infections, strokes, broken blood vessels in the brain, tumors, and epilepsy. Once the

	cause of the seizures has been identified and anticonvulsant medications are indicated, there are many medications that can be used to control seizures, the two most common being Potassium Bromide and Phenobarbital.
Encephalitis	**Encephalitis** is inflammation in the central nervous system. Affected dogs can present with seizures, disorientation, and imbalance. Diagnosis is typically made using a cerebrospinal fluid tap, but MRI scans can also be helpful. We typically treat encephalitis with anti-inflammatory drugs and chemotherapy. This is a serious disease, and the prognosis usually runs from fair to poor, depending on the type of encephalitis.
Strokes and vascular accidents	**Strokes** and **vascular accidents** (broken blood vessels) can also affect dogs. Symptoms to watch for include seizures and loss of balance. Typically, we treat these conditions only with supportive care. If the dog is not eating and drinking, we give him nutritional support and IV fluids until he recovers, just as we do with humans. In most cases, dogs with these conditions do recover most of their faculties.
Myasthenia gravis	**Myasthenia gravis** is a neuromuscular disease caused by inappropriate action by the immune system. Affected dogs will demonstrate an inability to get around.

	They can walk normally for a few steps but as they go along, their gait becomes stilted and they will actually lose all muscular control and tone, and collapse. These dogs may also regurgitate due to a megaesophagus. Treatment consists of medications and supportive care, and the disease carries a variable prognosis.
Old dog vestibular disease	**Old dog vestibular disease**, technically known as *canine idiopathic vestibular disease*, is an affliction that we see in older dogs, in which they are completely off balance and tend to roll over and over and over. Their eyes will dart back and forth rapidly. Old dog vestibular disease is usually self-limiting or goes away in five to ten days.

- Remember, if you have any doubts or worries about your dog's condition, get her to your veterinarian or to an emergency-care clinic right away. It could save her life.

Armed with the knowledge of how to spot potential problems and how to interpret what your veterinarian is diagnosing, you are well on your way to keeping your dog young and healthy for a long time.

CHAPTER FIVE

You and Your Vet

ONE DAY I had a very interesting case come into the clinic. He was a four-month-old chocolate Lab named Snickers, and he was suffering from what we call an "intra-hepatic shunt," an abnormal blood vessel structure surrounding a dog's liver. Basically, Snickers's blood did not properly flow through his liver to be detoxified. This was causing the dog severe problems, including lethargy, dementia, seizures, and inadequate growth. That little Lab was just not a happy puppy, and his chances of living a long, normal life seemed very bleak, indeed.

We correctly diagnosed the condition, but that was only a first step: we and his owners still faced a series of very complicated decisions. First of all, the shunt was within the dog's liver, making surgical correction difficult if not impossible. Unfortunately, an intra-hepatic liver shunt is a condition that was previously treated only with diet and medications, leaving the dog with a limited life expectancy. But Snickers's owners wanted the absolute best chance at getting as good a quality of life as they could get for their dog, even if the treatment was experimental. Our surgeons then directed Snickers and his family to the University of Pennsylvania, where doctors were developing a new approach to repairing this type of liver shunt. It was still in an early stage of development, but the procedure, at least in the eyes of the Penn surgeons, showed great promise. The new technique involved a delicate procedure whereby the surgeons use interventional radiology techniques to place a disc into the abnormal vessel in the liver. The disc gradually swells, thus occluding the vessel and forcing blood to be rerouted through the liver in a more normal fashion. We were all intrigued. There were no guarantees, of course, but this new technique seemed to offer Snickers at least a chance.

Snickers underwent the procedure, and it worked as planned. Three days later the pup was back home and enjoying good health. He still needed to take medication and eat a special diet, but he felt great. Thanks to the specialists at the University of Pennsylvania and their commitment to medical research, Snickers now has a chance at a potentially longer, happy life.

Snickers's case highlights several important things that you as a dog owner need to know about veterinary medicine today. First of all, as Snickers's owners quickly discovered, modern veterinary medicine has become almost as specialized as human medical care. Indeed, most of the specialties that we have in human medicine now have their counterparts in animal medicine. For disorders of the brain or central nervous system, you can take your dog to a veterinary neurologist. For skin and coat problems, you can see an animal dermatologist. For cancer, you should consult a veterinary oncologist. If your dog suffers from hip dysplasia or tears a ligament in the knee, you may need a veterinary surgeon. And if your dog has a chronic condition such as arthritis, you may want to consult with a veterinarian who specializes in alternative methods like acupuncture. In my view, this is good news. The trend toward specialization has brought some remarkable advances to veterinary medicine, and the result is better care for all of our animals.

The story of Snickers also highlights an essential truth for all of us dog owners: in this age of specialization, it is especially important that we find and work with a good primary-care veterinarian whose advice and counsel we can trust. Finding the right vet is crucial: you are going to entrust your beloved pet to this person; you need to feel totally comfortable that your dog is going to be in competent and caring hands. With Snickers, the primary-care vet realized that the shunt was beyond his expertise, so he sent the dog's owners on to more qualified specialists. We, in turn, made the right diagnosis and then did the necessary research to get Snickers even more specialized care. In this case, the system worked, in large measure because Snickers's owners relied on a good primary-care vet in the first place. I urge you to do the same.

In this chapter, I will show you how to find a vet or a team of vets that is right for you and your dog. I will explain what to expect from a first visit, and I will give you tips on how to build a strong working relationship with your vet, so that your dog gets the best possible care. I will also discuss the complicated issue of cost. All of this will set, the stage for Chapter Eleven, a comprehensive look at what you as an owner need to know about wellness care and disease prevention. There, I will lay down everything you need to know about your dog's checkups, vaccinations, flea and tick control, heartworm prevention, weight management, and spaying and neutering issues. The first crucial step, though, is finding the right vet for you and learning how to work with him or her in the most effective manner. These are essential first steps in helping your dog lead a full, healthy, and happy life.

How to Find a Vet Who Is Right for You

Let me be candid: all veterinarians are not created equal. Vets have widely differing levels of training, and we each have our different strengths, areas of focus and expertise. When looking for a vet who is right for you and your dog, there are many criteria to consider and many different kinds of vets to choose from. It can be confusing. So before you start your search, let me answer some of the critical questions that my clients frequently ask me.

Q: Dr. Dondi, can I rely on one veterinarian to handle all of my dog's health-care needs?

A: Probably not. In the old days, and in some communities still today, the local vet did almost everything himself. He treated farm animals like cows and horses, and he also treated the family cat, dog, bird, and gerbil. Those days, for better or worse, are almost gone. Today, there are veterinarians who specialize in cows and horses, and others who specialize in dogs and cats. As in the example above, there are veterinarians with even more specialized areas of interest. In general, I think this is good news. You might find a vet today who can treat thoroughbred racehorses as well as your poodle. Generally speaking, though, I think that you are better starting out with a vet whose specialty fits your precise needs. As your dog grows older, he will almost certainly need to see a specialist from time to time, just as we humans do. So no, over the years you probably cannot rely on one vet alone for all of your dog's health-care needs.

Q: Dr. Dondi, are there vets who specialize in healthy animals and others who treat only animals who have something wrong with them?

A: Not exactly. Many primary-care vets today are general practitioners, and they build their practices, primarily, on taking care of healthy animals. Their business is wellness care, meaning routine visits for vaccinations, heartworm tests and prevention, puppy exams, and the like. Their clients do, of course, bring in their dogs when they are sick or injured, and many of these vets do have an excellent array of diagnostic skills and equipment. But many general practitioners don't have the time to treat critically ill animals, and more and more they refer those dogs to their network of specialists.

I am on the other side: I rarely see a healthy animal. In my field of emergency and critical care, we mainly treat animals who are very sick or injured. We do not do vaccinations or "wellness care." So if your pooch needs his ears checked or his teeth cleaned, I'm not the vet to see. But I can tell you this: if your dog gets hit by a car or becomes seriously ill, your best bet is to get him to me or a vet with similar expertise. (As a precaution, I always urge people to ask their primary care vet for the name, address, and phone number of a reliable emergency clinic—and then to keep that information in their wallet and by the phone in case of emergency. See Chapter Twelve: "A Concise First-Aid Manual.")

Q: Do generalists and specialists have comparable training?

A: Only up to a point. In a typical career track, all veterinarians go to veterinary school, after which they take a test to become licensed in general practice. Most specialists, by contrast, get the same comprehensive education in animal care, but then go through several additional years of training. After graduating from veterinary school, they usually do an internship or practice for a while, then go back into a residency program where they train in a particular specialty of veterinary medicine such as internal medicine, surgery, cardiology, oncology, or emergency care. After that, they must pass a test to earn board certification in their field. Only board-certified individuals can legitimately call themselves specialists in a particular field.

Q: Given everything you've said, Dr. Dondi, am I better off with a sole practitioner or a group practice?

A: Good question. In my experience, this is almost entirely a matter of personal preference. In fact, I can offer strong arguments on both sides. If you go to a sole practitioner, you are guaranteed to see the same vet every time you go in. (Unless he or she is on vacation.) And that vet will get to know you and your dog well over the years. That is all to the good.

On the other hand, relying on a sole practitioner can have its drawbacks. It may take longer to get an appointment. And it probably means that one doctor will be making almost all the decisions on his or her own and doing most of the medicine and surgery on his or her own, as well. In the event of a complicated problem, the sole practitioner has no one else close by to ask for a second opinion or to bounce off an alternative approach. In my view, two heads are almost always better than one. So one of the great strengths of a multi-doctor practice is that it offers you a broader range of information and expertise. That can be especially valuable if your dog is sick and needs serious intervention: you have a team of doctors right there to help. Also, as your dog gets older, he will have a variety of different needs, and a multi-doctor practice may enable you to handle those needs under the same roof.

Q: Sounds good. But are there downsides to group practices?

A: It depends. The main complaint that I hear from my clients who visit large, multi-doctor hospitals is the continuity of care, or lack thereof. Now, that is not to say that all large practices lack continuity of care. But some people dislike not getting to see the same doctor every time they make an appointment, and this is a more likely possibility in a large hospital. If this idea bothers you, then a multi-doctor practice may not be for you.

Q: Is cost a part of that decision?

A: It might be. Some group practices have larger facilities, a bigger staff, and more diagnostic equipment. This means that their overhead might be higher, and this can be reflected in the fees that they charge. If cost is an issue for you, you may do better sticking with a smaller hospital. I'll have more to say about cost issues and how to handle them in a moment.

Q: This all sounds pretty confusing, Dr. Dondi. For a first-time dog owner, where is the best place to start?

A: I'm old-fashioned. I believe the essential first step is to find a primary-care veterinarian whom you like and respect, a person who can become your trusted family advisor for years to come. As with your own family doctor, your vet will be the anchor of your dog's well-being, both in sickness and in health. So whether he or she comes from a solo or a group practice, you need to find a vet who has the intuition and patience to get to know your dog, his specific physical and emotional makeup, and his specific health-care needs. Just as importantly, you need to find a vet who has the willingness to listen to your concerns and to give you guidance when it comes to health care, nutrition, exercise, behavior and training. If you find a good primary-care vet, you won't need to worry: if your puppy or adult dog develops health problems, he or she will make sure you get the best possible treatment, either in their clinic or from a qualified specialist that they know and trust. But I would add one caveat.

Q: What's that?

A: It is essential that *you* the dog owner make the effort to learn all you can about how to take care of your dog—and about how to work effectively with your vet. The better informed you the owner are, the better rapport you will have with your vet. And that, ultimately, will mean better health for your dog.

The Selection Process

Now let's get down to specifics: how do you find a vet that is right for you and your dog? As a first step, you can consult your local phone book, but that is not going to give you real firsthand information. Instead, I suggest you begin by asking your friends and neighbors about their experiences with vets in your area, to get their opinions and maybe a referral or two. You can also call a local kennel club for advice. From whatever sources you tap, develop a short list of potential vets, then get to work on the phone. But don't call just one practice; call several. Then glean as much information as you can over the phone.

I have a doctor friend who says this: the most important person in his office is the telephone receptionist. She sets the tone for every relationship between doctor and patient. There is truth in that. So when you call a vet, pay attention to how the phone is answered, whether you're put on hold for a long time, and how long it takes to get an appointment. These are all factors you need to consider in evaluating whether that vet is right for you.

If you do find a vet who sounds promising, set up an appointment to meet and see how you like him or her. When you go in, pay close attention to the conditions in the clinic. Is it clean and inviting? Does it run on schedule? Also, is it a nurse or the doctor who comes in and takes your pet's temperature, heart rate, and respiratory rate? Also, notice if the nurse or vet takes an accurate weight for your dog and puts it in his medical record. They should; it's important.

During the examination process, pay close attention to how the vet handles your dog. Does he or she put your pet at ease? Is he or she able to interpret the actions of your dog in an appropriate way? If your dog is nervous, does the vet perceive that and find ways to relieve the tension? There are no hard and fast rules here; a lot of medicine is intuition, and vets either have it or they don't. Now, even if you are going in solely for vaccinations or a first visit and your dog has no history of health problems, the vet should still do a complete, head-to-tail physical exam. If he or she doesn't, you are not getting your money's worth.

Throughout your session with the vet, notice how much over-all time he or she spends with you and your pet and whether he or she asks you thoughtful questions. This is key: a veterinarian should try to elicit all the information he or she can; he or she needs that to properly care for your pet over the long term. If he or she is not willing to take the time, then this is NOT the right vet for you. If, on the other hand, the vet works hard to glean as much information as he or she can, and if he or she works just as hard to address your concerns and earn your trust and confi-dence, then rejoice: this could be the right vet for you.

Cost

At the end of every visit, though, there comes a reality check: the bill. Have no illusions: taking proper care of your dog is *never* cheap. In evaluating whether a veterinarian is right for you or not, I urge you to be very clear in your own mind about what you are willing and able to spend on pet care. Some own-ers are perfectly happy to spend a king's ransom on their ani-mals; others have to be much more careful. If you are on a tight budget, seek advice from local humane societies or dog rescue groups; they usually know where to get good care at econom-ical prices. Also, some humane societies have veterinarians on staff or bring them in once or twice a week to offer low-cost medical services. That can result in considerable savings. Also, as I will explain in a moment, there is now pet insurance and other ways to handle pet health-care costs.

If you find a vet you really like, my advice is this: discuss cost in an open and forthright manner with the doctor. Some veteri-narians (though not all) will work with you to design a wellness program that addresses your dog's needs and suits your budget, too. Also, many elective tests and procedures can be quite expensive, so it is always best to ask about the price of those in advance. (A set of hip X-rays can easily run you $300, and surgeries $2,000 or more.) Being clear with your vet about money will help you avoid unnecessary conflicts and enable you to work together in a harmonious way for the good of your dog.

Building the Relationship

Once you have found a veterinarian you like, I urge you to be as open as possible with the doctor. Bring forth all the concerns that you have about your dog's health care, and address them fully. Beyond that, seek your vet's advice about nutrition, vaccination schedules, housebreaking the dog, and whatever other issues arise during the life of the dog. "Doctor, we're about to have a baby. How might the dog react to having a newborn in the house?" Or, "We're thinking about getting a kitty. Can you suggest ways that will help the cat get along with our family dog?" Or, "We're flying to Florida next month and we want to bring the dog along. What kind of preparations do we need to make?" Or, "Doctor, our beloved animal is now fifteen years old and is clearly suffering. Can you give us some guidance about how to handle his final days?"

My point is this: your vet should be your closest advisor regarding the health and well-being of your dog. He or she should also be your first and best source of information about how to care for your animal. I give you plenty of good information and advice in this book, but your own vet will know your specific dog. Rely on his or her advice and counsel. Likewise, if you spot any new physical or emotional issue with your dog, be sure to alert your vet in a timely manner. Remember: early detection can save your dog's life.

In building your relationship with the vet, I have one final suggestion: give the doctor honest feedback. If, for instance, the vet suggests a particular food and your dog winds up not liking it, tell the doctor. Likewise, if he or she refers you to a professional trainer, and you don't have a positive experience, tell the doctor. You are giving him or her information he or she needs to know. More importantly, you are protecting the basis of trust and confidence that is at the heart of a healthy relationship between vet and owner.

Questions to Ask Your Potential Veterinarian

Do you have someone in the hospital overnight with the animals?

Do you board dogs?

How do you handle emergencies?

Do you have weekend or evening hours?

Who covers the hospital when you go on vacation?

Can I take a tour of the hospital?

What type of anesthesia do you use? (Inhaled Isoflurane or Sevoflurane are best.)

Who does dental cleanings?

Are dogs placed on IV fluids while they are anesthetized for surgery? (They should be.)

Do you administer pain medications after routine surgeries? (They should.)

Do you run bloodwork in the hospital or send it out to a lab? (In the hospital means your dog gets results faster.)

Is your hospital accredited by the American Animal Hospital Association (AAHA)? (This is an extra credential that can help ensure that the hospital is following a little higher standard.)

Handling the Cost

In many veterinary offices across the United States, you will find a rack of brochures in the waiting area offering specific guidance about rabies vaccinations, dental care, dog training, and what to do about fleas, ticks, and heartworm. In recent years, brochures have appeared on a new subject: pet insurance. So far, not many of my patients use pet insurance, probably no more than 5 percent, but the trend is growing. And I do find myself signing more insurance forms. But it is not yet like some human insurance plans: you cannot go into the vet's office and expect to have everything covered or have it cost only a small co-pay. You will need to pay your veterinarian in full, then file for reimbursement with your insurance company.

Plans vary, so be sure you read any policy *very* carefully before you enroll. For more information, you can consult these Web sites:

www.nationalpetinsurance.com

www.petinsurance.com

www.petshealthgroup.com

www.petcarepals.com

There are other ways to cover routine and unexpected pet-care costs. Some veterinarians now offer clients a special dog-care credit card that covers veterinary expenses and allows clients to pay over time. These are like Visa or Mastercard plans for your dog, with comparably high interest rates. Another way individuals can cover pet-care costs is by setting up a separate savings account dedicated to that sole purpose. It's sort of like a college fund for your dog, to be used down the road just in case he needs it. If you start when the dog is a puppy and have the discipline to put in just five dollars a week, by the time the dog is eight years old you will have more than $2,000, counting interest. That money is enough to at least take the edge off of some unexpected disaster or illness.

Wellness Plans

A growing number of group veterinary practices, modeling themselves after HMOs, offer wellness plans. The premise is straightforward: in exchange for paying a monthly fee, clients get discounts on routine prevention and care, including annual checkups, vaccinations, deworming, and heartworm prevention. Some plans also offer discounts on dental care and spaying and neutering, and some will even allow you to spread out payments in the event your dog suffers a major illness or accident. There are downsides, though. Most of these plans do not cover hereditary problems, preexisting conditions, or many catastrophic illnesses. Nor do they cover services or procedures done outside their own clinic. So is this a perfect solution? I'd have to say no.

My best advice? Be realistic and evaluate what you are willing and able to pay *before* you ever get a dog. And be coldly realistic. Having a dog is *not* cheap. When evaluating what it will cost you, add in food, shelter, toys, treats, health care, and any possible grooming costs. Do you travel a lot? If so, then you'd better add in the cost of boarding, too—and it runs in the neighborhood of $25 a day or more. So if you're planning ten days in Hawaii or the Caribbean, add in at least $250 to board the dog. See what I mean?

But here's the bottom line, what you want to avoid at all cost: taking on the responsibility and joy of having a dog and then not having enough money to properly care for it. In such a case, your dog might wind up in a shelter—or worse. And just ask yourself: how would you feel then?

CHAPTER SIX

DogAge Nutrition

WHEN I WAS a veterinary student at the University of Florida, I spent three weeks doing an externship at the Angel Memorial Animal Hospital in Boston. It's an enormous facility with a very large intensive-care unit that's busy all night long. It was a perfect place to gain hands-on clinical experience. One night in the ICU, we got a call about a little pit bull puppy named Ajax who had eaten four ounces of baker's dark chocolate. Now that's a hefty amount of chocolate for a twenty-pound puppy to ingest, and it could be potentially toxic.

We told the owners to bring Ajax in right away, and it's a good thing we did: the little pup was in terrible shape. Chocolate toxicity can cause symptoms ranging from vomiting and diarrhea to hyperexcitability, seizures, and cardiac arrhythmias. Well, that little puppy was bouncing off the walls, quite literally. We immediately swung into action. The treatment for chocolate toxicity starts with making the dog vomit, then giving him activated charcoal orally. The charcoal helps bind whatever is in the dog's system and carry it out. We then put the dog on IV fluids to help flush out the system. Throughout this treatment, we monitor the blood pressure and heart rate and watch for seizures. Essentially we wait, because there is no antidote for chocolate poisoning. As soon as we started the treatment, little Ajax vomited up a large load of chocolate. That was a good sign. The intern on duty and I then gave him activated charcoal, put in an IV catheter, put him in a cage, and started the IV. Everything seemed to be on course, and we planned to check his heart rate and blood pressure every two hours. Everything by the book.

Soon, though, we had an unexpected problem: Ajax was going nuts in his cage. He was bouncing around, dislodging the IV, and getting himself wrapped in the tubing. We gave him valium to try to calm him down, but it had little effect. Ajax kept bounding around his cage and barking, barking, barking. Reluctant to give him any more sedatives, the intern on duty finally said, "I can't take this anymore." The nurses agreed: "Just let him out. The ICU is an enclosed area. Let him out and see if that will calm him down."

So we let Ajax out and he ran around and around in circles, and the only time he stopped was to poop out more chocolate. That pit bull puppy ran around in circles for a good hour, until he exhausted himself and finally collapsed and slept like a baby. By the next morning he was fine. But I will never forget the expression on his face as he ran around that night: it was pure excitement! He was so crazy, running as fast as he could, all over the ICU, for a full hour. All that from four ounces of baker's chocolate!

I tell this story to make an important point about your dog and people food: watch out! First and foremost, be sure to keep certain people foods far away from dogs. To a dog, chocolate is toxic. So are coffee beans, because of the high degree of caffeine in a handful of beans. Chocolate-covered espresso beans are double trouble. Onions can cause hemolytic anemia. So be careful what you feed your dog: his life may depend on it!

Toxic foods	
Chocolate	Raisins
Onions	Macadamia nuts
Coffee beans	Any form of alcoholic beverage
Grapes	Moldy yogurt

Levels of Chocolate Toxicity

5-lb dog: 5 oz of milk chocolate (four average candy bars) or ½ oz of baker's chocolate

10-lb dog: 10 oz of milk chocolate (more than one jumbo candy bar) or 1 oz of baker's chocolate (one square)

20-lb dog: 20 oz of milk chocolate or 2½ oz of baker's chocolate

30-lb dog: 1¾ lb of milk chocolate or 3½ oz of baker's chocolate

40-lb dog: 2½ lb of milk chocolate or 4½ oz of baker's chocolate

50-lb dog: 3 lb of milk chocolate or 5½ oz of baker's chocolate

60-lb dog: 3¾ lb of milk chocolate or 6¼ oz of baker's chocolate

75-lb dog: 4¾ lb of milk chocolate or 8½ oz of baker's chocolate

Chocolate toxicity is one of the most common questions I answer. I include this chart as a reference in case your dog gets into the Halloween candy or breaks into the pantry.

In this chapter I will tell you everything you need to know about making sure your dog gets a proper diet. I will also lay down twelve rules that will guide you through the complicated issues involved in proper dog nutrition. Along the way, I am going to tackle several familiar food controversies head-on: People food or dog food? Wet food or dry? What about table scraps? My dog loves to eat bones; should I let him? Should pregnant or lactating dogs have a special diet? Should older dogs have a special diet? Should I let my dog eat grass? My dog has put on a few extra pounds; that's not a problem, is it? I'm addressing these issues for one simple reason: properly managing your dog's food and weight is an essential component of Dr. Dondi's DogAge Wellness Program, and it is absolutely key to helping your dog lead a longer, healthier, and happier life. Now, here are Dr. Dondi's twelve rules of proper nutrition:

Rule No. 1: Remember Ajax. We all enjoy giving our dogs treats, and some forms of people food are not at all harmful. But you and every member of your household must understand what kinds of treats you can give and what kinds you can *never* give. Study that list of foods that are toxic to dogs.

Rule No. 2: Keep your dog slim. It's true: slim dogs live longer, healthier, and happier lives. Numerous scientific studies have shown that if your dog is overweight, he or she is more prone to suffer from osteoarthritis, joint pain, and even lameness. And that is just the beginning. In a very significant fourteen-year study done by the Pet Nutrition Research Department at the Nestlé Purina PetCare Company, researchers found that Labrador retrievers with optimal weight and nutrition lived, on average, a full 25 percent longer than their littermates who ate to their fill. Based on this research, the folks at DogAge estimate that dogs with a noticeably tucked-up waist may live as much as 1.8 years longer than heavier dogs. These are very telling results, and one of the main reasons that I have made correct nutrition a cornerstone of Dr. Dondi's DogAge Wellness Program.

In sum, there is no escaping the truth: giving your dog proper meals and snacks—and watching his weight—are among the most important things you can do to help your dog stay healthy and live longer.

UNDERFED   **IDEAL**   **OVERFED**

Diagram provided by Nestlé Purina PetCare, © Nestlé

Dog food or people food? If it doesn't adversely affect your dog's stomach and it's not toxic, technically there is no reason you can't feed table scraps. But you should know that there are several downsides. If you feed your dog people food, he is going to develop a taste for it and then demand it, because it's obviously more palatable than his dog food. Also, it may make your dog more prone to begging at the table—and more finicky about eating dog food. Feeding your dog only people food can also lead to your dog receiving too many calories or an unbalanced diet. Why? Because it is very difficult to build an appropriately balanced diet for your dog using people food You need to carefully balance proteins and carbohydrates, and make sure that your dog gets a proper range of nutrients. Most formulated dog foods, by contrast, go to great lengths, under government regulation, to make sure that your dog receives a good balance of proteins, carbohydrates, nutrients, and vitamins. DogAge says that dogs who are not fed people food may live up to six months longer than dogs of comparable size and breed who are fed people food.

Then there is the problem of toxicity. As I mentioned,

chocolate, coffee beans, and onions can do real damage to a dog. Different breeds, too, can be especially sensitive to certain foods. For instance, schnauzers and shelties are prone to hyperlipidemia, a disorder that can be dangerous and can cause pancreatitis if a dog is fed something high in fat. So, if you let your schnauzer or sheltie lick the bacon grease off the bacon cooker (you'd be amazed how many people let their dogs do that), it can have tragic consequences. Spicy foods can also be trouble. In some dogs, spicy foods can trigger gastrointestinal upset.

Many foods that are seemingly benign can also cause problems, as I learned firsthand. I once treated a two-year-old Labrador retriever who, at his owners' holiday party, ingested two planks of Nova Scotia salmon. Two full planks of it. He was a yellow lab and already obese. But eating all that salmon brought on a terrible case of pancreatitis. I don't know if the dog had an underlying condition like hypothyroidism or hyperlipidemia, because I'd never seen him before. But that poor guy was in our hospital for close to two weeks and, sadly, in the end did not make it. His pancreatitis was too severe for us to save him. By now the lesson should be clear: beware of people foods, especially those that are high in fat. And be especially careful if you have schnauzers and shelties: they seem to be the ones who are most prone to problems.

If you are determined to feed your dog people food, make sure that it is high in protein, low in calories, and low in fat. And please limit the quantity. I am guilty of anthropomorphizing my feelings onto my own dogs, and frequently do things to "doctor" up their food; but I try to do so in a safe manner. I use a few teaspoons of canned dog food or small amounts of boiled rice. I limit the quantities for sure because my Hannah has a little bit of a weight problem and can do without the extra calories. Because of her weight problem, Hannah's DogAge is a little bit older . . . but because I've been pretty stringent about her nutrition, she's younger overall. Her DogAge is 28.5; that's 12.2 DogAge years younger than the average rottweiler her calendar age. I'm happy about that!

Rule No. 3: Make sure you choose a high-quality dog food. You have to feed your dog a well-balanced diet, and the safest way to achieve that is to feed her a high-quality commercial-brand dog food. Generic foods, in my opinion, are not closely monitored or regulated enough to provide all the appropriate nutrients that a dog needs. Most name-brand, over-the-counter commercial diets are, and in a satisfactory way. That said, there are important differences among the store brands, the premium brands, and the super-premium brands. Read their labels and you will find a significant difference in the type of ingredients that are used by the manufacturers. Generally speaking, the more expensive the dog food, the higher the quality of ingredients and the fewer the number of fillers. Also, super-premium dog foods tend to be more nutrient-dense and calorie-dense than the lesser brands. That means you can feed a smaller quantity to your dog which, depending on the dog, may be a plus or minus. If you have a dog that is not satiated with the amount of food you provide, he or she may be driven elsewhere to find other food. You have to find the right balance. A further word about the super-premium brands: they cost more, but for many dogs I think they are worth it. These are the higher-end dog foods that are sold only in specialty stores. Most of them use only organic ingredients, and they use no preservatives, no by-products, and much less filler than the cheaper brands. It is an oversimplification, but you could say the super-premium brands are like filet mignon, whereas the cheaper brands are more like fast food.

Wet food or dry? The main difference between wet food and dry is that wet food has a much higher moisture content. That means it is less nutrient-dense and has less filler. In terms of quality, much depends on the brand. Some wet brands contain higher amounts of fat, and most wet foods, but not all, contain higher amounts of protein, as well. What it comes down to, ultimately, is owner (and sometimes dog) preference. A lot of people simply don't like the smell of canned dog food. Wet food is also more inconvenient at feeding time, and more expensive. Most dogs prefer canned food over dry, but I don't recommend one form over another, unless the dog has a specific problem that needs to be addressed with a dry or soft food. At one time or another, most people have heard that dry food is better for a dog's teeth than wet food. I say it all depends on whether your dog chews his food or not. Most dogs swallow the kibbles whole and only chomp a few of them. (Have you ever noticed what dry dog food looks like when your dog throws it up? It looks like whole pieces, doesn't it?) Therefore, your dog's teeth don't reap as much benefit from dry food as you have been told.

How often should you feed your dog? I recommend feeding your dog twice a day, not just once. That keeps him from getting too hungry, and keeps his metabolism even throughout the day. It can also decrease unnecessary bloating of the stomach by providing two smaller portions of food at different times. Just make sure the twice-a-day feeding does not give your dog too many calories per day. To do this, estimate your dog's caloric requirement and decide what quantity of food he should get per day. (You can also look on the back of the dog-food bag for recommended daily feeding allotments.) Now divide this total amount by two and feed that amount twice daily. You can pick a timeline that best fits your and your dog's schedule for feeding.

Rule No. 4: Treat overweight dogs with a multipronged approach. After my dog Hannah became overweight, I moved forcefully on several fronts. First, I put her on a restricted-calorie diet, based on a prescription food that you can't buy over the counter because it is too restricted in calories. If a dog food is sold over the counter, dog owners can use it at their discretion. Prescription diet foods are more restrictive, and must be used with guidance from a vet. I also changed Hannah's treats—radically. No more biscuits. None. Depending on the brand, a single biscuit might contain more calories than an entire limited-calorie meal. Instead, I gave my dieting dog a baby carrot or two green beans. Sometimes I'd remove some of the day's allotment of kibble and keep it aside to use as treats throughout the day. I also increased her daily exercise, of course. (See Chapter Seven on proper exercise.) The result? She lost weight and probably extended her life.

Rule No. 5: If your dog is overweight, count calories. I actually have a weight-loss formula for determining how much food to serve your dog. Take the dog's weight in kilograms and multiply that by 30. Then add 70. That gives you the maintenance caloric requirement for your dog, meaning the daily caloric intake that will maintain his current weight. Then you calculate 70 percent of the maintenance requirement and feed your dog *only* that amount of calories. You can calculate the right amount by checking the back of the dog-food bag; it tells you how many calories there are per cup of food. Be tough: give your dog that 70 percent and no more. Your dog will thank you during those extra years of his life!

Let me give you an example. Take a twenty-kilogram dog and multiply by 30. This gives you 600. Plus 70 gives you 670 calories as the maintenance caloric requirements. Now multiply 670 by 70 percent and you get 469 calories. This is the number you use to determine how much dog food to feed. You may be able to find out how many calories per cup your dog food contains by reading the label, or you may have to call the company for that information. Either way, feed only that amount of dog food per day and your dog will lose weight! Once your dog reaches his or her goal weight, you can begin feeding them according to the instructions on the dog-food bag. Make sure to keep a close eye on your dog's weight, though. If she begins to put on the pounds, the recommended daily allotment on the bag is too much! If this happens, I suggest you cut the total amount by a quarter and see how that goes. Use this system to arrive at the amount of dog food needed to maintain your dog's desired weight.

Rule No. 6: Many dogs require special diets. Puppies, of course, have special nutritional needs. Many puppy formulas, therefore, are rich in protein, fat, and calories, because these are needed for growth. Working breeds also need food that is higher in protein and calories, while formulas for senior dogs tend to have less protein. Likewise, small-breed puppies need a food richer in calories than large-breed puppies do, because their metabolism is so much higher. Small-breed pups also need to be fed frequently throughout the day.

Large-breed puppies, on the other hand, need to be fed a good-quality diet in quantities that keep their growth rate under control. There have been studies that show that feeding a large-breed puppy 80 percent of what it normally would eat will limit its rate of growth but won't keep it from growing to its full potential. This can reduce excess fat and reduce the chances of your dog developing cartilage defects and other common problems, such as hip dysplasia. With large breeds especially, it is best to keep the dog's maintenance weight on the low side.

Pregnant Dogs. Pregnant dogs should be fed a puppy-formula food. It has more protein, and higher calories and nutrient density. Many people ask me if they should give calcium supplements to their pregnant dog. I say no: do not give your dog calcium supplements prior to the birthing process. In pregnant dogs, there is a natural process that utilizes the calcium stores in the mother's bones to produce milk for the baby. If you give the dog calcium supplementation prior to whelping, it does not allow her body to activate that natural process. The result is not good: after the mother has her puppies and begins to lactate, she can't keep up with her needs and develops eclampsia. That's where the blood concentration of calcium is low. As a result, the dog can start having tremors and seizures. That is something that I also see in dogs that have large litters of puppies, or just small dogs that have puppies. I have not seen it that commonly in larger dogs, but I frequently see it in Chihuahas, Yorkies, and Maltese. Giving calcium supplementation before whelping only worsens the tendency.

Older Dogs. I believe that older dogs with joint problems can benefit from foods with added supplements such as glucosamine and chondroitin. In recent years, many manufacturers have also started putting fish oil and other additives into their foods, and that's good. I have seen research saying that supplements such as fish oil and the omega fatty acids it contains can improve your dog's coat and decrease the kinds of inflammation that often cause various skin problems.

Rule No. 7: Be Careful With Alternative Diets. Pet nutrition is in vogue today, and we're seeing a lot more products and a lot more information on home-cooked and other alternative diets. One new trend is raw-food diets. The thinking here is that dogs are wild animals, or were wild animals, and in the wild they eat other animals, muscle tissue, grass, that type of thing. None of the food that they eat in the wild is cooked or has preservatives. There are companies now that are making raw-food diets that contain raw meat, raw vegetables, and even ground bones.

Caution: I have some serious reservations about raw-food diets. A recent study cultured salmonella from a significant number of the raw-food diets, suggesting that raw foods, though commercially available, were not entirely safe. I myself have treated dogs who suffered from salmonella or bacterial endotoxemia that they got from raw-food diets. I also worry about toxoplasmosis and other parasites and infections that can be passed in a raw diet. I don't agree with the whole-bone concept either, because of the potential for damage to the GI tract. If owners want to feed a diet of whole foods prepared at home, I suggest that they consult a good nutrition book for dog food recipes, and that they cook the food.

Dog owners need to seek out reliable information about any new diet. I strongly recommend that you consult the DogAge.com Web site for the latest information. There are many other Web sites that also offer good advice about a wide range of dog foods. Many also sell food directly to the consumer. Always keep this in mind: food labels are well regulated, and brand-name manufacturers have to put their food through detailed trials to identify the quantity of crude fiber, crude protein, and other ingredients. By carefully reading labels, you can become very educated about dog food, and build a proper nutritional regime for your dog.

Understanding Pet-food Labels

Caloric Statement
Pet-food labels provide the pet owner with a great deal of information. They do not, however, tell everything that a consumer might wish to know about a particular pet food. It is still necessary and important to rely on the manufacturer's testing and research and upon the company's overall reputation to assure that the pet food is of high quality and provides complete and balanced nutrition.

Dog-food labels may also have a statement of the calorie content of the product. This statement must appear away from the guaranteed analysis and be under the heading

---

"Calorie Content." Calories are stated in terms of metabolizable kilocalories per kilogram of food, and may also be expressed as calories per unit of household measure, such as per cup or per can.

Manufacturers may determine the calorie content of their product through calculations based on laboratory analysis of the product, or through feeding-trial procedures established by the Association of American Feed Control Officials (AAFCO).

Additives

Two types of additives are included in pet-food products: those that are nutritional and those that add other benefits to the food, such as preservatives.

Nutritional additives include vitamins, minerals, fats, and amino acids. Many are added in pure form, which may have advantages of cost, availability, and stability. They also permit the supplementation of a product to increase single nutrient levels without disturbing the levels of other nutrients in the diet.

An animal's body cannot distinguish between vitamins that occur in natural ingredients and those that are produced synthetically. The use of synthetic nutrients helps achieve the high degree of nutritional balance found in good-quality pet foods.

The pet-food label lists a number of ingredients that do not necessarily provide nutrient benefits, but that do have a specific purpose in the diet. These types of additives are detailed below:

- Antioxidants—Ingredients such as BHA, BHT, or mixed tocopherols are added to the fats in pet foods in extremely low levels to prevent rancidity and, thus, to prevent the unpleasant odor, loss of palatability, and destruction of vitamins that can occur when fats go rancid.

* Chemical preservatives—Preservatives are used in semi-moist pet foods to prevent spoilage from mold and bacterial growth. These include such ingredients as propylene glycol (not for use in cat food), sorbic acid, and potassium sorbate. All ingredients of this type must be approved by the FDA.
* Flavoring agents—Flavorings are a convenient way to make products more appealing to dogs and cats. Some may have complicated chemical names, but others such as garlic and onion are also used as flavoring agents.
* Coloring—Colors are added to some pet foods to help maintain a consistent product appearance, because the color of natural ingredients can vary, or to distinguish between flavors in a multiparticle food. Artificial colors used in pet foods are the same as those approved for use in human foods.

Current Label Requirements

Label requirements can be broken down into a number of elements. One part of the label that will be referred to in the following discussions is the principal display panel. This is defined as the part of the label that is most likely to be displayed, presented, shown, or examined under normal and customary conditions of display for retail sale.

One important and basic requirement that applies to the entire label is that no statement can appear anywhere on a label that makes false or misleading comparisons between that product and any other pet food.

Product Name

This must be shown on the principal display panel. Where a flavor designation is made, such as "beef flavor," the words "beef" and "flavor" must be in the same size, color, and type of lettering. The source of the beef flavor must be shown in the ingredient list. This might be beef, or beef and bone meal, or similar beef-source ingredients.

If the product name includes the words "beef dinner," "beef dish," or words of similar meaning, the following conditions must be met:

- The named ingredient(s) in the product must be at least 25% but less than 95% of the total ingredients.
- If more than one ingredient is listed in a product name, each ingredient must be at least 3% of the product's weight.
- For the purpose of this provision, water sufficient for processing is excluded when calculating the percentage of the named ingredient(s). However, such named ingredient(s) must be at least 10% of the total product.
- The source must be shown in the ingredient list, and in this case it would be beef.
- Ingredients listed in the product name must be listed in the same order of predominance by weight as in the ingredient statement.

When the product name includes only the word "beef," such as "XYZ Beef Dog Food," this means that beef must constitute at least 95% of the total product. For the purpose of this provision, water sufficient for processing is excluded when calculating the percentage of the named ingredient(s). However, such named ingredient(s) should constitute at least 70% of the total product. If the name is "XYZ Beef, Liver, and Chicken Dog Food," these ingredients must constitute at least

95% of the product, with more beef than liver or chicken, and more liver than chicken. Liver and chicken must each constitute at least 3% of the formulation.

The words "dog food," or similar designations must appear conspicuously on the pet-food label principal display panel.

Any picture or other type of representation of a product on a pet-food label cannot misrepresent the contents of the package.

Guaranteed Analysis
Certain nutrient guarantees are required on the label of all pet foods. These are:

% Crude protein (minimum amount)
% Crude fat (minimum amount)
% Crude fiber (maximum amount)
% Moisture (maximum amount)

If the manufacturer desires to list any additional guarantees, such as vitamins and minerals, in the units defined by AAFCO, these will be shown after moisture.

The reason for the word "crude" is that the minimum or maximum amount shown is determined by lab assay, and is not the amount actually utilized by the animal. Consequently, figures given in the guaranteed analyses do not necessarily indicate nutritional balance or product quality.

The best way to evaluate potential product performance is through statements on the package (such as "complete and balanced nutrition for all life stages substantiated by feeding trials"), by the reputation of the manufacturer, and by past product performance.

Ingredient List

All ingredients used in manufacture of the pet food must be listed in the ingredient list on the label. The ingredients must be listed in descending order of predominance by weight. No reference can be given to ingredient quality or grade in the ingredient list. The names of all ingredients must be shown in letters that are the same size, color, and type.

If meat and/or meat by-products are used in the pet food, and if the animal species is other than cattle, hogs, sheep, or goats, then the source must be designated. For example, if the meat is from horses, the label should state "horse meat" or "horse by-products."

Here is an example of a pet-food product Guaranteed Analysis and Ingredient List:

Purina ONE® Brand Dog Food
LIFELONG HEALTH Chicken & Rice Formula

GUARANTEED ANALYSIS

Crude Protein (Min)	26.0%
Crude Fat (Min)	16.0%
Crude Fiber (Max)	3.0%
Moisture (Max)	12.0%
Linoleic Acid (Min)	1.4%
Calcium (Ca) (Min)	1.0%
Phosphorus (P) (Min)	0.8%
Selenium (Se) (Min)	0.30 mg/kg
Vitamin A (Min)	13,000 IU/kg
Vitamin E (Min)	100 IU/kg
Glucosamine*(Min)	400 ppm

*Not recognized as an essential nutrient by the AAFCO Dog Food Nutrient Profiles.

INGREDIENTS

Chicken, brewer's rice, corn gluten meal, whole-grain corn, poultry by-product (natural source of glucosamine), whole-grain wheat, beef tallow preserved with mixed-tocopherols (source of Vitamin E), natural flavor, dicalcium phosphate, chicken cartilage (natural source of glucosamine), salt, potassium chloride, calcium carbonate, choline chloride, L-Lysine monohydrochloride, vitamin supplements (E, A, B-12, D-3), zinc sulfate, ferrous sulfate, manganese sulfate, niacin, calcium pantothenate, thiamine mononitrate, copper sulfate, riboflavin supplement, pyridoxine hydrochloride, garlic oil, folic acid, calcium iodate, biotin, menadione sodium bisulfite complex (source of Vitamin K activity), sodium selenite.

Directions and dog-food label provided by Nestlé Purina PetCare, © Nestlé

Rule No. 8: Be very careful when switching your dog's food. As consumers, we often see sales and grab the best bargain. Many people do this with dog food. But watch out. Rapidly changing dog foods can cause various gastrointestinal problems, especially diarrhea. To avoid that, gradually mix in the new food with the old—I usually tell dog owners to mix it in over a ten-day period. So if you feed your dog two cups of food per day, on the first day you would feed 1¾ cups of the regular food and ¼ cup of the new food. Then gradually increase the new food and decrease the old until the dog is completely on the new food. Just be gradual enough to avoid any gastrointestinal upset. Please note: if you are changing the diet to a different nutrient density or protein or fat content, it might not matter how gradually you make the change; it may cause gastrointestinal upset in any case. If the problem continues, you have probably chosen the wrong food.

Rule No. 9: Work closely with your vet regarding nutrition. Begin when your dog is a puppy. After a year, you should move the dog from puppy food to adult food. After that, you can put most nutrition issues on automatic pilot. But if your dog develops a problem such as frequent vomiting or diarrhea, or weight gain or loss, you should work extremely closely with your vet, first to diagnose the problem and then to effectively treat it and provide nutritional support to the dog. As your dog ages and goes through different life stages, you will again want to consult with your vet about changes in the dog's food and supplements.

If your dog becomes overweight, you should consult your vet if you put your dog on a rigorous diet and he or she still does not lose weight. In that case, your dog may have a thyroid problem. First, though, make sure that no one else in the house is feeding the dog or that he is not helping himself to cat food or the other dog's food when you're not looking. If you have controlled your dog's intake and he still does not lose weight, see your vet.

Rule No. 10: No bones! Let me tell you a cautionary tale. One day a friend of mine took my dog, Hannah, to a company party of about twenty-five people. When no one was looking, dear Hannah scarfed down the remnants of a huge lunch of barbecue ribs. As soon as she arrived home, I could see that her stomach was enormous. I knew that if I took an X-ray, her tummy was going to be full of bones. I decided against taking her into surgery that night, because I knew there was a possibility that the bones would pass through her system and not cause serious damage. I knew the signs to watch for and kept a vigilant eye over the next few days, knowing that we still might need to go to surgery. So Hannah got only water for the next twenty-four hours and I prayed.

Hannah is a dog who has little sense, especially when it comes to food. I imagine she would eat until she burst—she is that driven by food. In this case, she was so uncomfortable and her stomach was so distended that she just lay down groaning and did not move for hours. Then she began passing what seemed like concrete, and she did that for several days. When I started her back on food, I gave her a bland diet and bulked it with rice so that, hopefully, it would bind any of the bones and carry them through. Luckily, she came through just fine.

Nevertheless, I have a rule: I just don't give bones to my dogs—and I recommend that you adopt the same rule. Over and over I see dogs come into our clinic with bone-related problems. Sometimes they come in with marrow bones lodged around their lower jaw; they get them up and over their canines and we can't get them off. We have to anesthetize the dog and use the "Jaws of Life" (hedge trimmers) to get the bone off. Time and again we have to surgically remove bones from dogs' stomachs and intestines. It keeps me in business, but my heart aches every time.

A couple of months ago, we had a two-year-old mastiff, a huge dog who, unfortunately, was very ill. In fact, he died just as he came into our waiting room. It turns out that the dog had ingested a large bone a little more than forty-eight hours earlier. He had even seen a vet, who X-rayed it and said, "Yes, the bone is there. You can have us take it out right now or see if it causes a problem." The vet told the owner that nine times out of ten, the bone dissolves or passes through and doesn't cause a problem, which is true in most cases. The owner decided to wait. In this case, though, the bone had perforated the dog's stomach, and it wound up killing him. I don't think that the vet did anything wrong by saying you have the option to wait. In fact, I would have said the same thing. But the lesson is clear: if you don't want to risk being the unlucky one out of ten, don't feed your dog bones in the first place.

Rule No. 11: Let them eat grass. Many people think that dogs eat grass in order to calm their stomach or to induce vomiting. Maybe. But in springtime my dogs love to eat grass even when they are blooming with good health. I think it's because the grass tastes good. Yes, dogs sometimes eat and eat grass until they vomit, and maybe they do so in search of relief. But I also believe that dogs often eat grass because it tastes so good, green and fresh. So I say, let them eat grass—as long as they are not eating toxic plants along with it. Obviously, though, you want to monitor the habit. If your dog starts acting abnormally—if eating grass is a new thing or is done obsessively, or if he stops eating, starts to vomit, develops diarrhea, begins to strain to defecate but can't, or becomes lethargic—something is wrong. Also, if the dog can't get comfortable while lying down, or is stretching and groaning, these can be signs of abdominal pain. In all these instances, go to the vet. Or at least call for advice.

Rule No. 12: Never leave a chicken on the counter. I learned this one the hard way. I bought one of those lovely baked chickens from the store, and put it on the counter for a moment as I prepared the rest of dinner. I turned away from the chicken for about half a second to pick up the phone and turned back to find that it had disappeared. In the other room I saw Hannah attempting to devour the entire chicken before I noticed or could get to her, whichever came first. I commanded her to "Drop that chicken!" but could only watch as she inhaled it even faster as I approached. Although Hannah suffered no ill effects (thank goodness) and I had salad for dinner that night.

CHAPTER SEVEN

Good Exercise

ONE AFTERNOON, a Dalmatian was brought into the hospital with a racquetball lodged in his throat! Poor guy!! He was in the middle of a happy game of catch with his owner, he jumped up to grab a throw, and—*kerplunk!*—the ball slid right down his throat, like a pitch disappearing in the catcher's glove.

The owner, a fireman, arrived at our clinic in a complete panic. That ball was lodged so tightly in his dog's throat that there was nothing he could do. The dog could barely breathe, and by the time he got to me he was almost dead. He just lay limp and blue on my examining table. Knowing we probably had only a few seconds to save him, I reached my hand into his mouth. I could feel the ball but I couldn't get ahold of it—it was too slippery to grasp. Luckily, there was a crack in the ball, and I was able to push my finger through and get ahold of it. As soon as his airway cleared, the Dalmatian took a huge deep breath and gave me the biggest, most grateful grin I've ever seen. We were all relieved; he was going to live.

I had another patient come in because he had swallowed one of those hard-rubber jingle balls. This time, the ball had gotten lodged in the oropharynx, the back of the mouth, and the dog could breathe but couldn't swallow. His owners actually brought him in for drooling; they had no idea that he had swallowed the ball. This dog was wide awake, so I had to anesthetize him to try to get the ball out. This ball was also too slippery to grasp, so I actually had to maneuver the ball around until a little hole in it was visible. Then I managed to guide a pair of forceps into the hole and extract the ball. The dog recovered nicely and, being the eternal optimist, I would like to think that he learned his lesson, but I'm sure he did not. My point is this: almost every week I treat dogs who have run into trouble while out playing or exercising. Therefore, in this chapter I am going to highlight the need that all dogs have for exercise, but I am also going to identify some of the dangers of certain forms of exercise and the type of injuries they often lead to. I am not trying to be a party pooper. Staying away from danger is an important part of Dr. Dondi's DogAge Wellness Program. As I and every other dog owner knows, one of the great joys of dog ownership is playing with your four-legged pal. But as you will see, careless play or exercise can land you and your dog right in the emergency room, and that's no joy for either of you. So now let's get down to business: how do you establish a safe exercise routine?

Understand your dog's individual needs. Regarding exercise, there are no hard-and-fast rules, no magic formula that fits all sizes and breeds of dog. Every dog, like every human being, has different exercise needs and different athletic abilities. My dog Hannah, for instance, has nerve damage in her left back leg. This prevents her from engaging in vigorous forms of exercise, but she does just fine with milder forms like walking. I plan her daily exercise with those limitations in mind. But make no mistake: all dogs, young or old, big or small, need some form of exercise or play every day. Some dogs will stay happy and healthy with a good daily walk outside. Others crave Frisbee, a long hike, playing ball, or a cooling swim, especially in the summer heat. And still others live for a daily romp at the dog park, running and roughhousing with other dogs. So with a new puppy or a new adult dog, your first job is to figure out what type and level of exercise makes your dog happy and keeps him well-balanced, physically and emotionally.

This is not hard to do. Take him out on the lawn or to the park and see if he likes to fetch a tennis ball or a rope toy or a Frisbee. Or take him to the dog park and see how readily he plays with other dogs. Take him for a mountain hike or to the beach for a swim and a long walk. With each of these activities, pay close attention to how long it takes your dog to get a good workout and even to wear himself out. (Just be careful not to overdo it, especially in warm temperatures.) That will give you a good idea how much exercise he needs to feel happy and healthy—and how much exercise might be too much.

In this vein, it is also helpful to understand the natural tendencies of your dog's breed. A small poodle, Chihuahua, or papillon, for instance, may be very content with a daily walk or two on the leash and some ball-playing inside, while working or herding dogs like Border collies or Australian shepherds may need much more active exercise in order to feel good physically and mentally. If those dogs don't get enough exercise, they often get very restless and hyper. German short-haired pointers, too, require loads of physical activity, and so do Weimaraners, which have tremendous energy and athletic ability. Whippets and greyhounds are a different story. They might seem to be born to run, and you might imagine that whippets and greyhounds need long, hard runs every single day. But no. Once they are mature, they can be very content lazing around the house. My mom has three whippets and all they want to do is stay curled up on the couch under a blanket. She'll take them out into the yard and they may zip around a little bit, but they are basically house dogs, couch potatoes, and they have not suffered any emotional problems from staying in. Young greyhounds and whippets, though, may need to run to feel happy and healthy.

In my experience, the most challenging breeds when it comes to getting enough exercise are the herding breeds: Border collies, Australian shepherds, and Australian cattle dogs. If these breeds get plenty of rigorous exercise, fine: they stay happy, balanced, and mentally healthy. But if they are housebound, and their energy and natural herding instincts find no healthy outlet, watch out: they can get frustrated and destroy the house, or exhibit other neurotic tendencies. In fact, one example comes immediately to mind. In our area of northern Virginia, there was a sweet Border collie who developed an unusual habit. If let outdoors unsupervised, she would round up the neighborhood children and sequester them in a circle in the middle of the street. Any "strays" would be nipped in the ankles to keep them in place. It was hard to blame the dog. That was the only avenue she had to express her natural instinct. Nonetheless, it was terrifying for the kids, and it caused much embarrassment to her owners because it was interpreted as an aggressive act. Needless to say, she is no longer free to roam. I only hope that her owners found a safer form of exercise and play. The bottom line is this: no matter what your dog's breed is, you still have to take the time to understand your individual dog's exercise needs.

Exercise two birds with one stone. By that I mean find an exercise routine that works well for your dog and for your own exercise needs, too. And here I have good news: what is good exercise for your dog is usually very good exercise for you, as well. Most doctors recommend that we humans get at least thirty minutes of quality exercise every day. That does not necessarily mean powerhouse mountain climbing, kick boxing, or a Schwarzenegger-like weight-lifting routine. Vigorous walking for thirty minutes is great. So is thirty minutes of playing fetch with your dog. So I urge you to take good care of yourself and your dog at the same time. Go for a walk together. Or a hike in the mountains. Go to the beach and take your dog for a swim— or swim together. Go biking together (but see my caution below). Or play catch or Frisbee together (again, see my cautions below). Your pooch will get her exercise and you'll get yours. My best rule of thumb? Make sure that your dog gets fifteen minutes of play or exercise, three times a day.

Playmates and dog-walkers. If you live alone, or if you and your spouse both have full-time jobs, you still have to make sure your dog gets a healthy walk and some playtime every day. How do you do that? Let me offer a few suggestions. First, consider getting the dog a playmate. When there are two dogs in the house, they can entertain each other and they rarely lack for exercise. They find their own ways to play and blow off steam. Second, if the dog is home alone and you're busy all day, you might want to hire a professional dog-walker. Third, if you have children, by all means enlist their help with the dog's exercise and playtime. It's good for the dog and good for building your children's sense of responsibility. Fourth, many of my single friends, who have no children, hire responsible neighborhood kids to take their dog out for a romp. (Let me repeat one word: *responsible*.) No matter what option you choose, the aim is the same: to make sure that your dog gets adequate exercise and playtime every day. You won't regret it—as the DogAge Test makes clear, proper daily exercise will extend the life of your dog.

Be careful: some activities can be dangerous. No matter what form of regular exercise you choose for your dog, there are always risks involved. As I mentioned, I've had dogs rushed to my clinic with a seemingly harmless ball lodged in their throat. And I can't tell you how often I've treated dogs with torn cruciates or injured backs from what seemed like harmless exercise.

Now, how to exercise your dog safely? My general advice is to use common sense. Sports injuries can happen with any activity. It's usually something that just happens—an accident. That said, I do want to set forth a number of primary points of concern. Here we go:

Frisbee

It's a beautiful sight, isn't it: seeing an athletic dog in the park or at the beach chasing after a soaring Frisbee and then leaping into the air to catch it. But there are risks to playing Frisbee with dogs, and I see them frequently. One injury I often see is a backbone injury called traumatic prolapse of an intervertebral disc. This is a condition in which a cartilage disc that sits between two vertebrae in the back slips out of place and puts pressure on the spinal cord, causing weakness in the hind legs or even paralysis. This injury can happen easily when playing Frisbee because of the dramatic stress placed on the spine when leaping and twisting in the air and then coming down hard onto the ground. These motions can be traumatic enough to pop a disc out of place. In many cases, the problem can be corrected with surgery, followed by a prolonged period of restricted activity and acupuncture treatments. Unfortunately, though, the damage to the spinal cord is sometimes too great and the dog winds up permanently paralyzed. Needless to say, that's a miserable outcome. Not to mention costly: back surgery can cost you up to about $3,500. Pretty expensive for a Frisbee romp in the park. Consider yourself forewarned.

Another common problem associated with very vigorous activity is FCE, or fibrocartilaginous embolism, a spinal-cord injury that is kind of like the injuries caused by a stroke. We also see muscle strain and ligament tears, especially in the knees in dogs who play Frisbee or engage in aggressive ball-playing. Just like people, dogs frequently tear their anterior cruciate ligaments, or ACLs. The solution is usually an expensive surgery (at least $2,000), followed by a long process of healing, about eight weeks of physical therapy, and a lifetime of being extra careful.

Leaping for a Frisbee can also put strain on a dog's hips. But contrary to what some people might think, it does not cause hip dysplasia. That malady is actually a malformation of the cox-ofemoral joints. Strenuous exercise will sometimes create abnormal friction or pressure on the joint, and this may lead to inflammation and the onset of osteoarthritis or degenerative joint disease. In terms of hip dysplasia, though, dogs are either born with it or they're not.

Let me make my point here as clearly as I can: When I see dogs jumping high in the air to catch a Frisbee, I cringe because I know the potential problems. If you ask their owners to deny their dogs the enjoyment of playing Frisbee, they say it interferes with their quality of life. Okay. But I think that there are safer forms of exercise.

Bicycles

I also get nervous when I see a dog owner riding a bicycle with his dog tethered on a leash and running alongside. Let me tell you: that is rarely a happy dog. Just imagine what you'd be experiencing if you were on a leash and were forced to run alongside someone on a bicycle. Well, the dog is experiencing the same thing. Nevertheless, the dog is in that obedience frame of mind and she can't exactly say, "Hey, I can't go any faster or farther!" So when running alongside a bike, a dog can easily be pushed beyond her limits, and that makes me very nervous. It can lead to heatstroke, muscle injury, ligament tears, and more. There are other risks, too. I've seen leashed dogs running alongside a bike and then, out of the blue, the dog spots a cat or a squirrel and everybody goes flying. All of this is common sense, and you would think that people would be more careful, but no. I see the frightening results all the time, right on my operating table.

Playing With Sticks

For reasons that go beyond simple logic, kids and dogs seem to be almost mystically attracted to sticks. Most dogs love to chase sticks, and many dogs love to chew them. So I am not about to oppose all forms of stick play. I just want to say, as your mother probably did: be careful when you play with sticks. They can be very dangerous. I've treated dogs who have impaled themselves on sticks, and I've seen other serious injuries resulting from stick throwing. So fetch is fine. But why not toss tennis balls or rope toys instead?

Toys

Some toys do worry me. Over the years, I have taken parts of rubber toys and nylon bones out of the intestines of too many dogs. These are toys that are supposed to be chew-proof, but there are some dogs who apparently do not read the label. I have treated several dogs who have chewed off the end of the nylon bone and then had the bone bit wind up obstructing their insides. Nylon rope toys are safer than sticks, but they can be dangerous, too, if ingested. Even seemingly harmless stuffed animals can lead to problems. I once treated a little Chihuahua who had swallowed the eye of a teddy bear. Not pretty. The problem, of course, usually has more to do with the dog and its tendencies than with the toy, but the lesson is the same: you have to be very, very careful. Be sure to watch them when they play with toys.

Swimming

Many dog owners love to take their dogs to the beach. They throw a ball out into the water and the dogs run and swim after it—if they can swim and if they enjoy the water. Not all dogs do. Some dogs, like people, are more comfortable in the water than others. In fact, there are certain breeds that love to swim and others that don't, although most dogs can learn to swim if they have to. So rely on your dog to show you his abilities and his limits. The good news is that swimming is one of the best forms of exercise for dogs. It's easy on their joints, it uses their muscles well, and it's physically taxing. If you want to see a zonked-out dog, take him to the beach to play for a day. And watch him sleep soundly all night long!

The only real problem that I have seen associated with swimming is a condition that I affectionately refer to as "Swimmer's Tail." It seems that every spring, I see five or six labs who come in with what their owners describe as nebulous pain. At home, the dog can't seem to get comfortable, cries when it sits, and is holding its tail down. On physical exam, I find that the base of the tail is extremely painful to the touch. When I ask if the dog had a full day of jumping into the water to swim the day before, the answer is invariably, "Yes." I surmise that when the dog jumps into the water repeatedly, the tail slaps against the water again and again, and this causes soreness. X-rays are typically normal, and the dog returns to normal after a few days of analgesics and exercise restriction. I'm sure if you asked the Lab, he'd say that "Swimmer's Tail" is a small price to pay for a full day of fun.

Watch out for dehydration. There is no mystery here. When you take your dog out for exercise, be sure to take plenty of water along. Most dog parks have water taps available, but I always carry a couple of bottles of my own if we are going to be out for a prolonged period of time. I always keep a water dish in the car, too, and there are handy collapsible bowls that you can buy that are ideal for long hikes or runs. Be especially careful, of course, in hot weather.

Breathing problems and heatstroke. Every summer I treat dogs for heatstroke, and it is one of the most serious and deadly conditions that I see. Dogs who are dark in color, thick-coated, and/or overweight are especially at risk, and so are the so-called brachiocephalic breeds: the bulldogs, Boston terriers, French bulldogs, and pugs. These smoosh-faced breeds tend to have a lot of extra soft tissue in their airways, and that makes them prone to breathing problems and heatstroke, especially in hot weather. So be very careful when you exercise them; if they start to pant excessively, stop! Likewise, be careful in the heat if you have a black Labrador, a rottweiller, or any other dark-coated dog. Hot temperatures can hit them especially hard. Vigorously exercising them in the summer is just not a smart thing to do. During the summer, my dark-coated Hannah goes on only short walks with me or her dog-walker, and we walk her in the shade only. Active exercise should be done in the mornings or in the evenings when—and only if—it's cooler. The reason is simple: breathing problems and heatstroke can be life-threatening. So know your dog, know the characteristics of her breed, and plan your exercise and play routines accordingly.

How to spot heatstroke. Most dogs brought into my clinic with heatstroke have a similar story. Their owner takes them out for a run or walk in warm or hot weather and they simply give up on the walk. They lie down and will not get up. That is a clear sign of overheating or, worse, of heatstroke. Pay close attention, too, if dogs pant excessively while outside or come back from the walk, lie down inside, pant excessively, can't get comfortable, and then become lethargic. The onset of heatstroke is usually pretty dramatic—you'll know that something is wrong. If, for instance, your dog lies down on the walk and will not get up, get him to an emergency clinic. Likewise, if your dog has been locked in a hot car, and you see excessive panting, discomfort, or collapse, get him to a clinic right away. You can pour cool or lukewarm water over the dog to cool him down. Give him drinking water and get to the nearest emergency clinic ASAP.

What does the vet do for heatstroke? Each case is different, but typically we provide the dog with IV fluid therapy and we slowly cool him down. The most common secondary effect of heatstroke is a condition we call disseminated intravascular coagulation (DIC). In layman's terms, this is a process in which the blood begins to form clots in the vessels, thus using up the clotting factors and causing bleeding into the tissues. Death occurs from organ failure associated with thrombosis (blood clots) and severe bleeding. It is obviously a very serious condition, and a lot of dogs don't survive it.

Will a summer haircut help avoid heatstroke? Not necessarily. Many dogs may be more comfortable with less hair in the summer heat, but you still have to be very careful when it comes to heatstroke. If you have a thick-coated or longhaired dog, it can help in summer to shave their coats, but it won't prevent possible problems if it's 95 degrees outside. If you have a shorthaired dog, I see little to gain by close-cropping its hair in summer. Dogs expel most of their heat through panting, so shaving their coats shorter isn't going to allow them to cool themselves any better.

Exercise for the Overweight Dog

Always be careful with an overweight dog, especially regarding exercise. If your vet tells you that your dog is overweight and you should increase his activity, it does not mean that you should take him out and make him run along the bicycle for two miles. Use common sense. How would you feel if somebody asked you to go out and run a few miles cold turkey? For many of us couch potatoes, that would not be a happy prospect. Instead, gradually increase the amount and intensity level of the dog's physical activity and exercise. Remember, too: exercise doesn't have to be difficult or taxing in order to be effective. A brisk walk through the neighborhood is a very effective way to exercise your dog. The exercise should also be fun and engaging for the animal: throwing a ball, throwing a stick, or playing tag. My Georgia loves to play tag and, of course, she's always "it." I tag her and then I run and hide. She'll actually play hide-and-seek, too. I say, "Georgia, I'm going to go hide," and she'll run to the opposite end of the room so I can go hide. Then she runs around the house to find me. It's good exercise for both of us, and she loves it.

Exercise for the Aging Dog

I have written about injury and disease rehabilitation in an earlier chapter, but I do want to say a few words about aging dogs and dogs recovering from injuries. As always, common sense is your best guide. But try this: use the DogAge Test to determine your dog's biological age in human terms; that will help you picture his condition properly. If your dog is over sixty years in DogAge years, or people years, would you take him out running? How about an all-day hike? I didn't think so. You should always try to make your dog's daily exercise appropriate to his age and physical condition. I used to live next door to an elderly man who had an ancient Jack Russell terrier named "JR." He was eighteen years old, and was as crotchety as they come, but with his owner he was as gentle as a lamb. Every day at 7:30, 12:30, 3:30, and 8:30, like clockwork, you would see the two of them tottering down the street. You could set your watch by them. Their pace was slow but steady as they made their way around the block and down the alley. JR had a special little "hitch in his git along" that made my neighbors and I smile as we watched them walk. I think that those daily walks were what kept old JR, and his owner for that matter, going as long as they did. To me, the two of them are proof that exercise can keep you younger. So like JR's owner, try to keep your dog as active as he has the ability to be. This can help him, and possibly you, to live a longer life.

Examples of Good Exercise	
Walking	Swimming
Hiking	Hide-and-seek (Georgia loves this game)
Jogging (if the weather is good and your dog is fit)	
	Tug-of-war
Fetching a ball or toy	

CHAPTER EIGHT

Dog Safety

FREDDY, A HEARTY, 150-pound bullmastiff, had a devilish habit: he loved his owner and he loved to rummage through her laundry. In fact, he liked to do more than just rummage. The first time I saw Freddy he was only a year old and he was in dire straits. He had not eaten in four days, and the poor guy had been vomiting for a full two and half days. His owner had no idea what was the matter. Well, we did some testing and found that Freddy's gastro-intestinal tract was completely blocked. So we rushed him into surgery, and lo and behold, what did we find? Panty hose!

Ah, that Freddy. Who knew what strange hunger lurked inside that dog? I didn't, that's for sure. The surgery was successful, Freddy recovered nicely, and of course I assumed that Freddy—and his owner—would learn their lesson. In fact, I urged the woman to henceforth store her laundry in a secure hamper, tucked away in a closet. And, stupid me, I thought that was the end of the story.

Six months later, Freddy was back in my clinic. Same symptoms. This time Freddy had not gobbled down panty hose. No, this time it was a long, satin nightgown, very chic, too. In surgery, we extracted it from his intestines in big, wadded-up pieces. It was not pretty. Nor was it cheap: for a dog of Freddy's size, these surgeries run from $3,000 to $4,000 each. Upon Freddy's discharge from the hospital, I gave his owner some stern counseling about dog safety, and this time I felt certain that she would follow my advice and establish a secure system for her laundry. For the sake of Freddy—and her wallet.

Alas, a year later, the happy couple was back. Same symptoms. "What happened?" I asked. "Didn't you take precautions?"

The poor woman blurted out her tale of woe. Yes, she had taken to putting all her laundry in what she thought was a secure hamper. And she kept the hamper in her closet—behind a closed door. But Freddy was determined; there was just no curbing his appetite for her laundry. Somehow he had figured out how to turn the knob on the closet door, open it, and then have free access to the treasures inside her hamper. This time it was another nightgown. And another costly surgery. By now, Freddy had become a $12,000 bullmastiff.

"You know, this is ridiculous," I told Freddy's owner. "*He* is not going to learn from his mistakes. *You* are the one who has to learn the lesson. Do you realize he could die from one of these episodes?" I told her to go to the hardware store straightaway and buy a dead bolt for the closet door. I told her that it would be a worthwhile investment: about $1.39 to save another $3,000 or $4,000 in surgery. Good heavens, it was simply common sense.

Four months later? Yes, the woman called me again in a panic. "I just caught Freddy in my closet! He had my bra in his mouth, and when I yelled at him he just went right ahead and swallowed the whole thing! Right in front of me!"

I didn't know whether to laugh or cry. When she arrived at the clinic with Freddy in tow, the woman was absolutely beside herself. I gave her three options. One, another surgery. Two, I could try to pull the bra out with an endoscope. Or three, I could try to make poor Freddy vomit up the bra. At this stage, the woman confessed that she had run out of money. Even the endoscopic procedure was too expensive for her now. She told me to try to make Freddy vomit. It was our only option. If it failed, she could not afford another surgery.

Well, luck was with us. I gave Freddy a dose of apomorphine, a drug that induces vomiting. Ten minutes later, Freddy brought up the entire bra that he had swallowed, right there on our clinic floor. Talk about a fortuitous upheaval: it saved his owner a lot of money and it probably saved Freddy his life.

What can you say? By the age of three and a half, that poor animal had suffered more trauma than most dogs suffer in a lifetime—and in my eye very little of it was his fault. I'm sure his DogAge, had I calculated it, would be significantly older than his calendar age. Sure, he had a weird taste in snacks, but it was up to the owner to take responsibility and protect her dog. Sad to say, though, I see cases similar to Freddy's more frequently than I care to admit. And the root cause is always the same: dogs suffer senseless accidents and illnesses for only one reason: their owners failed to adequately "dog-proof" the pet's environment. Folks, you do not need to be Einstein. Take the time to study this chapter, then get busy and make your home and yard safe for your dog. If need be, lock away your hamper! It may save your dog and your wallet.

How to Dog-Proof Your Home

The first step is to take into consideration the specifics of your individual dog. Is it a puppy? Or is it an adult rescue dog that is new to your family? What history of the dog do you know? If you have a puppy, you can count on him to chew anything and everything. If you think there is something he will not chew on, he definitely will. And if you think there is something that he would NEVER eat, you're wrong: puppies will try to eat *everything*. Therefore:

Get anything that is valuable out of harm's way. If you have expensive shoes, and your dog can get into your closet, put those shoes away safely, up on a shelf. Also, it's best not to introduce old shoes, socks, or clothing as chew toys for your dog, because later your dog won't be able to discern the difference between play shoes and your brand-new running shoes. Even if your dog doesn't play with shoes, it is always a good policy to make sure that your closet door closes securely. You might not need a dead bolt, like Freddy's owner, but at least make sure the door latches shut. Beware of any door that can simply be pushed open.

Beware of small objects that sit on the floor. For instance, those little triangular rubber doorstops are invitations to disaster. Puppies can chew them and—worse—they can swallow them. Anything that sits on the floor that is movable or could be ripped up should be taken up and put out of reach.

Consider crate-training your puppy. There is a lot to be said for crate-training. It facilitates housebreaking, and puppies are usually safer and easier to train if you keep them in a large crate or cage while unsupervised. The crate also keeps puppies from ingesting things they shouldn't. And it keeps your home safer. If you don't like the idea of crate-training, try letting the dog have the free run of one room, such as the kitchen or bathroom. You can put up a baby-gate to keep the puppy from roaming. But beware: if your pup is teething he might start chewing the bottoms of bathroom or kitchen cabinets. That can be costly, of course. Many people are willing to give their puppies free run in the house. But I can tell you this: those dogs tend to be harder to housebreak than those who are crate-trained. Let me add a safety concern, though, about crate-training: if your puppy is a chewer or shredder, do not put towels or blankets inside the crate. These can be chewed up and swallowed. And you, dear owner, will wind up with a Freddy story of your own.

Carefully store all medications. Whether you have a puppy or an adult dog, you have to be very careful about all medications. Think of it this way: your dog is just like your child—you have to protect him from medications and other toxic substances. How do you do that? First of all, keep your medications locked up. And I mean *all* of them. For instance, you might think that Advil, Tylenol, and other nonsteroidal anti-inflammatory drugs are not dangerous. Wrong: they are very toxic to dogs. Some of the popular anti-inflammatories are more toxic than others, but they are all dangerous. Also, since most of them taste bitter, the manufacturers coat them with either a coating with no taste or one that tastes good, which makes them even more appealing to dogs. Advil, for instance, has a sugar base, and I have seen dogs who will gnaw on an Advil bottle as gleefully as if it were a rawhide bone. They don't know it's an Advil bottle; they chew it because it's there and seems like a toy. But then out comes the Advil, and those pills taste so good. I have treated lots of dogs for Advil toxicity. For your protection and that of your dog, I include here a list of common toxic substances.

Acetone (nail polish remover)
Ammonia
Antifreeze
Bleach
Charcoal lighter
Chocolate (all varieties)
Deodorants
Detergents/soap
Furniture polish
Gasoline
Ibuprofen
Kerosene/fuel oil
Lead
Lime
Lye
Organophosphate insecticides
Paint thinner
Phenol cleaners
Rat poison
Rubbing alcohol
Strychnine
Turpentine
Tylenol

Safety in Your Yard

Before your dog ever sets a paw in your yard, you should go over it with a fine-tooth comb and remove anything that could be ingested, especially anything toxic. If you move into a new house, do the same thing. This applies if your dog is a puppy or an adult dog. If your dog is going to be unsupervised outside, your yard should be properly fenced, using wood, chain-link, or electronic fencing, depending on your needs and taste. Pay attention to the height of the fence. Sometimes people think it's cute if their dog can stand up on its hind legs and look over the top of the fence. But this can be dangerous. I have seen several dogs who have caught their collars on the top of the fence; they wound up hanging themselves by the collar. Also, I recommend on outdoor dogs that you use a "breakaway collar," the kind specially designed to release if significant pressure is applied. These are an effective way to prevent strangling accidents.

Toxic Plants

Aloe	Branching Ivy
Amaryllis	Buckeye
Asian Lily	Buddhist Pine
Asparagus Fern	Caladium
Autumn Crocus	Calla Lily
Avocado	Castor Bean
Azalea	Ceriman
Bird of Paradise	Charming Dieffenbachia
Bittersweet, American/	Chinaberry Tree
European	Chinese Evergreen

Christmas Rose	Iris
Clematis	Japanese Show Lily
Cordatum	Japanese Yew
Cornstalk Plant	Jerusalem Cherry
Cutleaf Philodendron	Kalanchoe
Cycads	Lace Fern
Cyclamen	Lacy Tree
Daffodil	Lily of the Valley
Day Lily	Macadamia Nut
Devil's Ivy	Madagascar Dragon Tree
Dumbcane	Marble Queen
Easter Lily	Mauna Loa Peace Lily
Elephant Ears	Mexican Breadfruit
Emerald Feather	Mistletoe, American
Emerald Fern	Morning Glory
English Ivy	Mother-in-Law
Fiddle-Leaf Philodendron	Narcissus
Flamingo Plant	Needlepoint Ivy
Florida Beauty	Nephthytis
Foxglove	Nightshade
Fruit Salad Plant	Oleander
Glacier Ivy	Onion
Gladiolas	Orange Day Lily
Glory Lily	Panda
Gold Dieffenbachia	Peace Lily
Gold Dust Dracaena	Philodendron Pertusum
Golden Pothos	Plumosa Fern
Heartleaf Philodendron	Precatory Bean
Heavenly Bamboo	Queensland Nut
Holly	Red Emerald
Horsehead Philodendron	Red Lily
Hurricane Plant	Red-Margined Dracaena
Hyacinth	Red Princess
Hydrangea	Rhododendron

Ribbon Plant	Taro Vine
Rubrum Lily	Tiger Lily
Saddle Leaf Philodendron	Tomato Plant
Sago Palm	Tree Philodendron
Satin Pothos	Tropic Snow Dumbcane
Schefflera	Tulip
Spotted Dumbcane	Variable Dieffenbachia
Stargazer Lily	Variegated Philodendron
Striped Dracaena	Warneckei Dracaena
Sweetheart Ivy	Wood Lily
Swiss Cheese Plant	Yucca

The doghouse. If your dog is going to be housed out in the yard (not my favorite option), be sure that he has proper shelter against heat, rain, snow, and ice. Make sure, too, that your dog always has adequate water while outside. Use a water dish or receptacle that cannot be tipped over. Make sure to check it twice daily to ensure that it is adequately filled. This will help to protect your dog against heatstroke and dehydration. In the winter, the water bowl should have a mechanism to keep the water from freezing. Again, check this on a daily basis to make sure that it is working. These measures may well make his DogAge younger and extend his life.

Toxic substances. Be especially vigilant about removing toxins such as rat poison, fertilizers and pesticides, ant and roach traps, snail or slug bait, antifreeze, cleaning materials, cans of paint or varnish, even cleaning supplies. Use the checklists at the end of this chapter; they will alert you to many items that you probably did not realize were dangerous. For instance, some of the most serious problems I've seen came from rose fertilizers. I've treated dogs who actually ate the dirt under the rose bushes after they were fertilized. So it must smell good or taste good—and it can make your dog very sick. Even the runoff from fertilized garden plants after a rainstorm can be dangerous if your dog drinks it. Every so often, too, I see a golden retriever who has ripped open a bag of fertilizer and had himself a toxic meal, for no good reason. I've seen it with snail bait, too. So be careful and check those lists.

Antifreeze is also extremely toxic. If you have an air-conditioning unit outside or even in a window box, it is important to check it every month, to make sure there are no leaks or pools of water gathering underneath. Your dog might drink the runoff and become very sick. If you work on cars in the yard or in the driveway, make sure you dispose of the antifreeze properly or use a nontoxic antifreeze. Any brand with ethylene glycol in it is toxic. I see way too many cases where owners change the antifreeze in their car radiators, then leave the old fluid in a bucket somewhere. Along comes the family dog, he's thirsty, and the next thing you know he's drinking out of the bucket. *Any dog who ingests antifreeze has to be taken to an emergency clinic immediately.* Antifreeze is deadly to dogs.

[If your dog ingests and antifreeze, as a stop-gap measure, try to induce vomiting. To do that, on the way to the animal hospital take a syringe or an old-fashioned turkey-baster and fill it with hydrogen peroxide. For small dogs, inject 3 to 5 ccs into their mouths (about a teaspoon) every five or ten minutes, until they vomit. For big dogs, inject 15 ccs (about two tablespoons) at similar intervals. Do not administer more than three doses of hydrogen peroxide.]

Once at the hospital, we do everything we can to empty their stomachs. Then we give them activated charcoal and put them on a twenty-four-hour infusion of ethyl alcohol (grain alcohol) for a seventy-two-hour period. The ethyl alcohol finds the ethylene glycol in the dogs' system and prevents it from damaging the kidneys. Immediate action is needed to save these dogs. An ounce of prevention is worth a mountain of cure.

Dog Safety in Your Vehicle

Cars. There is no room for error here: you have to dog-proof your car just the way you would child-proof your car. To do that effectively, begin by carefully assessing your individual dog. If she tends to be rowdy, jumpy, or nervous in the car, the best thing to do is to restrain her in a carrier, if she is small enough to fit comfortably inside. That keeps the dog safer and it keeps you safer while you drive. You can concentrate on the road, not on your dog. For large dogs, always put them in the backseat; that is the safest means of travel. If you have a large dog who is also prone to be rowdy, you should consider one of the restraint systems or seat belts that are now available for dogs. You can find them in pet stores or on pet supply sites on the Internet.

Pickup Trucks. Now here's my view: never, never, never transport your dog in the back of a pickup truck—even if the dog is leashed or held with restraints. You can buy cross-ties that keep the dog from going to either side of the truck, but even those are not foolproof. Now I realize that a dog in the back of a pickup is as traditional in the United States as apple pie. But I don't care: this is DANGEROUS. I have treated way too many dogs who were riding in the back of the truck (even many who were leashed) and then spotted a squirrel or cat and jumped over the side. The result is never pretty. In fact, those animals suffer terrible damage—if they survive at all. So I feel strongly about this.

Beware of open windows. Dogs love to hang their heads out of windows. But I do have my safety worries. With the window rolled fully down, many dogs can fall out of cars on sharp turns or jump out to chase a cat or another dog. So I recommend that the window never be rolled down more than halfway. Also, if you have electric windows, watch out: your dog's paw can easily hit the up button and roll his neck up into the window. That can be deadly. If you do let your dog hang his head out, make sure you lock the windows into position and watch closely when rolling them up.

Seat belts. Here is another worry. Many dogs get anxious when left alone in the car and they will chew right through your seat belts. And, believe me, seat belts are not cheap to replace. Also, dogs left alone in the car can get wrapped up in a shoulder belt and end up strangling themselves. The poor dogs have no idea what they're doing, and when they get stressed out, anything can happen. So, if you can, unfasten shoulder belts when you leave the car and tuck the waist belts out of harm's way.

Beware of heat. My dogs, for their whole lives, have traveled with me—except in hot weather. If it's cool out, they ride in the back of my SUV, and I am always careful to provide them with ventilation and bowls of water if needed. But I will tell you this: if the temperature is above 70 degrees Fahrenheit, never, never, never leave your dog alone in the car. Even a few short minutes can lead to big trouble. Why? Because dogs get overheated much more easily than we do. In fact, a bulldog can get overheated at 70 degrees. They have so much redundant soft tissue in their upper airways that even moderate activity on a cool day can make them overheat. And they cannot expel the heat they need to by panting. So never, ever leave a dog alone in a car in warm temperatures. It's dangerous!

Dog Safety in Airplanes

Most airlines require a valid health certificate for your dog, issued seven to ten days before travel. So before flying, you must go to your vet and get a complete physical exam for your dog. Also, the airlines have strict rules about how animals need to be housed for air travel. These include specific guidelines for crate size and water containers. (I recommend the large water bottles designed for rabbits. Unlike a typical dog dish, they do not spill during turbulence.) Also, the airlines will not let dogs travel on the plane if the temperature is more than 75 degrees Fahrenheit. The risk here is the time the plane spends on the tarmac, when the air-conditioning is not functioning. For animals traveling in the cargo area, most of the airlines do a good job of making sure that the temperature and air pressure in the hold are completely safe for dogs or other animals. Some airlines even have trained personnel to monitor the animals throughout the flight.

Even if you follow these rules, there are still risks. We recently treated two tiny, six-week-old Yorkshire terrier puppies who were shipped here from Vietnam. These puppies traveled in the cargo bin. This was not unusual; puppies are often shipped this way. Well, tiny dogs like that have a rate of metabolism that is as fast as a hummingbird's. They need to eat every two hours or so just to maintain themselves. In this case, the Yorkies' travel time was more than thirty-six-hours, point to point, and when they arrived in the United States they had not eaten for who knows how long. When they were rushed to our clinic after the flight, both dogs were weak and suffering from dehydration and hypoglycemia. Both dogs, I'm sad to say, did not survive the ordeal.

Sedation. Your dog might need to be sedated for air travel: always consult your vet. When I dispense tranquilizers for dogs, I give owners several test doses and ask them to try them out first at home, where they can carefully observe the animals. I do this because you never really know how an animal is going to react. Some of the most common sedatives are very effective; they will chill anybody out. But they have a wide range of dose levels, and different dogs will react with varying sensitivity. In fact, you can give two dogs of the same weight the exact same dose, and one dog may be significantly affected while the other won't be. It just depends on the individual dog and his metabolism. That is why I urge owners to try test doses. Then, if the dog becomes too sedate, they can get the dog to a veterinary facility to be checked out. This is an important precaution. You certainly do not want to give a dog medication he has never had before, then put him in a crate and put him on an airplane where no one is going to see him for several hours. Also, if your dog was sedated five years ago and did fine, do not assume he will react exactly the same way this time. Do the trial test. Better safe than sorry.

Safety in Boarding Your Dog

Step One: If you are going out of town and need to board your pet, ask friends, neighbors, and veterinary hospitals about a reputable kennel or boarding facility. But don't take their word for it. I urge you to personally check out the facility before you make a reservation for your dog. Tour the facility, meet the people who will be caring for your pet, see where the dog will be exercised, find out how often your dog will be taken outside, and see what their sanitation protocols are. Also ask about its policies for responding to medical emergencies. I really prefer a facility that has someone looking after the dogs 24/7. In sum, make sure that you are totally satisfied by the facility and how your dog will be cared for. Also, remember that boarding can be traumatic for your dog, so you want to find a place where you know she will be comfortable and happy.

Step Two: Make sure that your dog's vaccinations are complete and up-to-date. Most reputable kennels require a full set of vaccinations; have your dog's shot record available. Most kennels require vaccination against kennel cough. But beware: Your dog must be vaccinated two weeks before the boarding period. It takes two weeks to become effective. Some kennels will tell you, "It's okay. We'll vaccinate him when he arrives." But those shots will do nothing to protect your pet. Nor will it protect other dogs if your dog has kennel cough.

Step Three: Plan for an emergency. Make sure your kennel has a medical release form for you to sign, and be very clear about what treatment you will and will not agree to. I also urge you to go a step futher: in an emergency, you might not always be reachable. So make sure the kennel has access to a credit card and your authorization to use it. If you are off traveling in India and your dog suddenly needs emergency surgery, you want to know that your dog is properly covered. Most veterinary hospitals will require proof of payment before they will treat a dog. I would also alert your vet in advance of travel. Tell him or her where your pet is being boarded and specify what sorts of treatments you are willing to authorize in your absence. Have the vet keep that information in your pet's permanent file.

Step Four: Prepare an overnight bag containing everything your dog will need during his stay. Include an adequate supply of your dog's regular food. Also, include all medications that your dog takes or may need during his stay. You should label them clearly, including proper doses. I also recommend that you buy those little week-long pill dispensers and pre-fill them, so that there is no question about whether or not the dog has received his proper medication on time. Some of the dispensers are marked by the day, and some have different slots for morning and evening doses. These are ideal for pets on several medications. Also, provide the kennel with a detailed guide describing each pill (in case the bottles open and spill), what it is, what the dosage is, and how often it should be given. One more thing: some kennels will allow you to bring in a favorite toy or blanket, while others will not. Check in advance.

The Checklists

The issue of dog safety is extremely important, as the stories of Freddy and other dogs make starkly clear. Also, we have covered a huge amount of ground in this chapter, and I know that much of the material will be hard to remember. So here are some helpful checklists for you to use and keep close at hand.

Travel Checklist

Enough dog food for entire stay.

Vaccination records.

Current medical records.

Medications needed for entire stay.

If you are crossing a border or flying with your pet, you will need a health certificate issued by a licensed veterinarian within seven days of travel.

If you are flying with your pet, check climate conditions for your arrival and departure dates to make sure that temperatures coincide with airline regulations.

Extra leash and collar.

Checklist for Boarding Your Dog

Dog food—make sure that you include enough for the entire stay.

Medications—I recommend filling a "day of the week" dispensing container for this. Make sure that you include a list of what each medication looks like and its dosage.

A current copy of your dog's vaccination record and pertinent medical records.

ALL CONTACT NUMBERS! If you are unreachable, appoint a representative who can act in your stead to make decisions.

Authorization/consent form for treatment in case of emergency.

Credit card number for treatment in case of emergency.

Specified emergency clinic or veterinary hospital and contact numbers for these.

Personal effects, if allowed.

Chew bones or treats.

CHAPTER NINE

Finding the Right Dog for You

IN CHAPTER EIGHT I covered a wide range of things to do to make sure that your dog is safe at home, in the yard, and while traveling. But there was one larger safety issue that I did not touch on at all: making sure that you have chosen a dog that is right for you. Some breeds are just not well-suited to a particular home or family environment, and that can make your life extremely difficult, especially when children are involved.

I once had a family in my veterinary practice that had a wonderful dog, a Lab mix. She was a sweet, sweet dog who loved to play with the kids, and she lived a long, happy life as a member of this family. When this beloved dog died, the entire family felt a painful sense of loss, as we all do when we lose a pet. Sometime later the mom came to me for advice. She said the family was ready to get a new dog; could I help guide them to a proper choice?

As the mom explained to me, the family planned to go to the local shelter and rescue a dog who needed a home. That sounded fine to me; I always applaud people who adopt an animal in need. Still, the mother told me she had some serious concerns. She had three small children, ranging from four to ten years of age, and they were used to having a sweet, friendly dog in the house. How could she be sure that a dog rescued from the shelter would safely fit into the family home?

I understood her concern, and despite the wonderful experience they had had with their first dog, I urged her to avoid breeds with a tendency toward aggression (chows, shar-peis, rottweilers, etc.). Not that all dogs of these breeds are aggressive. I happen to have an unbelievably benign rottweiler, but certain breeds do have tendencies. I told her the family might be safer with a Labrador or a golden retriever. These dogs tend to be gentle in nature and patient around small children. With them, I said, you can rarely go wrong.

Nonetheless, Mom soon returned to my office, straight from the shelter, with their new dog, Cinnamon. The shelter had posted Cinnamon as a Chow-Lab mix, but she looked mainly chow to me: the puppy had the telltale black tongue of a chow. I gave Cinnamon a thorough check-up and assured the family that she was in good health. Within two weeks, though, Mom had Cinnamon back in my office. The dog was growling at the kids if they approached her when she was playing with her toys. Also, the dog had a specific chair that she liked to sleep under, and when one child approached her while she was napping, Cinnamon lashed out and bit her. I was very concerned by this behavior. Cinnamon was a puppy. If she was exhibiting these tendencies at thirteen weeks of age, I could only imagine what she would be like when she reached maturity. I strongly urged the mother to take Cinnamon back to the shelter and tell the folks there to find the dog a home where she could be raised without children.

The family was torn by my advice. Mom saw the dangers, but to a certain degree her kids had already become attached to Cinnamon. The family also felt a certain sense of responsibility for Cinnamon's well-being and did not want to return her to an uncertain future at the shelter. In the end, they chose to keep her. One month later, Cinnamon bit one of the children again. Again, though, they chose to keep her. This time, at my urging, they sought help from a professional dog trainer who specialized in aggressive behavior. They ended up sending Cinnamon to an obedience boot camp, where she stayed for an entire month. Then, for most of the following year, the family and Cinnamon both worked intensively with the private trainer, learning how to control the dog's dominance and aggressive tendencies.

Today Cinnamon remains with the family, but they constantly work on obedience with her. They don't let the neighborhood children play with her unsupervised, and she is in a controlled environment. I respect the family's commitment to Cinnamon. Frankly, though, I think they picked the wrong dog at the shelter. And they had been warned: they had telltale signs from the beginning that Cinnamon was not going to be good with kids. Nevertheless, they chose to spend a great deal of time and money on obedience training, and I know that their heart was in the right place. A year later, I asked Cinnamon's mom if she was happy about their decision to keep the dog. She answered, "We love Cinnamon, but it would have been easier to pick a different dog from the start."

You should choose a breed that is well-suited to your family, your house or apartment, and your living conditions. And if you have small children, you have to be especially careful. The risks otherwise are just too great. Let me be blunt: some dogs get along well with small children, but others do not. Some dogs get along fine with cats, some do not. Some dogs are well-suited for living in small apartments in the city, while some dogs do much better in the country, with plenty of room to run in the yard or adjoining fields. The key, always, is to get the right fit. If a dog is not well-matched to its home environment, it can be a recipe for disaster. Some problems can be addressed through proper training, as I'll explain in Chapter Ten. But if you have a German short-haired pointer and you want to keep it in a small apartment in the city, you are just asking for trouble—and for a very un-happy dog.

The lesson here is simple: *before* you bring a dog home, hon-estly confront a crucial question: is this the right dog for you? Does it fit well with your desires, your family situation, your home environment, and your lifestyle? If so, great. If not, save yourself some heartache and keep on looking.

The Selection Process

So how do you choose a dog that is a good fit for you? Before you start looking, answer these simple questions: Where do you live? Do you have a yard? Are you going to be walking this dog on a leash or not? Do you have children in the house? How many hours are you typically gone during the day? Do you plan to hire a dog-walker? How many people are in the house? Do you have neighbors nearby? What type of personality are you looking for in a dog? What type of hair coat do you prefer? Are you or anyone in the fam-ily allergic to dogs? How much maintenance, as far as grooming goes, are you willing to do? Do you want a large dog or a small dog? Why do you have that preference? (Some people's idea of what they're going to get from a small dog or a large dog is much different from what they actually get.) Now, if you have a particular dog or breed in mind, I urge you to zoom in on these important issues:

◆ Does the size of the dog match your living conditions? A Border collie who needs plenty of exercise will simply not be happy in a small apartment, unless someone in the family can take him out every day for some activity. *Twice* a day. Even then, the situation is less than ideal.

◆ Does the temperament of the dog suit your needs? For

instance, having a German shepherd, a rottweiler, or a pit bull in the house might be a suitable security measure, provided he is properly trained. But if you have small children in the family or in the neighborhood, this might be a dangerous idea.

- Is this an indoor or outdoor dog—and do you have the suitable home environment to make sure he's happy? Likewise, will he be happy if he's alone outside all day in the yard, or is this a social dog who prefers to be inside around people? Does this fit with your living situation? An Alaskan malamute is not the right dog for you if you live in Florida and are planning to keep him in the yard all the time.

- Be realistic about money. Proper nutrition, grooming, veterinary care, and boarding your dog, when necessary, are all costly. And some breeds cost more in grooming and upkeep than others do. Do you have the financial resources to properly care for this dog? Also, dogs do get sick and have accidents; can you handle the cost of emergency care?

Breed Characteristics and Predispositions

With dogs, as with people, genetics are not necessarily destiny. Golden retrievers are usually gentle souls, but that doesn't mean you won't run into one who bites. Likewise, you might find a chow that is wonderful, even around small children. Still, after years and years of working with dogs and counseling their owners, I know that different breeds do have predictable temperaments to a certain extent—and you ignore them at your own risk.

To facilitate your search, I have included a list of the most common breeds and their usual characteristics of temperament, behavior, predisposition to disease, and other problems. Likewise, most libraries, bookstores, and pet shops have vast shelves of books devoted to specific breeds, and there are many breed-specific Web sites on the Internet, as well. Read and visit them! For first-time dog owners especially, doing this kind of research is essential to the process of choosing a dog who's right for you. Also, talk to friends or neighbors about their dogs. Ask veterinarians, too, about specific breeds and the usual tendencies they display. This can be very helpful in clarifying your decision.

Where to Find the Right Dog for You

Once you have decided on a particular breed or mix of breeds, you have many options about where to look for a specific dog who will be right for you. Let me go over some of those options, highlighting their relative merits and disadvantages:

Professional Breeders. Professional breeders specialize in developing purebred, high-quality animals. So if you want a purebred, show-quality papillon, poodle, Welsh terrier, Jack Russell, German short-haired pointer, Doberman, borzoi, English springer spaniel, or other purebred, you can find a professional breeder via the Internet or the American Kennel Club (AKC), which licenses professional breeders and holds them to very high standards.

Going to a reputable breeder may give you important advantages. Because they know the characteristics of the breed and the specific parents of a given dog, breeders can give you an accurate description of a dog's probable temperament, and size. Also, there are many breeders who will guarantee that your dog has no health problems or genetic predispositions. If they prove wrong, they may give you another dog or refund your money. For example, some breeds are prone to hip problems. A reputable breeder specializing in those dogs will certify the hips, meaning that they guarantee that the dog's parents and grandparents have not shown evidence of hip problems. Also, if you are looking at a puppy, most breeders will introduce you to the parents, so that you can get some idea what the puppy will be like in terms of size, color, and disposition.

With professional breeders, you can observe the setting in which the dogs have been bred and raised, and you can ask essential questions. Do they have any history of parvovirus or distemper in their kennel? Did the dog's parents produce litters before? Were there any congenital problems? Good breeders generally maintain tightly controlled environments for their dogs, and offer high-quality animals. So while it costs substantially more money to get a dog from a breeder, you may get some important guarantees. Also, in contrast to dogs in shelters, these are dogs that don't *need* homes; many people will be eager to buy them.

What to Ask Your Breeder

Do you have the mother and father of the puppies on the premises? Can we meet them?

Have these dogs ever had a litter together? If so, were there any problems?

Have you ever had a problem with parvo or distemper virus in your kennel?

Do you keep medical records on all your dogs? Can I see them?

When was the mother of the puppies last vaccinated?

Are your dogs on heartworm preventative?

How often do you deworm your adult dogs?

Have the puppies been examined by a veterinarian?

Are all the puppies in this litter healthy? Did any of the puppies in the litter die? How old were they? Do you know the cause?

Do you have your dogs vaccinated by a veterinarian, or do you do it yourself?

What is your quarantine protocol for dogs coming onto the property?

Does this line have a history of inherited problems?

What food do you feed your dogs?

How do you go about selecting a new home for your puppies?

What is your health guarantee? What do you do if the puppy becomes ill within that period of time?

What is your return policy?

Pet stores. Beware of pet stores. Though there are some pet stores that maintain excellent standards and offer healthy, high-quality animals, there are far more that don't do this. Pet stores are also usually a stressful environment for the animals housed there. The dogs are held in close quarters, which combined with stress makes for a perfect environment for the spread of viruses and bacteria. The two most common problems that I see in pet-store puppies are coccidia and upper-respiratory infections.

Coccidia is a bacterial parasite that can cause pretty severe vomiting and diarrhea. Take my little Chihuahua, Chili Beyoncé, for example. Her previous owners purchased her from a pet store. She was seemingly healthy at first, but within a few days she stopped eating and became very ill. She was infected with coccidia and probably parvovirus. The people who bought her, bless their hearts, had no idea what they were in for. Though initially they consented to her treatment, they soon realized that her care was going to be too much for them and turned her over to me. She came through her illness and is healthy now, but it was touch and go for a week or so, and I wasn't sure that she would make it.

Now Chili Beyoncé is a strong pup. Her DogAge (4.8 years— remember, DogAge is expressed in human terms, so she's like a preschool child) may be a little older biologically because of this early turmoil, but she's still about half a DogAge year younger than other teacup Chihuahuas her calendar age.

Upper-respiratory infections are generally caused by viruses, and can also have serious consequences. If one puppy is infected, it is very easy for the others to become infected due to the close quarters. And because of the incubation period for some illnesses, it is possible for a puppy to appear healthy when it is purchased, then come down with something five to seven days later. On the plus side, most pet stores provide a trial period for their customers, giving you a specified period to see if this is the right dog for you, your family, and your home environment. If you are going to purchase a puppy from a pet store, make sure that it comes with at least a two-week "healthy pet" guarantee. Also ask what their quarantine procedures are. A responsible pet store should observe at least a two-week quarantine period, during which all new animals in the store are housed away from the ones who have been there for more than two weeks, to limit the spread of illness.

Some pet stores are affiliated with "puppy mills," breeders who raise large numbers of many breeds and sell them specifically to pet stores. Their driving motivation is profit, not to produce healthy, high-quality animals. The best advice I can give is "an ounce of prevention," meaning do some research about the pet store and where it gets its animals.

Shelters. Many shelters and humane societies do marvelous work, rescuing hundreds or thousands of dogs each year and finding them homes. I applaud them, and adopting a dog from a shelter is certainly an admirable thing to do. But let's be clear: you will know little about the animal you are bringing home. In fact, many families give up their dogs to shelters precisely because these dogs have exhibited difficult behavioral problems or they don't relate well to children or other animals in the home. So caveat emptor—buyer beware.

There are also health concerns associated with dogs coming from shelters. The dogs are held in close quarters with a questionable vaccine history or no history at all. As a result, these animals can be highly stressed, and are more prone to succumbing to viruses and infections. It is also possible that the dog you pick up may seem perfectly healthy while at the shelter, but will get sick a week after you bring her home. The result can be a devastating and costly experience. If you do take a dog home from a shelter, always take him straight to a good vet. The vet will do a thorough physical exam, looking for underlying physical problems. Unfortunately, your vet will be unable to tell from a physical exam what your new dog has been exposed to, and therefore will be unable to predict what you can expect health-wise over the next two to three weeks. He or she will, however, be able to give you a list of signs to watch for, just in case. One of the most heartbreaking things that I've seen is a new puppy adopted from a shelter who comes down with parvovirus five days after going to its new home. Invariably, the family has to wrestle with the decision to pay for intensive treatment with no guarantee of survival, or to euthanize the puppy.

Breed-rescue organizations. These organizations specialize in rescuing and finding homes for one particular breed of dog. I think they're great. You can go and get the exact breed of dog you're looking for, plus you get a dog that needs a home. Most breed-rescue organizations are very conscientious about pursuing appropriate medical care for their dogs, and they'll even go as far as to assess the dog's temperament to ensure that it goes to the right new home. People who love their particular breed run these organizations, and they take great care to put the dogs in proper homes.

Other options. There are many other ways to find a dog to adopt. You can usually find ads in your local newspaper posted by families whose dog has given birth to a litter of puppies. Many pet stores and humane societies run periodic adoption fairs. And, of course, there are the stray or lost dogs who wind up at your back door or find you in more unusual ways. I have had people bring a dog in and say, "We were driving along the highway, and there he was, sitting in the rain. We felt so sorry for him! We'd like you to check him out for us because we think we're going to keep him."

Evaluating Temperament

Let's say you go to a professional breeder or a shelter and you see a puppy who appeals to you and seems to fit your desires and home environment. Great. But how can you tell if that dog has a temperament that will be compatible with what you want? Is there anything you can do to assess that *before* you take him home on a permanent basis?

Yes. If you are interested in a particular puppy, watch how he or she plays with the other puppies in the litter. Watch for signs of dominance. These include standing on top of the other puppies, mounting other puppies, or placing its head and neck above the others' heads and necks. Dominant puppies also tend to be more vocal during play. Also, if it seems to be the most active puppy in the litter, you're going to have your hands full when you get him home. My rule of thumb is this: "Don't take the most reserved, don't take the runt, and don't take the most active puppy of the litter. Take the middle-of-the-road puppy. He'll grow into the more even-tempered dog." I find that this system works out well most of the time.

There are also a few tests you can do to evaluate a dog's temperament. Especially if the dog is a puppy, flip it onto its back and hold it in your arms. No dog likes to be on its back, but a dominant dog will put up a big fuss until it is returned to the upright position. A more desirable response is this: the puppy struggles a bit, but then, realizing that you're going to hold him there, gives up and relaxes. If a puppy gets so distressed while being held on his back that he becomes quite vocal—or so upset that he urinates or defecates—then you know you have a problem dog on your hands.

Here is another test: give the dog a rawhide bone or other toy to chew on, then take it away. Then give it back, take it away, and give it back. In the process, watch for growling or aggressive movements. That will tell you how the dog might react to kids. You can do the same thing with food. If she submits, you can feel more comfortable with the idea of bringing this dog into your home. That said, I still don't recommend ever letting babies crawl around the dog-food dish; that's just asking for trouble.

Now, to summarize: there are many different places you can go to find a dog who is right for you, and there are a few simple things you can do to check a dog's underlying character and temperament. My basic advice is this: use your common sense. Do your research. Ask questions. Gather as much information as you can about any dog who you might want to take home. Most puppies are cute and loving and will rustle our hearts, but please, use your head as well as your heart. As we saw with the case of Cinnamon, this is a very serious decision, one that can carry heavy costs and heavy risks, especially if you have small children in the house. So let Dr. Dondi offer you one last pearl of advice:

Choosing the right dog is a decision best made by knowledgeable adults—NOT by your children! I'm sure you catch my drift.

Predispositions

How do you know if a particular breed may be the right dog for you and your family? One factor to consider is the breed's predispositions to various diseases. I hope the following table will help.

How to Read This Table

I have divided breed predispositions into two categories: "Most Common Conditions," and "Less Common Conditions." All of them are believed to have an inherited basis, or are known to have a predilection for this breed ("breed predisposition"). This means the disorder occurs more commonly in this breed compared to other breeds, or more commonly than in the general dog population.

The most popular breeds, like cocker spaniels and poodles, tend to have the most disorders. That's because a larger number of dogs is affected, and there is therefore more opportunity to recognize that breed's predisposition to a particular disorder. Also, there is likely to be more indiscriminate breeding of these more popular breeds.

The good news: where serious disorders are common to a breed, most professional breeders go to great lengths to eradicate them. The reason is simple: those disorders can seriously affect the health of your pet, and may require medical or surgical intervention.

Breed and Characteristics	Most Common Conditions	Less Common Conditions
Basset hound: laid back, easy-going, can be "barky"	**Basset hound thrombopathia:** disorder of small blood cells called platelets or thrombocytes. **Seborrhea:** an inherited disorder of the skin in which the outer layer of the skin, the sebaceous glands, and part of the hair follicles are hyperproductive.	**Elbow dysplasia:** several conditions that affect the elbow joint. **Glaucoma:** a leading cause of blindness in dogs. **Intervertebral disc disease:** occurs when the jelly-like inner layer of the spinal cord protrudes into the vertebral canal and presses on the spinal cord. **Patellar luxation:** a condition in which the kneecap slips out of the groove. **Prolapsed gland of third eyelid** ("cherry eye"): the base of the gland (embedded in the cartilage) flips up and is seen above and behind the border of the third eyelid. **Von Willebrand disease:** a common, usually mild, inherited bleeding disorder.

Breed	Most Common Conditions	Less Common Conditions
Beagle: energetic, can be diggers and barkers, sometimes stubborn	**Pulmonic stenosis**: partial obstruction of normal blood flow, most commonly due to a malformation of the pulmonic valve.	**Cataracts**: any opacity or loss of transparency in the lens of the eye. **Cervical vertebral instability**: compression of the spinal cord in the neck (cervical) region. **Corneal dystrophy**: an inherited abnormality that affects one or more layers of the cornea. **Epilepsy**: seizures are the result of a disturbance in the electrical activity of brain cells. **Glaucoma**: a leading cause of blindness in dogs. **Intervertebral disc disease**: occurs when the jelly-like inner layer of the spinal cord protrudes into the vertebral canal and presses on the spinal cord. **Retinal dysplasia**: abnormal development of the retina.

Breed	Most Common Conditions	Less Common Conditions
Bichon frise: friendly, very energetic	**Cataracts:** any opacity or loss of transparency in the lens of the eye. **Congenital hypotrichosis:** hair loss at birth or by a few months of age, due to faulty development or a complete absence of some or all of the hair follicles from which the hairs normally grow. **Hemophilia B (factor IX deficiency):** bleeding disorder of varying severity that is due to a deficiency in specific clotting factors. **Patent ductus arteriosus:** the ductus does not close.	None

Breed	Most Common Conditions	Less Common Conditions
	Urolithiasis: crystals in the urine combine to form stones called **calculi** or **uroli.**	
Boston terrier: very energetic, generally friendly	**Brachycephalic syndrome:** respiratory difficulties.	**Cataracts:** any opacity or loss of transparency in the lens of the eye. **Cerebellar hypoplasia:** the cells of the cerebellum do not mature normally before birth, causing clinical signs relating to poor balance and incoordination. **Glaucoma:** a leading cause of blindness in dogs. **Hydrocephalus:** an abnormal buildup of cerebrospinal fluid (CSF) in cavities (the ventricles) in the brain. **Keratoconjunctivitis sicca:** an eye disease caused by abnormal tear production. **Mitral valve disease:** a defect in the mitral valve (the left atrioventricular

Breed	Most Common Conditions	Less Common Conditions
		valve) causes a backflow of blood into the left atrium. **Patellar luxation**: the kneecap has slipped out of the groove. **Pyloric stenosis**: a narrowing (stenosis) of the pylorus, the region of the stomach through which food and liquid pass into the small intestine.
Boxer: energetic, generally intelligent	**Aortic stenosis**: a partial obstruction to the flow of blood as it leaves the left side of the heart (the left ventricle) through the main blood vessel (the aorta) that carries blood to the rest of the body. **Corneal dystrophy**: an inherited abnormality that affects one or	**Atrial septal defect**: a defect or hole in the muscular wall (the septum) that separates the right and left atria, two of the four chambers of the heart. **Demodicosis**: a mite that is present in small numbers in the skin of most healthy dogs. **Hip dysplasia**: a loose fit at the hip joint. **Hypothyroidism**: a decrease in normal thyroid hormone activity.

Breed	Most Common Conditions	Less Common Conditions
	more layers of the cornea.	**Pyloric stenosis**: a narrowing (stenosis) of the pylorus, the region of the stomach through which food and liquid pass into the small intestine. **Von Willebrand disease**: a common, usually mild, inherited bleeding disorder.
Chihuahua: intelligent, can be timid and nervous, may be difficult to housebreak, need socialization	**Patellar luxation**: the kneecap has slipped out of the groove.	**Color dilution alopecia**: a poor, patchy coat progressing to widespread permanent hair loss. **Glaucoma**: a leading cause of blindness in dogs. **Mitral valve disease**: defect in the mitral valve (the left atrioventricular valve) causes backflow of blood into the left atrium. **Patent ductus arteriosus**: the ductus does not close. **Pulmonic stenosis**: is partial obstruction of normal blood flow, most commonly due to a malformation of the pulmonic valve.

Breed	Most Common Conditions	Less Common Conditions
Cocker spaniel: generally laid back and friendly	**Retinal dysplasia:** abnormal development of the retina. **Seborrhea:** an inherited disorder of the skin in which the outer layer of the skin, the sebaceous glands, and part of the hair follicles are hyperproductive.	**Autoimmune hemolytic anemia:** the immune system destroys red blood cells prematurely, faster than new ones can be produced. **Cataracts:** any opacity or loss of transparency in the lens of the eye. **Chronic hepatitis:** a slowly progressive liver disease. **Distichiasis:** extra eyelashes grow from abnormal follicles on the inside edge of the eyelid. **Epilepsy:** seizures are the result of a disturbance in the electrical activity of brain cells. **Glaucoma:** a leading cause of blindness in dogs. **Hypothyroidism:** a decrease in normal thyroid hormone activity. **Immune-mediated thrombocytopenia:** a reduction in platelets.

Breed	Most Common Conditions	Less Common Conditions
		Keratoconjunctivitis sicca: an eye disease caused by abnormal tear production.
Dachshund: bright, moderately energetic, can be nervous	**Intervertebral disc disease**: occurs when the jelly-like inner layer of the spinal cord protrudes into the vertebral canal and presses on the spinal cord.	**Hyperadrenocorticism**: a common endocrine disorder in dogs. **Hypothyroidism**: a decrease in normal thyroid hormone activity. **Mitral valve disease**: defect in the mitral valve (the left atrioventricular valve) causes backflow of blood into the left atrium.
Doberman pinscher: moderately energetic, can be nervous and aggressive	**Cardiomyopathy**: disease of the heart muscle. **Intervertebral disc disease**: occurs when the jelly-like inner layer of the spinal cord protrudes into the vertebral canal and presses on the spinal cord.	**Chronic hepatitis**: a slowly progressive liver disease. **Cervical vertebral instability**: compression of the spinal cord in the neck (cervical) region. **Demodicosis**: a mite that is present in small numbers in the skin of most healthy dogs.

Breed	Most Common Conditions	Less Common Conditions
	Von Willebrand disease: a common, usually mild, inherited bleeding disorder.	**Hypothyroidism**: a decrease in normal thyroid hormone activity. **Panosteitis**: a common disease that causes pain and lameness in young dogs.
English bulldog: laid back	**Brachycephalic syndrome**: respiratory difficulties. **Hip dysplasia**: loose fit at the hip joint. **Pulmonic stenosis**: partial obstruction of normal blood flow, most commonly due to a malformation of the pulmonic valve. **Ventricular septal defect**: a hole (or defect) in the muscular wall of the heart	**Aortic stenosis**: a partial obstruction to the flow of blood as it leaves the left side of the heart (the left ventricle) through the main blood vessel (the aorta) that carries blood to the rest of the body. **Demodicosis**: a mite that is present in small numbers in the skin of most healthy dogs. **Distichiasis**: extra eyelashes grow from abnormal follicles located on the inside edge of the eyelid. **Entropion**: a defect of conformation in which there is a sagging or rolling-out (eversion) of the eyelids.

Breed	Most Common Conditions	Less Common Conditions
	(the septum) that separates the right and left ventricles.	**Hydrocephalus**: an abnormal buildup of cerebrospinal fluid (CSF) in cavities (the ventricles) in the brain. **Hypoplastic trachea**: abnormal growth of the rings of cartilage that make up the trachea, resulting in a narrowed airway. **Hypothyroidism**: a decrease in normal thyroid hormone activity.
German shepherd: moderately energetic, intelligent, can be nervous or aggressive	**Degenerative myelopathy**: a slowly progressive loss of coordination in the hind limbs, with increasing weakness. **Exocrine pancreatic insufficiency**: a gradual wasting away (atrophy) of the acini.	**Hip dysplasia**: loose fit at the hip joint. **Lupus erythematosus**: an autoimmune disorder, which means that the body mounts an inappropriate immune response to some part of itself. **Seborrhea**: an inherited disorder of the skin in which the outer layer of the skin, the sebaceous glands, and part of the hair follicles are hyperproductive.

Breed	Most Common Conditions	Less Common Conditions
	Hemophilia: a bleeding disorder of varying severity that is due to a deficiency in specific clotting factors. **Panosteitis:** common disease that causes pain and lameness in young dogs.	
German short-haired pointer: very energetic, generally intelligent	**Hip dysplasia:** loose fit at the hip joint.	**Aortic stenosis:** a partial obstruction to the flow of blood as it leaves the left side of the heart (the left ventricle) through the main blood vessel (the aorta) that carries blood to the rest of the body. **Lymphedema:** abnormal lymph flow; lymph fluids accumulate and cause swelling in the affected tissue. **Von Willebrand disease:** a common, usually mild, inherited bleeding disorder.

Breed	Most Common Conditions	Less Common Conditions
Golden retriever: generally sweet and laid back	**Aortic stenosis:** a partial obstruction to the flow of blood as it leaves the left side of the heart (the left ventricle) through the main blood vessel (the aorta) that carries blood to the rest of the body. **Hip dysplasia:** loose fit at the hip joint. **Retinal dysplasia:** abnormal development of the retina.	**Atopy:** the canine equivalent of hay fever. **Cataracts:** any opacity or loss of transparency in the lens of the eye. **Distichiasis:** extra eyelashes grow from abnormal follicles located on the inside edge of the eyelid. **Entropion:** a defect of conformation in which there is a sagging or rolling-out (eversion) of the eyelids. **Epilepsy:** seizures are the result of a disturbance in the electrical activity of brain cells. **Hypothyroidism:** a decrease in normal thyroid hormone activity. **Von Willebrand disease:** a common, usually mild, inherited bleeding disorder.

Breed	Most Common Conditions	Less Common Conditions
Great Dane: laid back	**Cardiomyopathy:** disease of the heart muscle. **Cervical vertebral instability:** compression of the spinal cord in the neck (cervical) region. **Gastric dilatation-volvulus:** the stomach becomes distended with air, and then while dilated, twists on itself. **Hip dysplasia:** loose fit at the hip joint.	**Aortic stenosis:** a partial obstruction to the flow of blood as it leaves the left side of the heart (the left ventricle) through the main blood vessel (the aorta) that carries blood to the rest of the body. **Demodicosis:** a mite that is present in small numbers in the skin of most healthy dogs. **Entropion:** a defect of conformation in which there is a sagging or rolling-out (eversion) of the eyelids. **Hypothyroidism:** a decrease in normal thyroid hormone activity. **Tricuspid dysplasia:** causes backflow of blood into the right atrium, also known as tricuspid regurgitation.

Breed	Most Common Conditions	Less Common Conditions
Labrador retriever: moderately energetic, intelligent and sweet	**Hip dysplasia:** loose fit at the hip joint. **Retinal dysplasia:** there is abnormal development of the retina.	**Atopy:** the canine equivalent of hay fever. **Diabetes mellitus:** a disruption of the body's ability to use carbohydrates/sugars. **Entropion:** a defect of conformation in which there is a sagging or rolling-out (eversion) of the eyelids. **Epilepsy:** seizures are the result of a disturbance in the electrical activity of brain cells. **Intrahepatic portosystemic shunt:** abnormal blood flow in the liver. **Panosteitis:** common disease that causes pain and lameness in young dogs. **Seborrhea:** an inherited disorder of the skin in which the outer layer of the skin, the sebaceous glands, and part of the hair follicles are hyperproductive.

Breed	Most Common Conditions	Less Common Conditions
Maltese: laid back, can be nervous, can be difficult to house-break	**Patent ductus arteriosus**: the ductus does not close.	**Cryptorchidism**: one or both of a dog's testicles have not descended into the scrotum. **Hydrocephalus**: an abnormal buildup of cerebrospinal fluid (CSF) in cavities (the ventricles) in the brain.
Miniature pinscher: moderately energetic, can be nervous	None	**Corneal dystrophy**: an inherited abnormality that affects one or more layers of the cornea. **Legg-Calvé-Perthes disease**: a disease of the hip joint in young (four to twelve months) small-breed dogs. **Mitral valve disease**: defect in the mitral valve (the left atrioventricular valve) causes backflow of blood into the left atrium. **Small-dog encephalitis**: a genetic condition causing inflammatory brain lesions.

Breed	Most Common Conditions	Less Common Conditions
Pomeranian: high energy, can be barky and nervous, can be difficult to housebreak	**Patent ductus arteriosus:** the ductus does not close.	**Hydrocephalus:** an abnormal buildup of cerebrospinal fluid (CSF) in cavities (the ventricles) in the brain. **Patellar luxation:** the kneecap has slipped out of the groove. **Tracheal collapse:** a narrowing of the inner diameter of the trachea, which fluctuates with the stage of the respiratory cycle.
Poodle, Toy: intelligent, moderately energetic	**Patellar luxation:** the kneecap has slipped out of the groove. **Tracheal collapse:** a narrowing of the inner diameter of the trachea, which fluctuates with the stage of the respiratory cycle.	**Autoimmune hemolytic anemia:** the immune system destroys red blood cells prematurely, faster than the rate at which new ones can be produced. **Cryptorchidism:** one or both of a dog's testicles have not descended into the scrotum. **Diabetes mellitus:** a disruption of the body's ability to use carbohydrates/sugars.

Breed	Most Common Conditions	Less Common Conditions
		Distichiasis: extra eyelashes grow from abnormal follicles located on the inside edge of the eyelid. **Glaucoma:** a leading cause of blindness in dogs. **Hydrocephalus:** an abnormal buildup of cerebrospinal fluid (CSF) in cavities (the ventricles) in the brain. **Immune-mediated thrombocytopenia:** reduction in platelets. **Legg-Calvé-Perthes disease:** a disease of the hip joint in young (four to twelve months) small-breed dogs. **Mitral valve disease:** defect in the mitral valve (the left atrioventricular valve) causes backflow of blood into the left atrium.
Pug: sweet, laid back	**Keratoconjunctivitis sicca:** an eye disease caused by abnormal tear production.	**Atopy:** the canine equivalent of hay fever. **Brachycephalic syndrome:** respiratory difficulties.

Breed	Most Common Conditions	Less Common Conditions
		Entropion: a defect of conformation in which there is a sagging or rolling-out (eversion) of the eyelids. **Exposure keratopathy syndrome:** chronic irritation of the surface of the eye (the cornea) because of increased evaporation of tears and increased corneal exposure. **Pug encephalitis:**
Rottweiler: moderate to low energy, can be aggressive	**Hip dysplasia:** loose fit at the hip joint. **Von Willebrand disease:** a common, usually mild, inherited bleeding disorder.	None
Shih Tzu: laid back	**Cataracts:** any opacity or loss of transparency in the lens of the eye.	None

Breed	Most Common Conditions	Less Common Conditions
	Intervertebral disc disease: occurs when the jelly-like inner layer of the spinal cord protrudes into the vertebral canal and presses on the spinal cord. **Pannus**: a slowly progressive disorder of the cornea.	
Siberian husky: moderate to high energy, can be aloof	**Cataracts**: any opacity or loss of transparency in the lens of the eye. **Corneal dystrophy**: an inherited abnormality that affects one or more layers of the cornea. **Hip dysplasia**: loose fit at the hip joint.	**None**

Breed	Most Common Conditions	Less Common Conditions
	Pannus: a slowly progressive disorder of the cornea.	
Weimaraner: very high energy	**Hip dysplasia:** loose fit at the hip joint. **Tricuspid Valve Dysplasia**: a congenital malformation of the tricuspid valve.	None
Yorkshire terrier: high energy, can be nervous and difficult to housebreak	**Cataracts:** any opacity or loss of transparency in the lens of the eye. **Cryptorchidism:** one or both of a dog's testicles have not descended into the scrotum. **Hydrocephalus:** an abnormal buildup of cerebrospinal	None

Breed	Most Common Conditions	Less Common Conditions
	fluid (CSF) in cavities (the ventricles) in the brain. **Legg-Calvé-Perthes disease**: a disease of the hip joint in young (four to twelve months) small-breed dogs. **Patellar luxation**: the kneecap has slipped out of the groove. **Protein-losing enteropathy**: an inherited immune-mediated disease of the intestines. **Tracheal collapse**: a narrowing of the inner diameter of the trachea, which fluctuates with the stage of the respiratory cycle.	

CHAPTER TEN

Basic Training

I WAS RECENTLY in New York City chatting with a charming couple who had adopted an adult standard poodle named Max. They had visited a breeder and immediately fallen in love with Max, and the dog was indeed adorable. From the moment they got him home, however, they had a little problem: Max was running their lives. If the couple was sitting on the couch and Max wanted attention, he would stand in front of them and bark incessantly. If that didn't work, he would grab one of their forearms with his mouth or climb on top of them. Max was hyperactive and at times destructive, and he had no concept of the word "no." He would often jump defiantly onto the couch and stare right at them as they asked him to get off as if to say, "What are you going to do about it?"

After a few weeks of this, the couple was fit to be tied. They'd look at each other and say, "What have we done?" Finally they called in a professional trainer. The trainer spent some time with Max and the couple in their home, saw how they interacted, and then sat the couple down to give them his assessment. "Look," he said, "the main problem is that this dog is dominant over you. And it's your fault. You have allowed him to be dominant. I am sorry to say that you are the ones who need the training, not Max."

Luckily, this story has a happy ending. After getting over the initial shock and their own embarrassment, the couple worked diligently with the trainer, and they, in turn, applied the lessons to Max. The entire training process took only a month or so, and once they "got it," Max "got it." Now the couple tells me that Max is the best-behaved dog in the world. They just had to learn some basic obedience guidelines and how to establish the proper hierarchy. This meant, simply, that they had to teach Max one basic fact of life: *they* were the dominant dogs, not him.

In this chapter, I will explain the fundamentals of good dog training: how to establish an appropriate hierarchy, how to housebreak your puppy, how to stop dogs from begging at the table, and much more. I will also discuss the behavior patterns that should alert you that your dog, like Max, needs serious professional training. Let me emphasize that I am not a professional dog trainer. The pros have skills and expertise that I just don't. There are a number of excellent books on training, covering leash training, voice, hand and whistle commands, show training, and how to deal with problem dogs. I urge you to read one or two of them. Also, see the list showing how to teach basic commands (see page 183). Training your dog to respond to your commands most of the time can make your dog 1.3 DogAge years younger! Just remember this: whether you have a little Chihuahua or a big rottweiler, the principles of good dog training remain the same.

An adult dog. Let's say you have just adopted an adult dog from the shelter, humane society, or pet shop as a new addition to your family. How do you assess what kind of training the dog needs? First of all, it depends on how experienced you are as a dog owner. If you do have experience with dogs, you will probably be able to recognize whether or not your new dog is dominant or submissive, well trained or not. If you are a novice dog owner, your vet or a professional dog trainer can help you make that determination. You can also consult books. If the dog seems like a handful and you have little experience, you may want to consult an animal behaviorist or a dog trainer.

A puppy. I recommend that you put a new pup through puppy kindergarten and then obedience classes, to train you, to train the puppy, and to socialize him, as well. Socialization to me is just as important as training. A dog needs to learn how to deal with different situations, because life isn't predictable. The more socialized he is, the more confident he will be and the better he will be at handling difficult or stressful circumstances. In addition, early obedience training can make you more able to control your dog, thus avoiding potentially dangerous situations.

Where do you find puppy and obedience classes? You can find dog-training schools in many cities and towns; check your yellow pages. Also, many large pet stores and boarding facilities offer dog-training classes. You can also contact your local humane society or animal shelter for recommendations. Obedience classes are generally affordable. They allow you to work with a trainer while socializing your dog to other dogs. In a class, a trainer may be able to identify dogs who need help in one specific area or another. The training process can teach your dog to channel his energy as well as give him an activity to concentrate on (and make him tired). It can make your dog a safer pet and one who is much more pleasant to have in your home. In a larger sense, obedience training can help to structure the bond and hierarchy between you and your pet.

Establishing a hierarchy. To do this, you must be consistent. First decide what YOUR rules are, then stick to them. You will have to be clear and consistent in your enforcement of those rules. (But don't forget to be loving and sweet when you are not enforcing the rules. You want your dog to think of you as the "benevolent dictator," not the "wicked queen.") If you do not want your dog to be on the couch, enforce that all the time, not some of the time. If you are not consistent, your dog will not understand what is desirable behavior and what is not. If you tell your dog, "No, don't get on the bed," and then he jumps on the bed anyway, that's defiant behavior and he is expressing dominance over you. In that case, it is up to you to take steps right away to reestablish the proper hierarchy and to make clear the rules that you want the dog to follow. Use your voice, your posture, and your body language to let your dog know that you mean business. Here are some examples of easy things that you can do to establish yourself as the *dominant dog*: don't let your dog walk through a doorway in front of you; make your dog sit before receiving his food or treats; don't always entertain "fetch" when your dog brings you the ball—*you* determine when it's playtime; and don't let your dog get the best spot on the bed.

Establishing the hierarchy is the cornerstone of all dog training. Beyond that, what kind of rules and practices you enforce depends on what type of relationship you want to have with your dog. I know people who want their dog to sleep on their bed and don't care if things get chewed up, and I even have a few clients who don't much care if the dog goes to the bathroom in the house. To each his own, I suppose, but that is certainly not my style nor my advice to you. I have a very close relationship with my dogs Hannah, Georgia, and Chili, and I will admit that I indulge them at times. But they all know their boundaries, and when it matters, there is never any question as to who says what goes down. I do. And they know it. In our family, this makes for a very strong, happy, and safe relationship. When I take them to the dog park or have people over to visit, I can be sure that my dogs will always be on their best behavior.

Building Trust. Once you have established the proper hierarchy, you have to gain your dog's trust and confidence. This is key to building a relationship with your dog. Do this by combining consistent behavior with tender loving care. In this regard, physical contact is extremely important. Petting your dog can convey love and comfort, and generally provides pleasure to both pet and owner. You can also use this touch to make your dog less sensitive to things that she may encounter in life.

Along with physical contact, activities can help you build a stonger bond with your dog. Depending on what your dog likes to do, walking, running, going to the park, playing fetch, hiking, or just sitting on the floor watching TV are all activities that you and your dog can do together. Just spending time at home with your dog is important. Have you ever noticed that when you move from one room to another in your house, your dog tends to go along with you? My dogs are all lying around me downstairs as I write. In the morning, I often sit on the floor for ten minutes or so and play with them before I start my day. It always seems to get me out the door on a happy note.

Talk to your dog. I believe strongly in the importance of talking to your dog. I talk to my dogs all the time, and when my clients bring their dogs in, I talk to them, as well. I ask them questions, and even answer for them sometimes. Frequently, my clients with deaf dogs will remind me that the dog can't hear. I simply reply, "I know, but it makes me feel better." Seeing my facial expressions and sensing that I am comfortable allows my patients to feel more comfortable themselves.

But do they understand? I have long believed that some dogs (though not all) understand *exactly* what I say, and there are now some studies that confirm my belief. Researchers at the Max Planck Institute for Evolutionary Anthropology in Leipzig, Germany, tested a Border collie named Rico, and found that he knows the names of dozens of play toys, and can even find the one called for by his owner. According to Julia Fischer, who led the study, Rico's vocabulary is the about the same size as apes, dolphins, and parrots trained to understand words. Rico was even able to identify a new word. The researchers put several known toys in a room along with one that Rico had not seen before. From a different room, Rico's owner asked him to fetch a toy, using a name for the toy that the dog had never heard. Rico was able to go to the room with the toys and, seven times out of ten, bring back the toy he had not seen before. The dog seemingly understood that because he knew the names of all the other toys, the new one must be the one with the unfamiliar name. A month later, Rico still remembered the name of that new toy three times out of six, a rate that the scientists said was equivalent to that of a three-year-old child. Thank you, Rico, for confirming my own belief!

Obeying commands. Talking to your dog is also important because it trains your dog to *listen* to you. When you say "Come!" or "Down!" you want your dog to understand and to obey. In order to do this they must be listening to you. One primary component of all professional dog training is teaching your dog to obey simple voice commands. (See the list on p. 183.) But no animal (or human) wants to hear an unbroken litany of commands; they also want to hear affection. So if during the day you talk to your dog in warm, affectionate tones, and you give him an affectionate scratch at the same time, he will certainly pay more attention the next time you change tone and give him a stern command. In essence, through voice and touch you are creating a system of communication between yourself and your dog, and at the same time you are building the relationship and reinforcing the proper hierarchy.

Housebreaking

Ah, now the fun really begins. If your dog is going to live in your house, as opposed to out in the yard, it is essential to teach him proper bathroom manners. This can be one of the most stressful periods in a dog owner's life, but it is also a good opportunity to establish the necessary hierarchy and get the larger training process off to a strong start. To make this process work smoothly, I urge you to start by getting your expectations in order. Specifically, you have to know what kind of learning is age-appropriate for your dog. Breeds and individual dogs vary in their learning process, but generally speaking we can distinguish at least six different periods of dog development:

- Birth to Seven Weeks. This is a period when puppies should remain with their mother. She can quite competently manage her offspring and begin the teaching process. Puppies who are taken away during this period, to a pet shop or a new home, may have trouble developing into well-adjusted, mature dogs.

- Seven to Twelve Weeks. This is a period of socialization and exceptional learning potential. Whatever the puppy learns during this period will be deeply imprinted in her psyche, so this is an optimal time to begin the training process. At the same time, you want to avoid any trauma or undue distress during this period; it, too, will be permanently imprinted on the dog's psyche. For that reason, most vets usually do not like to perform elective surgeries during this period, and recommend that puppies stay with their mothers until eight to ten weeks of age.

- Twelve to Sixteen Weeks. This is an unsettling period when puppies begin to be PUPPIES. In an instant they go from "sleep, eat, poop, sleep, eat, poop," mode to "run around like mad, chew everything in sight, eat everything in sight, never sleep, never listen, and oh-my-I-can't-control myself!" mode. Puppies generally begin to lose their baby teeth at four months, and any object that can fit into their mouths appears to be fair game. Though it is a trying time for an owner, it is also a time of laughter and high spirits. Puppies are pure joy. This age is the perfect time to begin basic obedience training.

- Four to Eight Months. Often referred to as the "flight instinct period," this is a time when your dog will test his independence and boundaries. He may go off on his own, ignoring your commands to "Come!" This is undesirable behavior, and you must be firm in counteracting it. Keep him on a leash until he fully gets the message. Allowing him too much freedom will only embolden his demands for independence and dominance.

- Six to Fourteen Months. By now your dog has entered adolescence, and she may be fearful of confronting unfamiliar territory. Some dog specialists refer to this as the "fear imprint period." My advice is to be kind and patient during this period, and continue the training with determination. Continued socialization is also key in this period.

- One to Four Years. With maturity, some dogs become aggressive, and you have to be on your guard for behavioral problems and major changes in your dog's mood or behavior. For more information about this period and how to cope with it, please see my later chapter on spaying and neutering.

Now, how does all this apply to housetraining? First of all, it indicates that the period of seven to twelve weeks is the optimum time to start housetraining. But you have to keep this in mind: puppies younger than twelve weeks old have only a limited ability to control their bladder. That means that they need to go to the bathroom frequently, so keep your expectations in line. If you have a favorite or expensive rug, pull it up or keep it off limits to the puppy. This will save you both unnecessary strife. Punishing a very young puppy for going on the carpet is unfair, and does nothing for the training process. During the night, when the body slows down, many puppies can go long stretches without having to pee or poop, but that is not true during the day. Remember these things: after they eat, they need to go. When they wake up, they need to go. After they run around playing for thirty minutes, they need to go. Get them outside during these times and you will have fewer accidents inside, and the housetraining process will become quicker and easier. Now, how do you teach your dog to wait until she is outside? Here is Dr. Dondi's essential primer on housetraining your dog:

1. Set up a strict routine. Dogs, like kids, feel more comfortable when they have a set schedule. Feed the dog at feeding time. Try to take walks at the same time every day. This will help your dog establish a schedule to follow.

2. As soon as he has finished eating, take him outside—and take him to the same spot each time. Be patient: you need to stay outside until he goes. Puppies are generally very oriented toward playing and not much else, so be prepared to stay outside for a good long time. When your puppy finally does go, make sure that you praise him. In training Chili these days, I have been using food as a reward. She is very food-oriented, and looks for her treat as soon as she goes. I have found that this cuts down on "chewing sticks and leaves nonsense time" outdoors, and allows her to get down to business quickly.

3. When housetraining your pup, never change his diet. Same food, same amount each time. Give him no table scraps, either. You want to make everything as regular and predictable as possible.

4. Accidents are going to happen—don't go haywire when they do. That does no good for the dog and no good for you. If you catch your puppy in the act, firmly say "No!" or "Stop!" and immediately whisk him outside. Go directly to his designated spot and wait for him to go. When he does go, praise him.

5. Here is a Dr. Dondi no-no: if you come upon an accident sometime after the fact, NEVER drag the puppy back to the scene of the crime and scold him. The dog will not make the connection between the punishment and his wrongdoing, or between the mess on the floor and his earlier urge to go. He will only become confused and hurt, and that will set back the housetraining process and undermine your bond and trust.

6. To clean up a mess, use a product designed to absorb urine odor, or use vinegar and water. Do NOT use an ammonia-based cleaner, as those can attract the dog back to the exact same spot.

7. Finally, smile. Accidents are a small price to pay for the many, many years of pleasure and camaraderie that your puppy is going to give you!

Crate-Training. Now, here is a tool that makes the entire process of housetraining go much, much smoother: the crate. I am a believer in crate-training, because it works with the natural instincts of the dog. Nature tells puppies to go to the bathroom outside of their nest. In nature, the mother cleans up all the urine and feces, to make sure that they do not attract predators. As the puppy is whelped, the mother teaches him to go to the bathroom away from the nest. The aim of crate-training is to build on those natural instincts. In essence, you turn the crate into the dog's nest. By keeping the dog in the crate at night and at times during the day when you can't supervise him, you encourage him to hold his bladder in the nest and not go until you take him outside. Your job is to nurture your pup's natural inclinations and add corrective discipline as needed. Here, step by step, is how you do it:

1. Select a crate that suits the size of your dog or puppy. You want a size that will allow your dog to stand up inside the crate and to easily turn around and make himself comfortable. However, it shouldn't be too big. If your dog can go to the bathroom on one end of the crate and get away from it at the other end, the crate is too big.

2. Present the crate to the dog as if it were both a treat and his new house. Let him inspect it. Maybe put his blanket inside, along with a few toys. You want the dog to think of it as his private sanctuary— *not* as his prison. Once you entice him to go inside, give him plenty of affectionate praise and several treats. Then let him out. Repeat this frequently, until the dog goes easily in and out, and until you can shut the door behind him without generating fear or panic. You can also give the dog a treat that will take some time to chew, such as a "Greenie" or peanut butter in a "Kong" toy to keep him occupied. That way he can settle in for a period of time without freaking out. If he panics, let him out right away. The goal, though, is to leave the dog in the crate for longer and longer periods of time and for him to feel comfortable being inside.

3. Accustom the dog to the idea that this is where he sleeps. Many people put the crate in their bedroom, so the dog will sense their presence throughout the night. As with children, do not treat bedtime as a time for negotiation. When you tell the dog to get into his crate, be firm and matter-of-fact. Maintain the hierarchy. The dog will not view the crate as punishment—unless you treat it as punishment. So if the dog is naughty, do not put him in the crate. Also, during the

day leave the gate to the crate open, so the dog can use it as his personal nesting area.

4. Watch out for power struggles. If the dog is confined and starts barking, do NOT let him out. That only rewards bad behavior. To the contrary, insist that the dog stop barking. If he does, praise him and then let him out.

5. Again, remember that accidents will happen. If the dog goes to the bathroom in his crate, treat it for what it is: an accident. He has already been punished enough by having to stay in the crate with his mess. Instead, let him out, take him directly outside, and clean up the mess. As the dog matures, he'll learn what he should do—and where.

Schedule for Puppies

7 weeks–6 months*

6:00	a.m.	Walk
6:30	a.m.	Feed, water, and walk
10:30	a.m.	Water, and walk
3:30	p.m.	Water, and walk
7:30	p.m.	Feed, water, and walk
10:30	p.m.	Walk

*Toy breeds should be fed 3–4 times per day.

6–12 months

6:00	a.m.	Walk
6:30	a.m.	Feed, water, and walk
11:30	a.m.	Water and walk
3:30	p.m.	Water and walk
6:30	p.m.	Feed, water, and walk
10:00	p.m.	Walk

---

12 months+		
6:00	a.m.	Walk
6:30	a.m.	Feed, water, and walk
3:30	p.m.	Water and walk
6:30	p.m.	Feed, water, and walk
10:00	p.m.	Walk

Socialization

I take my dogs everywhere. I take them in my car, I take them shopping, and sometimes I even take them to my clinic. My dogs have been socialized their whole lives, and they have learned how to interact properly with people and other dogs. They know what they are allowed to do, they know when they are allowed to visit with other dogs, and they have learned how to play happily with other dogs. Thank God, they have never been aggressive or attacked or bitten another dog, and this has not happened by chance. It happened because I took great pains to teach them. If you want to have a safe, comfortable experience with your dog, you have to do the same. Start early. Have them meet and play with other dogs, but only after they have received their first three sets of vaccinations. Unvaccinated puppies are at risk of contracting contagious diseases, so be careful. Use common sense— and a strong leash in the beginning.

Let me emphasize an important point here: even though my dogs are very well-behaved, if you put them on a leash or behind a fence they will still act like idiots. If they are restrained, they don't have to own up to their own actions. For instance, if they are in their yard behind a fence and another dog walks by, they can bark and raise a ruckus because they know there will be no consequences. It is only just a brief interaction, and they have the justification of protecting their property. They realize they are not going to get into a fight—thanks to the fence—so they can act however they want to establish and protect their territory. By contrast, I think that dogs usually interact much better when they are off the leash. Then they know that they have to be sociable or else they may have to pay the price. That said, if your dog has aggressive tendencies, I urge you to always err on the side of caution: keep her on the leash in unfamiliar situations, such as in a park where there are fifteen dogs running around.

If you have a new dog and want to begin the socialization process, take him first to a neutral territory where you can expose him to one or two other dogs whose temperament you know. Neutral territory will help to ensure that no dog has to feel protective of his surroundings. If you are unsure how he will react, keep the leash attached to the dog but let it drag on the ground. That way, if a problem arises, you can quickly grab the leash and bring the situation under control.

How to Spot a Dominant Dog (Or an Irresponsible Owner)

At the park and in other socializing situations, it is important to understand the posture and behavior of each of the dogs, but especially of a dominant dog. When he is on unfamiliar ground or encountering unfamiliar dogs, a dominant dog will raise its tail up in the air and its hackles—the hair over the shoulders and back—will stand up. If he sees an unfamiliar dog in the distance, a dominant dog will hold its head down and level with its back, like he is getting the other dog in his sights, then he will move slowly forward toward him. If they are in closer proximity the dominant dog will raise his head and try to put his chin over the other dog's head or the back of his neck. Be very careful of those dogs; they can spell trouble.

A submissive dog, by contrast, will respond to an approaching dog in a very different way. He will sit or roll over, exposing his belly, or he might lick the mouth of the other dog. His ears will tend to go flat back, his hackles will be down, and he'll tend to exhibit exaggerated tail wagging and wiggling, to show a friendly, nonaggressive demeanor. His tail might also be tucked beneath his legs, again to show submission. Learn to detect these signs from a distance, so that you can take steps to control the situation.

Surprisingly, perhaps, the issue of dominance and submission is not a function of size. I have seen Jack Russell terriers stand right up to a rottweiller and get themselves into a world of trouble. The terriers don't necessarily realize that they are midget-size; it is just their instinct to be pushy. So you always have to be careful going into a new situation, in particular one in which many dogs are running off-leash. The best precaution is to know your own dog well, know exactly how she will react if she is challenged, and have her well trained to obey your commands. If another dog then starts to get aggressive, you can give your own dog a command and bring the situation under immediate control. That will keep everybody safe.

Learn, too, to spot trouble in the making. You've probably seen it already: an uncertain owner with a big dog on the leash, struggling to keep the dog under control. It's a scary sight, and one that even experienced dog owners learn to dread. At any moment, that aggressive dog can break loose and attack whatever dog—or human—is in sight. In San Francisco, there was an infamous case in which two such dogs attacked a neighbor woman carrying groceries in the hallway of their apartment building. The woman was killed, and the dogs' owners ended up going to jail. Enough said, right?

Do dominant dogs sense their owner's uncertainty? Yes, dominant dogs are always testing their boundaries. They won't come when called, they won't listen to commands, they do whatever they want, and are constantly acting in an uncontrolled manner. They are not getting clear, strong direction from their owner, and the dogs simply do not know what to do. The worst part of it is that many of these owners have absolutely no clue that the master-dog relationship is out of control; they think everything is fine. Let me be emphatic: *this is a dangerous situation.* Dangerous for anyone in the vicinity—man, woman, or dog. If the out-of-control dog is also aggressive by nature, that can spell real trouble. If you are an outsider, stay clear. If you are the owner, you must recognize the danger and immediately seek professional obedience training for your dog. You will regret it one day if you don't.

Little dogs can be little monsters. It is not just big, aggressive dogs who need professional training. Even little dogs can be obstreperous and unpleasant companions. For instance, if you have a little terrier who keeps lunging forward on the leash, to the point that he hacks and coughs as he pulls, get him into obedience school. He needs to learn socialization. That will make him a more confident and pleasurable pet, it will strengthen your mutual bond, and it will save you all sorts of grief down the road. I believe all dogs, big and small, should be properly trained, either by their owner or by a professional trainer. Frankly, it drives me nuts when people come into my clinic with a dog that they can't control. Many owners do not even try to control their dog by commanding them to sit or stay; they think it's fine or cute that their dog is jumping all over me. It isn't. And it's not good for the dog, either.

How to Find a Professional Trainer

If your dog is difficult to control or is showing signs of dominance or aggression, please get him to a professional trainer. The younger the dog is, the easier he will be to train, so don't waste weeks or months hoping that the situation will improve on its own. It probably won't. To find a professional dog trainer in your area, you should first ask your veterinarian for a referral. Humane societies, breeders, and some rescue organizations might also be helpful in locating a trainer, but your vet will know your dog better than any outsider. You can also consult the Web site of the American Kennel Club, www.akc.org, for a list of professional trainers in your area. The AKC Web site is a fountain of useful information for dog owners. It lists basic training procedures and also has a list of the many cities and towns that have AKC dog clubs. If you contact the AKC club closest to you, you may get a good tip on where to find a professional trainer. The AKC can also steer you to reputable breeders to contact in your area. Breeders are, generally speaking, very serious dog people, and they will know most of the best trainers in your area.

Table Manners

As every parent in France or Italy will tell you, good training of children begins at the table. And it is not much different with dogs. If you are training your dog on your own, this is an excellent place to set down rules—and enforce them. As for exactly which rules to set down, all I can say is, "To each his own." Some of my clients practically set a place at the table for the family dog and give him scraps throughout the meal. That usually results in constant begging, something that some owners find cute. Other owners, by contrast, banish their dogs from the dining room during lunch or dinner. Whatever practice you endorse, be clear and consistent. If you allow the dog to beg at family dinners, he will do the same when guests come over. And if he does, don't blame the dog—it will be your fault. I also urge you to be careful about feeding people food to dogs. And no bones! (I discuss these topics at length in Chapter Six, "DogAge Nutrition.")

All this said, I do have some concrete suggestions about how to make family meals more enjoyable—for you and your dog.

Dr. Dondi's Guide to Proper Canine Table Manners

1. Set up clear rules for everyone to follow, all the time. If you do not want your dog begging at the table when guests come over, you have to train him not to beg at all. Period.
2. To discourage begging at the table, feed the dog at the same time that you are eating. It won't be as agonizing for him to watch you eat if he's not hungry.
3. Set physical boundary lines. If you don't want him begging at the table, don't allow him to go past the threshold of the dining room while you are eating. With a little effort, you can teach him that he can go into the dining room on a regular basis, but when you sit down to eat, he cannot cross that threshold.
4. If you do give your dog people food, put it in his dog bowl, not on a plate. That teaches him that his permitted treats will be in his bowl and that people plates are off limits. It should come as no surprise that dogs who are allowed to eat off plates will steal food off plates when you're not looking.

5. If you allow your dog to lick your forks and spoons, don't do it in front of your guests. They may not realize that you put them in the dishwasher afterward!

Let me add one last thought on the subject of table manners. You can train and train, but there are some dogs who just go berserk when they smell a fine meal. My Hannah is like that. She is well trained, and she knows I really mean business, but there is something about food that overrides all her circuits. Maybe it is because I got her as a stray, and she ate out of garbage cans for years before I got her. But if she smells a piece of steak on the counter, and I tell her "No!" she will look at me, then look at the steak and weigh the consequences. I can almost see her thinking, "I know I'm going to get in trouble, but it's STEAK!" Invariably, if it's within her grasp, the steak will win out.

Cats

It's the same with cats: the sight of a cat running away will almost always override a dog's circuits, and no matter how well you've trained your dog, she may well tear off after that cat. There are exceptions, of course, but I think chasing cats is a natural behavior that is hardwired into most dogs' brains. So what is it with cats and dogs? And what do you need to know about keeping the peace between cats and dogs?

For starters, I urge you to pay attention to a number of different factors. First, is your dog an adult or a puppy? In my experience, you're probably okay if you bring a puppy into a house where cats are already a part of the family. They will establish their own hierarchy. A normal puppy doesn't generally have it in his makeup to aggressively go after a healthy adult cat. If the puppy does try anything, an adult cat will usually shut the puppy down or at least remove himself from the situation. Kittens may actually engage in play with both puppies and adult dogs who are amenable. Most cats, however, will get stressed when a new puppy is introduced to the house. For this reason, it is important to give the cat a safe haven and ample time away from the puppy to ensure the success of the introduction. In most cases, though, harmony will eventually be established.

Adult dogs are far trickier to introduce into a house with cats. I had to do this with Hannah, my rottweiller, and I had no idea how she'd react. So when I came into the house for the first time with Hannah, I left the leash attached to her. I followed her around the house watching to see how she would react to the cats. Luckily she noticed them and just went on about her business. It made no difference to her that those cats were in the house. I was very fortunate. But here is an important point to remember: if you have other animals and are bringing a new dog into the house, leave the leash on him or her while inside for the first few days. It may come in handy if you need it.

Here is another important thing to keep in mind: some dogs and cats will NEVER get along, no matter what you do. One of my nurses has a dog who will literally eat through the drywall in the house to get into the room where the cat stays. The nurse adopted this dog as an adult, and in the beginning, when she was crate-training him, she noticed that whenever the cat would walk by, the dog would salivate. So she built a pen for the dog, far away from any contact with the cat. They figured, better safe than sorry.

If, as in this case, your dogs and cats simply do NOT get along, you have three options to consider. First, you can try obedience training for the dog and can keep him in a crate or pen when he's unsupervised until you figure out if things are going to work or not. Second, you can confine the cats to another part of the house and try to make sure that the cats and dogs never come face-to-face. Be careful, though: this is NOT a foolproof solution. Recently, I had a client with an adorable little Siamese kitty. Her fiancé had three big huskies, and they had already terrorized several cats in the neighborhood. What were they to do?

Well, the couple partitioned their house, with the three dogs on one side, the little kitty on the other, and, as far as they could tell, no avenues of communication between them. One afternoon, though, one of the dogs was able to open the door to the cat side of the house. All three dogs went in and attacked the kitty. She was in the ICU for two and a half weeks, and we didn't think she was going to make it. She did pull through, though, thank goodness, and some serious negotiations ensued. The woman refused to give up her cat, and the man refused to give up his dogs. So they took the extra precaution of putting dead-bolt locks on all the doors on both sides, and when no one is home the dogs are kept locked in a pen. All I could do was wish them good luck. (And you thought being a vet was only about shots and flea collars. . . .)

That brings me to the third option. If your cats and dogs (or dogs and dogs, for that matter) cannot work out a hierarchy on their own, and obedience training doesn't work, you might have to consider giving one of them up. Instinct is instinct, and I wish I could tell you that there was some magical way to teach everyone, to get along. Training has its limits. And you ignore those limits at your peril.

One last word on the dicey subject of cats and dogs: it is not always the dog that is the aggressor. We have two hospital cats named Hank and Tugger. During the day, they used to live in a large pen in the hub of the hospital, the ICU. Tugger is pretty docile, but Hank is a real tough guy. He will attack any dog who comes his way. We quickly separated the two kitties, because every time Hank saw a dog and couldn't get to it, he would beat the tar out of Tugger. Still, whenever Hank spotted a dog, he would stand up, arch his back, puff up his fur, and slowly walk over to the part of his cage that was closest to the dog. No matter how big the dog was, Hank wanted to get him. Of course we knew that there was no way that cat could *ever* be in a house with a dog. As I said, there are some cases where even the most gifted animal trainer is of absolutely no use whatsoever. Nature is nature.

Zelda, *Sit!*

How to Teach Your Dog Basic Commands

How do you teach your dog to sit, stand, stay, lie down, come, and heel? This can be a fun exercise and bonding experience for you and your dog. And a well-trained dog has a younger DogAge! There are techniques to follow that are usually very effective. Usually, but not always. Some dogs are just more headstrong, and may need some professional training. Always begin basic obedience training in a secure area where your dog cannot get out, or with a leash and collar attached. You can enroll in a class or practice at home. I recommend at least fifteen minutes daily on the weekdays and maybe two or three fifteen-minute sessions at home on weekend days. Here is Dr. Dondi's quick how-to primer on teaching your dog the basic commands.

Dr. Dondi's Basic Command Primer

1. The first step in training is to establish a hierarchy. This means teaching the dog that you are the boss. In the wild,

dogs develop their own hierarchy in the pack. The most dominant dog gets to eat first, sleep in the best spot, and basically gets to do what he wants to do, when he wants to do it. In order for you to establish this, you don't have to be mean, but you do have to be firm. You must be the dominant dog in your pack. You must let your dog know that when you say no, you mean NO! Using a firm tone and stern expression on your face will go a long way toward conveying that. Don't let your dog push you around.

2. Treats can be an especially effective way to get your dog's attention. Try to use very small, bite-size treats that are low in calories. The last thing you want to do is to create a weight problem for your dog while you address his need for obedience training. If your dog likes green beans or baby carrots (cut into small pieces; vegetables still have calories) those are perfect treats. If you must use commercial treats, make sure to get ones that can be broken into small pieces.

3. Successful training depends on your ability to communicate clearly what you want your animal to do. Your voice is key. Use a gentle but authoritative tone, and use the same simple commands over and over. How you use your body is also very important. Many professional trainers urge you to use hand signals, and that's fine. I prefer using voice commands along with hand signals. You can use a treat, affectionate words, and affection to reinforce to your dog that he has done a good job. If he behaves badly, you can reinforce a strong, verbal "No!" with a gentle but firm correction of the undesired behavior. I do *not* favor hitting any animal at any time.

4. Teaching your dog to sit is a good place to start. Have the dog stand next to you, facing in the same direction. Initially, you will need to show your dog what "sit" means. Here's how you do it. After saying "sit," put one hand under your

dog's chin to gently lift his head. At the same time, use your other hand to push down on his lower back until the dog is in the sitting position. Immediately follow this success with kind words of praise and a treat. Remember to say the command "Sit!" only once before helping your dog into the sitting position. Now perform this action several more times. Once your dog gets the hang of it, you will need to use physical coaxing less and less. If your dog has a momentary lapse and doesn't perform the command properly, don't say the word "sit" over and over while getting no response. It will desensitize him to the command and lessen the idea that you mean business. Say the command only once. If your dog does not go into the sitting position, gently help him to do so and praise him once he's there. Do that over and over, until your dog associates sitting with praise and reward. After a few weeks or months, depending on your dog, you will be able to drop the treat after every successful "sit." That said, it is still a good idea to periodically reward good behavior with a treat, to keep the incentive firmly planted in his head.

5. Now, let's teach the dog "down." As you prepare to teach any new command, begin the session with a few successful "sit" commands to get your dog into training mode. In teaching "down," you will have more success getting your dog to lie down from a sitting position than from a standing one. For this reason, ask your dog first to get into the "sit" position. Then, standing in front of him, close a treat in your hand so that he sees it. As you say "down," bring your hand down to the ground in front of your dog. You will be surprised at how many dogs will naturally lie down on their own to get the treat. If your dog does not do this, have him first sit, then give him the "down" command and gently coax him down by the collar while lowering the treat hand in front of him. Once he

is in the down position, give him the reward and words of praise. As you repeat this, lower the treat hand less and less until you are not lowering it at all—you are just using the verbal command and possibly a hand signal. As with "sit," eventually cut back the treat every once in a while, but always follow a successful command with some form of praise.

6. Now, we'll teach the dog "stay" And here it gets fun, because you get to combine commands. Again, start with commands that your dog has already learned to get him into training mode. Then have your dog lie down. Stand in front of him, maintaining close proximity and eye contact. Say the command "stay" and walk slowly backward. Here it is important to recognize your dog's ability and attention span, because you want to execute as many successful commands as possible to reinforce your training. If you have a hyperactive puppy, he will not be able to "stay" in position for a few minutes. In fact, you will be lucky if he is successful for a few seconds. For this reason, you will need to praise him while he is still performing the desired behavior. So, "sit," praise; "down," praise; then "stay" and back away for a few feet.

Before your dog has a chance to get up, give the release command "OK, come," allowing your dog to come out of the "stay" position and receive the reward of praise and a treat. If your dog gets up before receiving the release command, firmly say "no" and walk over and put him back into position. Give the "stay" command again and repeat the process. Eventually, your dog will get the hang of it, and you can gradually increase the time that you insist that he "stay."

7. Now comes the big one, the most important command to teach your dog: "come!" Every day I take my dogs to the dog park, where they are allowed to run around off-leash and

play. Every once in a while, a situation develops (such as a dog fight) in which I need them to be near me quickly. "Georgia, Hannah, come!" is all I need to say to bring them to my side. That keeps them out of trouble. Likewise, if they are out playing and I see a cat on the horizon, one "come!" and I've averted a major showdown. Teaching your dog to obey the command "come!" is essential—and it may even save his life. Here's how you do it:

I recommend you start gently, as soon as you get the dog. It is best to start in a confined area, like your living room. In an enthusiastic, playful voice, say "come!" If the dog comes, give him a treat and lots of praise. In the beginning, you might have to wave the treat in front of his nose and then move some distance away before you say "come!" Do this frequently and give him lots of treats. Then, slowly wean the dog away from the treats by only giving them randomly when he obeys the word "come!" Once your dog has gotten the idea of what "come" means, you can begin to reinforce your training. If you give the command and your dog fails to respond, go get him and bring him by the collar to where you were. Then you can dish out some praise. Be careful, though: if your dog fails to obey, and you have to go get him, do *not* reprimand him or even use harsh body language—he is liable to run in the opposite direction. That undercuts the lesson. That's why it is so important to always keep the training of this command positive.

Now, let's do this outdoors. When you are ready to teach this command off-leash, follow the same rules but do so outdoors in a fenced area that is safe for your dog. If you do not have a safe, fenced-in area, use a long utility leash as a training aid. Also, teaching "come!" is one area in which treats will be very effective, provided your dog is food-oriented. If he's not food-oriented, try a squeaky toy. Here's what to do. First practice the "come" command, leash attached, with your dog a significant distance away in a "down" position. Remember to release your dog with an "okay" before commanding him to come. If he does not respond, you can pull him to you using the leash and lots of friendly words of praise and end with a food reward. Next, allow your dog to walk freely, sniffing around with the leash attached but slack. When you are ready, command him in a friendly, playful voice by saying his name followed by "come!" Reward success with lots of praise and a treat. If your dog fails to come, gently pull him to you using the leash and friendly words. Remember to praise him when he reaches you. Eventually, most dogs will get to where you will not need the leash at all. Just make sure that you are in an environment where your dog is not exposed to potential danger: his life may depend on it.

8. "Heel!" If you have ever walked a big dog who pulls at the leash while on an icy sidewalk, you'll understand the need for the command "heel." I hope that everyone wants their dogs to be well behaved on the leash, and this is where "heel" comes in. To do this, always keep your dog on-leash and on your left as you walk. The proper heel position is when your dog's head and shoulder are aligned with your left hip. Professional trainers have many strict guidelines to follow to teach your dog to heel, but here is the method that I use. Start with your dog on your left side and say his name followed by the command "heel." Begin walking briskly, keeping the leash taut as you walk along so that your dog cannot sniff or stray. If he begins to lag behind use a gentle tug to get him back into proper position, and reinforce with "heel." If you can maintain eye contact with your dog during this exercise, it will keep his

attention better and make your training more successful. You can then begin to make quick left and right turns, using the leash to coax him along on right turns and your hip to nudge him into position on left turns. Stop and give the "sit" command frequently so that you can reward your dog with praise and a treat. This also helps to make training fun for both of you. As you move along, space your reward breaks further apart. You can use the "heel" command on a walk when you see another dog. That will help alert your dog to be on his best behavior.

9. Finally, there's the all-purpose command, "no!" There are all sorts of dog behaviors that you will find unacceptable: chewing shoes, getting on the furniture, begging, chasing cats, or barking inappropriately. This is when you have to bring out the howitzer: the command of "no!" When using this command, make sure that you say your dog's name followed by "no." You can modulate the volume and tone of your voice to fit the crime and thus drive home the necessary lesson. If your dog is begging at the table, a gentle no may be all that you need (depending, of course, on how obnoxious your dog is—you should see my Chihuahua). If your dog jumps on the furniture or chews your Manolo Blahniks, that may require a firmer "no!" with an exclamation point. But if your dog is about to ingest something toxic or gets away at the dog park, you'd better have a big, powerful, watch-it-buster "NOOOOO!!!" in your repertoire of commands. Here's the key: you have to teach it right from the beginning, and you have to mean business—no exceptions. No matter which tone of voice you use or how many exclamation points follow it, the dog has to understand that "no" means "no."

Separation Anxiety

There is one exception when "no" doesn't always work, even with much special training: separation anxiety. It's a difficult problem to solve, and training is not always an effective answer, at least not in my experience. Now, to the average reader, separation anxiety in dogs might sound like a trivial problem, or something that Jay Leno might make wisecracks about late at night. The truth is, though, many dogs suffer from separation anxiety, and it is a serious problem. I see it most often in dogs who have been rescued from shelters or shuffled from home to home. Many times, the anxiety manifests itself in undesirable behaviors that prompt the dog to be given up for adoption. So let's dig into it a bit.

The basis of separation anxiety is no mystery. The dog forms an emotional bond to a family or a person, and then he is abruptly taken away. If he goes to a shelter or rescue organization, the dog may form new bonds, to another dog or to a specific schedule that is maintained in the new environment. Then he is abruptly shifted again. This time the dog may experience an acute sense of loss and disorientation. In the new environment, the dog will create new bonds and adapt to the new routine. A couple of weeks or even months later, though, when those new bonds begin to strengthen, the dog might become nervous and even panicky that things are going to change again. He is afraid that these new bonds will once again soon be broken, and that he'll be torn away from his new family and environment. Separation anxiety rarely manifests itself right away when a dog joins a new family; it takes a little time to form new bonds. It is a reaction based on a fear of abandonment and a hesitancy to trust the new situation.

The symptoms of separation anxiety can be dramatic. The dog can act out in destructive ways and, when he is left alone at home, he may develop panic-type reactions. The dog may tear up the furniture, go to the bathroom in the house, or howl or bark incessantly. The problem can be very distressing to both dog and owner. I have even had owners request euthanasia because their dog's separation anxiety was such an uncomfortable ordeal. I know this problem well. I once had a whippet who developed severe separation anxiety. I believe that it was because my schedule was changing all the time and we moved a lot between the time I graduated from veterinary school and became established in my practice. While I was at the clinic, she'd be busy destroying my house. I tried keeping her in the kitchen, but she started destroying it. Even if I went to the grocery store for twenty minutes she'd freak out and rip out the linoleum. It got so bad that she began injuring herself trying to get out of the house. Modifying my schedule, remedial obedience training, and even medications did not help relieve her anxiety or her destructive behaviors. Finally, I was forced to place her in a home with a retired couple who took her everywhere they went, even to the golf course! And there she lived, happily ever after.

How do you treat separation anxiety? Sometimes remedial obedience training coupled with desensitization training can help. Crate-training and even medical management with antianxiety drugs can be used. Some people even modify their schedules so that a family member is always with the dog.

My whippet history was typical for a dog with separation anxiety. I had gotten her as an adult from a breeder. She had been kenneled for her whole life, and never seemed to fully relax in the home environment; she always seemed a bit wary of the surroundings. She was also a sight hound, and they tend to be very sensitive. The term "sight hound" applies to whippets, greyhounds, Russian and Irish wolfhounds, and a few others. They are called sight hounds because they are very visual. With their sensitive eyes, they are often used for hunting. By temperament, they have a tendency to get keyed into a schedule, a regimen that they like to follow every single day. Any change in schedule can make them feel off-kilter and, as in the case of my dog, even panicky.

Some of the medications we use to treat separation anxiety can be very effective. Some dogs also benefit from specialized training, to build the bond of trust to where the dog no longer feels she is about to be abandoned. I have to be truthful, though: there is no magic solution for separation anxiety. If you have a dog who gets distressed when left alone, my advice is to experiment. Some of my clients try to distract their dog with a long-lasting Greenie or a rubber toy filled with peanut butter. This may keep them busy and distracted for hours. Other clients hire dog-walkers to come in and play with the dog, take her for walks, and assure the dog that her master will be home in a few minutes.

I have one friend whose English springer spaniel used to howl when he was gone for more than five minutes. He tried toys and peanut-butter bones and even giving the dog a job: he told the dog to guard the door and inspect the baseboards while he was gone. Most of these tricks worked short-term, but the dog would still howl. Finally, he hit on a solution: the radio. This fellow often listened to the radio when he was home, especially during baseball season. So when he went out, he would leave the radio on and that seemed to calm the dog, probably because it was already a part of the daily routine in the house. Once or twice he tried leaving music on, but the dog was not as happy. Apparently the sound of human voices on the radio was more reassuring to the dog—especially, perhaps, if the home team was winning. If baseball fails, you can always try Mozart.

CHAPTER ELEVEN

Putting It All Together: Dr. Dondi's DogAge Wellness Program

CHILI BEYONCÉ is an adorable, teeny-weeny teacup Chihuahua, and her early life experience carries many important lessons for dog owners. That's especially true when it comes to puppies, vaccinations, and the importance of establishing a proper DogAge wellness program for your animal.

Chili came to our clinic in horrible shape, and I can tell you that her life was truly dangling by a thread. Teacup Chihuahuas are always small, but Chili weighed less than a pound, and was so tiny I could hold her in the palm of my hand. Dogs that small have very fast metabolisms, and they have to eat every three to four hours just to stay alive. Well, little Chili Beyoncé had not eaten a drop of food for days, and worse, she had been suffering from chronic vomiting, diarrhea, even seizures. That poor little girl was so sick, and her owners had no idea what was wrong with her or what to do about it. Finally, in a panic, they brought her in to our emergency service.

As we obtained her medical history, a disturbing story emerged. Four or five weeks before that, her owners had bought Chili and a brother of hers from a local pet store. The puppies seemed fine for about the first five days but had not been healthy since. From the beginning, neither of them had much of an appetite, and they both would intermittently vomit or have soft stools. Their owners didn't realize it, but both puppies had low blood sugar and, as a result, were having periods of dementia, unresponsiveness, and seizures. Her brother was doing a little better than she was, but little Chili just got weaker and weaker. Once we had her in intensive care, we did a battery of tests and found that things were relatively normal except for her low blood sugar. We checked her for intestinal parasites but found nothing significant. In the end, we could not pinpoint the precise cause of her suffering, but we had our suspicions. It is not uncommon to fail to uncover intestinal parasites on a fecal test if a puppy has been having a lot of diarrhea. The sample gets so diluted that few parasite eggs or organisms are contained within it. We went ahead and put her on antibiotics and an anti-parasite medication and prayed for the best. Luckily, it worked. After a few days, Chili began to get stronger, but she was still very ill and in need of intensive care. It was at this point that her owners were forced to make a very difficult decision. They had reached their limits both financially and emotionally, and they realized that they would be unable to even deal with her necessary aftercare if she were to leave the hospital. It was very sad.

By now, you readers know me well enough to know that I simply couldn't let little Chili go. She had been so brave! She had been in our ICU for several days, and the poor thing had endured more in the way of diagnostic tests and treatment than most of us will experience in a lifetime. She was frightened and understood none of it, but she never complained. Not once. I just couldn't let her go through all that and then die for nothing. I told her owners that from then on I'd take over her medical care, and if we could make her better, she could live with me or

I would find her a good home. It was a good proposal—far better than euthanasia—and her owners readily agreed.

Well, I took the pup in hand and, believe me, it was touch and go. She still had no appetite, and because her metabolism was so fast her blood sugar would drop to nothing. I had to force-feed Chili every two hours for about a week after she came home. I'd hold her and feed her baby food with a syringe. (Which is not the easiest thing to do with a three-quarter-pound Chihuahua puppy, let me tell you.) I spent much of my time sitting with her in my lap, offering her various things to try. I tried one kind of baby food, then another: chicken, lamb, scrambled eggs. I was making midnight trips to the grocery store, wandering down the aisles buying Vienna sausages, ground turkey, canned chicken—basically anything I could think of to get her to eat. I knew the stakes: if she didn't eat, she wasn't going to live, and I couldn't hand-feed her every two hours forever. Still she refused to eat on her own.

As you can imagine, I was a wreck; I just loved this little puppy. Then one morning I went over to my friend Sarah's house and brought Chili with me. I was crying at this point because my heart was breaking at my new baby's refusal to eat. I told Sarah that I was afraid that Chili really was going to die no matter what I did, because she had no interest in eating anything. Now Sarah is a real dog lover and spoils her dog rotten. Her response was: "I bet she'll eat chicken nuggets. Jesse loves them." As fate would have it, Sarah had ordered pizza the night before and it came with chicken nuggets. She walked right over to Chili with one, and to my surprise, that little Chihuahua just tore right into it! I was shocked and thrilled at the same time. We must have spent the next thirty minutes feeding Chili as many chicken nuggets as she would eat on Sarah's kitchen counter. For a few days, all Chili would eat was chicken nuggets and a little cheese, but then her appetite really kicked in. Soon she became a competitive eater: when she was around my other dogs, she ate more and more, and she even wanted to eat out of their bowls. I couldn't let her do that; it was too dangerous: the bigger dogs might get protective of their food.

Anyway, little Chili soon recovered all her strength, and I am happy to report that today she is a normal, healthy pup with high energy and an absolutely darling personality. I love her to pieces, and so do Hannah and Georgia. They act like her big sisters at the dog park and protect her, and she has the full run of the house. When I go out, I carry her along with me in a little purse that I use just for her. She rides in that purse like a little princess in her own private carriage.

Now, what lessons do I see in the saga of Chili Beyoncé?

Lesson One: Beware of buying puppies from pet stores. I don't want to generalize unfairly, but in my experience too many pet stores sell puppies from puppy mills that are out for profit, not to promote responsible breeding. See my earlier warning in Chapter Nine, "Finding the Right Dog for You." Dr. Dondi's best advice? Get your puppy from a reputable breeder or shelter, not a pet store. This is the advice I always give to my friends and clients. Breeders are more careful about proper screening and medical care, and you as an owner have many more guarantees when you buy from a breeder. You can get a dog from a reputable humane society or rescue group, but then get the dog to a good vet right away for a professional examination. It can save you enormous cost and headaches down the road. For more advice on how to find a dog that's right for you, please see Chapter Nine.

Lesson Two: Be vigilant. Typically we have a fourteen-day window when a puppy's prior exposures can catch up with him. And you never know what's in store. Puppies offered for sale in pet shops have been separated from their mother and siblings, and they have commonly traveled some distance and then been placed in an extremely stressful environment where they can be exposed to all kinds of things. Also, you can never be sure if the store has paid proper attention to cleaning and sanitizing to prevent communicable diseases. Most viruses have a seven-to-fourteen-day incubation period. So the puppy may be healthy when you see it, but you've got about two weeks to see if it is going to stay that way. Be alert during that time.

Lesson Three: If you spot a problem, act quickly. If your new puppy shows any signs of illness, take her to the vet immediately; don't wait a few weeks. All puppies should be isolated from other dogs for ten to fourteen days because of the potential for spreading kennel cough and other infections. I know it's tough to do, but it's for the best. Otherwise, everyone in the house could come down with kennel cough or, as in Chili's case, far worse.

Lesson Four: Be careful: buying a puppy is not just a financial decision, it is an *emotional* decision. Let's say you go to a pet store, fall in love with the cutest puppy you've ever seen, buy him, and bring him home. Ten days later you discover that the puppy you have now grown attached to has a severe illness that it contracted at the pet store. Now you are caught in a real pickle: like Chili's owners, you either have to spend a lot of money to try to get your puppy well, or you have to face the emotionally wrenching decision of returning the puppy to the pet store. Painful! And guess what? That pet store won't ease your pain. Most pet stores will *not* cover any of the medical expenses necessary to make your pet better. Instead, they will say you can bring the puppy back and they'll give you your money back. But who wants to do that? So you're stuck—and don't say I didn't warn you!

The Biggest Lesson: Check with the pet store to see what kind of health guarantee they give, how long the puppy is covered under the guarantee, and what their policy is on paying for necessary medical treatment. Whether you get your dog from a breeder, a rescue group, or a pet store, go right to the vet with all the paperwork you have. (More on proper vaccinations in a moment.) Then have a full physical exam done and get the puppy on a proper schedule of vaccinations and complete wellness care, as I will describe later in this chapter.

Now, Chili's story leads me into the heart of this chapter: how do you build an effective, long-term wellness program for your dog? What specific vaccinations does your puppy or adult dog need? Are all vaccines safe and worthwhile? What do you need to know about spaying or neutering your dog? What do you need to know about controlling fleas, ticks, and heartworms? What about proper dental care for your dog? And alternative medicine? In this chapter, I will answer all of those questions, and I will also go over the basics of good grooming and explain why this is so important to the health and longevity of your dog.

This is material that you need to know. When you combine it with the areas that we have already covered—the monthly home exam, proper nutrition, healthy exercise, dog safety, and how to find and work with a veterinarian who's right for you— you will be on the road to creating a sound and effective wellness program that will help your dog lead a longer, healthier, happier life. So let's get to it.

Dr. Dondi's DogAge Wellness Program

Puppies and adult dogs have different prevention and wellness needs, but puppies require the most attention. So let's start there.

Let's say you are the proud owner of a new pup. What do you need to know and what do you need to do first? As I said, take him to the vet right away. Even if you got the dog from a reputable breeder or shelter, have the vet give him a thorough physical exam and begin his vaccinations. During that first exam, the vet's trained eye may spot an underlying health or temperament problem that you didn't see when you chose your puppy. This is standard procedure. But I urge you to go much further. I urge you to work closely with your vet to create a comprehensive wellness care program designed to keep your dog healthy, happy, and safe for many years to come. Whether on the first visit or on subsequent visits, these are the issues you should cover in detail:

Regular visits. Each vet has his or her own preferences, and that's fine. But here is the gospel according to Dr. Dondi: initially, I recommend that your puppy gets his first vaccinations between six and eight weeks of age. Then the puppy should go back to see your vet every three weeks for three or four more visits. After that, take him in when he's six months old and again at one year. As the dog matures into an adult, I think you can scale back the routine visits to once a year. When your dog reaches six or seven years of age and becomes vulnerable to the various problems of aging, I recommend you bring the dog in twice a year for his wellness care.

Vaccinations. In my opinion, vaccinations given at the appropriate time are one of the essential pillars of a good wellness program. Your vet may have a different point of view, but most vets say this: **Vaccinations should be started between six and eight weeks of age and every three weeks after that, until the dog receives a full course of preventive treatment.**

The subject of vaccinations used to be quite simple: you went to the vet, got your dog his vaccinations and boosters—against rabies, distemper, hepatitis, parvovirus, coronavirus, kennel cough, and leptospirosis—and left feeling confident that your dog was protected for another year or more. But all that is changing. In fact, in recent years we have seen the emergence of a great deal of new thinking—and a degree of controversy—regarding the issue of vaccinations. Your vet will certainly have his or her own ideas on the subject. But right here let's explain the basics of what you need to know.

First, some history. Thirty years ago, veterinarians routinely administered only four vaccines: distemper, rabies, hepatitis, and leptospirosis. As veterinary medicine advanced, researchers developed a wide array of new vaccines, and many of them were absolute godsends. Take the case of canine parvovirus. Parvovirus was first identified in the late 1970s, and at the time it was causing a worldwide epidemic. Tens of thousands of dogs were dying from the infection and the resultant diarrhea and dehydration. In a full-scale counterattack, teams of veterinary researchers worked feverishly to come up with an effective vaccine, and they did so in the space of just three years. That work saved the lives of untold numbers of dogs around the globe. The same can be said for many other vaccines that were developed over the past thirty years.

However, with this wave of progress has also come confusion and controversy. Today, there are many basic types of vaccines and many varieties within those types. There are mountains of data about the efficacy and duration of action of each of those vaccines. And now into this mix comes another confusing element: today we are seeing a sharp rise in the incidence of autoimmune disorders in dogs. The cause remains under investigation, but many scientists believe it may be related to the growing number of vaccines. These scientists theorize that the combined effect of the vaccines is overkill: they are simply overwhelming the immune systems of more and more dogs. All of this has generated enormous controversy and a major rethink among vets about which vaccines to use and how frequently.

I'm sure we haven't heard the last word on this, but in 2003 the American Animal Hospital Association issued a new set of nonbinding guidelines regarding vaccines. The AAHA guidelines divide the gamut of available vaccines into three separate categories:

♦ The "must-give" vaccines (which they identify as rabies, parvovirus, canine adenovirus-2 for hepatitis, and distemper);

♦ A larger group of vaccines aimed at less virulent diseases, which vets can administer at their discretion (such as kennel cough and leptospirosis);

♦ And a third group of vaccines that were to be dropped altogether. These included vaccines that were found to be too dangerous (a vaccine against canine adenovirus-1, for instance, was found to cause serious visual problems in dogs) and vaccines that were designed to combat diseases whose incidence was deemed statistically insignificant. Coronavirus was a leading case in point.

Now, where does all this leave you, the responsible dog owner? Probably confused, right? (Many of us vets are confused by these vaccine issues; why shouldn't you be?) So my best advice is this: talk to your vet. He or she will have his or her own views and, hopefully, the best information available for your dog and your region. For your guidance, I have compiled a checklist of the most important vaccinations to administer or to at least consider. (See the chart on page 206.) You can also use the checklist to help keep track of what shots your dog has had and when he needs another round. Your vet will keep the same information, but it is best to keep your own record, as well. Now, also for your guidance, I want to take a closer look at most of the vaccines that I and other vets consider to be "must-give."

Rabies. There is no controversy or second-guessing here: you have to get your puppy or adult dog vaccinated against rabies and return for boosters at regular intervals. The reason? Rabies kills. If a dog or a person becomes infected with rabies, it is fatal. The virus enters the body through an animal bite, then moves through the nervous system to the spinal cord. Then it attacks the brain. In the short term, that often induces bizarre or aggressive behavior. Death comes within days and, believe me, it's not pretty. But here is the good news: rabies has been almost totally eliminated in the United States. Strict enforcement of rabies vaccination laws is the best way to keep it that way. The vaccine is almost 100 percent effective in preventing rabies.

When to start? Puppies should be vaccinated for rabies between four and six months of age, then again at one year. After that, laws vary from state to state. Some states require annual boosters, others require a booster only every three years. Ask your vet about your state's requirements. And follow them; it's the law. Also, be aware that the law requires that a rabies vaccination be administered by a licensed veterinarian. That means that pet stores and breeders are not allowed to give them.

Caution: I recommend that a licensed vet give all of your dog's vaccinations. As I've also said (but it's worth repeating), some pet shops, rescue and humane societies regularly sponsor low-cost vaccination clinics and special vaccination days. To be fully effective, vaccines must be refrigerated properly and maintained at certain temperatures. They also have to be administered before precise expiration dates. If the vaccines are not properly maintained, they can become unstable and lose their potency. That can spell big trouble for you and your dog. So take no chances. One more thing: some pet supply houses and

Internet sites will sell various vaccines direct to pet owners. Bad idea, for all of the reasons I have specified above.

Distemper. There is no controversy here, either: the distemper vaccine not only works, it's a godsend. Distemper used to disfigure or totally wipe out entire canine populations; today, we rarely see a case—the national vaccine programs have been that effective. This is one nasty disease. The distemper virus is spread via the bloodstream to the lymph nodes, where it proceeds to kill the all-important lymphocytes. These are cells that provide the dog with immunity to a wide range of viruses and diseases. Once the dog's autoimmunity is compromised, the distemper virus can attack the lungs and cause pneumonia. It can also attack the brain and cause encephalitis, seizures, and paralysis. And just to add insult to this array of injuries, it can attack the gastrointestinal system and weaken the dog via diarrhea and dehydration. Up to 80 percent of puppies who are infected with distemper die. Those who recover suffer lifelong afflictions such as blindness, lameness, or seizures. Instead of seeing those animals continue to suffer, many owners choose to have them humanely euthanized.

Kennel cough. Known formally as Bordetellosis, this is an upper-respiratory infection caused by the bacterium *Bordetella bronchiseptica.* I see it most frequently in dogs who have been kept in closed quarters in pet stores, kennels, and sometimes at breeders. It is transmitted through secretions such as saliva and mucus, so dogs who cough or sneeze can easily spread it to other dogs. There is a vaccination for Bordetellosis but it is *not* 100 percent effective.

Caution: the vaccine takes about two weeks to take full effect. This is important to keep in mind. Many kennels insist that any dog to be boarded must have the Bordetella vaccination. If your dog is not vaccinated, the kennel may administer the vaccine, but it will likely provide no protection to your dog. If your kennel does demand the shot, go to your vet and get it done at least two weeks in advance.

Leptospirosis. This is a serious disease caused by a bacteria that has many different strains. The bacteria is spread via the urine of many species of wild and domesticated animals, including cattle, raccoons, and skunks. If your dog happens to drink water that is tainted by infected animal urine, the bacteria will enter his bloodstream and replicate throughout the body. Typical symptoms to watch for are fever and chills, nausea, vomiting, diarrhea, and jaundice. From there it can lead to kidney failure and hemorrhaging in the lungs and intestines. Humans can also be infected with leptospirosis. But there is double good news here: the vaccines are very effective against specific strains, and infected dogs and people who are treated promptly with antibiotics usually make a full recovery. Still, who needs it? The upshot is not rocket science: get your dog vaccinated against leptospirosis if it is prevalent in your area.

Caution: Not all dogs react well to vaccines. For most dogs, vaccines are a safe and effective way to prevent disease. However, there are some dogs who have severe, sometimes life-threatening allergic reactions to some vaccines. If your dog has ever had a negative reaction to a vaccination, make sure that you notify your vet and have him or her make it a permanent part of the medical record. Also, always consult your vet before seeking any future vaccination for a dog with a history of allergic reactions.

Second Caution: Be extremely careful with dogs who have compromised immune systems. Dogs suffering from hemolytic anemia, lupus, and other immune-related disorders should *never* be given a vaccination except under strict medical supervision. Even then I have qualms about it. For a dog with immune-system problems, the risk of giving him a vaccine might, in fact, be higher than the risk of him contracting whatever disease the vaccine is designed to prevent. Fortunately for dog owners, there is another option to consider: titers.

Titers. A titer is a measurement of the levels of a specific antibody in the bloodstream. Let me explain its importance. When we give a vaccine to a dog, that vaccine contains certain disease instigators that we call antigens. These cause your dog's body to generate a powerful array of antibodies to combat these antigens and keep the dog from coming down with that disease. After we give the vaccine, we can test the dog's blood and see what level of antibodies remain in the blood fighting these antigens. Those measured antibody levels are called titers. In other words, years after the shots we can *try* to assess a dog's immunity to distemper, parvovirus, and other diseases by measuring those relevant titers.

I say "try"—unfortunately, this is not yet an exact science; we are not yet certain exactly how high a titer must be to provide protection against a specific illness. Nevertheless, these titers may be helpful in deciding whether a dog at risk should be vaccinated or not. Let's say, for instance, that your dog has shown an allergy to the parvovirus. Instead of automatically giving him a booster shot when he is due, you can check the relevant titer to see if he has a significant amount of parvovirus antibodies still in his system. Then your vet can make an informed guess about which is riskier: giving him the shot or his chances of contracting the disease. Perhaps one day soon our understanding of titers will be fully developed and we will be able to use them in a more definitive way. But we're not there yet.

Vaccination Reminders. Most veterinary practices will send you a timely reminder to bring your dog in for his vaccinations and boosters. Some do that for the heartworm test, as well. However, do *not* rely on those reminders. Veterinary offices can get busy, computers can break down, and reminders can get lost in the mail. Better safe than sorry: use the accompanying check-list to keep your own shot records and put reminders in your calendar well in advance.

Vaccination List

Disease	Age at 1st vacc	Age at 2nd	Age at 3rd	Revacc. Interval
Distemper	8–10wks	10–12wks	14–16wks	12mos.
Canine hepatitis	8–10wks	10–12wks	14–16wks	12mos
Parvovirus	8–10wks	10–12wks	14–16wks	12mos
Bordetellosis	8–10wks	10–12wks	14–16wks	12mos
Parainfluenza	8–10wks	10–12wks	14–16wks	12mos
Leptospirosis	10–12wks	14–16wks		12mos
Rabies	16wks	52wks		12–36mos
Coronavius	I don't recommend coronavirus			

Other Pillars Of Dr. Dondi's DogAge Wellness Program

Fleas

I'm sorry, but today there is absolutely *no* excuse for fleas. With the products we have available now, products that are both affordable and extremely effective, no dog or cat should have to suffer through a serious flea infestation, no matter what climate or environment you live in. If I see a dog with a bad case of fleas, I know I'm dealing with an owner who is either ill-informed or just downright irresponsible. And if you want to see Dr. Dondi's fur fly, bring me a dog with a bad case of fleas. For a concise guide to detecting and fighting fleas, see the box on page 209. Here, though, are the whys and wherefores:

Fleas are nasty little critters that thrive in moist, hot weather. Summer is their high season. Growing up in Florida, I saw them by the truckload. In fact, the Southeast is the flea capital of North America. Fleas bite because they thrive on blood: your dog's, your cat's, even yours. And they multiply like crazy—in your house, and maybe even in your bed. The bad news: if you see your dog aggressively scratching his ears, legs, or bottom, there is a strong chance that he has fleas, and you need to give it urgent attention. Or the problem will get worse.

How To Fight Fleas. There are three principal forms of flea control: flea collars; externally applied liquids such as Advantage or Frontline; and internal treatment with pills, the most popular form being a preventive called Program. Personally, I am no fan of flea collars, and most vets who I know aren't, either. The flea collars that I have tested have simply not been effective. Worse, they are loaded with chemicals, and if you or your kids handle the collar, guess where those chemicals wind up? Yep. On you and your family. I am also not a big fan of the over-the-counter products that mimic Advantage and Frontline. My experience is that most of them are less reliable in killing either adult fleas or their larvae.

Advantage is available only through licensed vets, and it is very popular with vets and dog owners. It comes in a single-use applicator, and you apply it to three or four spots on the dog's upper back, up where she cannot ingest or scratch it. I like it because it usually stops your house from becoming infested. Here's how: an adult flea must be present on your pet for at least twenty-four to thirty-six hours before it can lay eggs. Advantage kills almost all fleas on dogs within twelve hours, before they have time to lay eggs. That's good news. Also, Advantage protects your dog and your house against reinfestation for the following four weeks. Most people who use Advantage maintain it throughout the summer season in cooler climates and year-round in warmer ones. **Caution: Do not give Advantage to puppies under seven weeks old.**

Frontline is another popular treatment applied topically. It kills 100 percent of all fleas on your dog within eighteen hours, and it, too, keeps your dog flea-free for up to four weeks. There is one potential side effect to both Advantage and Frontline: some dogs do show allergic reactions such as hair loss. If this occurs, stop the treatment immediately and ask your vet about changing to a different product.

Program is a different type of system. It is an internal flea preventive, based on a single pill that you give once a month with food. The active ingredient in Program is lufenuron, a product that works through the dog's bloodstream. Whereas Advantage and Frontline kill virtually on contact, the lufeneron is passed to the flea only when it bites the dog. The lufenuron then sterilizes the biting flea, thus breaking the flea life cycle at its base. The result? An *eventual* wipeout of the entire flea population on your dog. More on that "eventual" in a moment.

I prefer Program for my dogs Hannah, Georgia, and Chili Beyoncé. Why? Because I'm all over my dogs. I hug them and kiss them and if there's any chemical product on their coat or skin, it will inevitably get onto me. No thank you. That's why I always recommend Program for families with small children. Another reason I like Program is that there's no toxicity. The manufacturers have done extensive tests on it and found no side effects, even in nursing puppies.

Caution: There are two downsides to Program. First, dogs who are allergic to fleas do not do well with Program. Why? Because the flea has to bite the dog in order to ingest the lufenuron, and just that single bite may cause a dog with flea allergies to have a bad reaction. The second downside: Program does not kill the adult fleas immediately, it only sterilizes them. (That's where the "eventual" comes in.) As a result, in the short run your dog and your house may still be crawling with adult fleas. What to do? For a serious infestation, I recommend that you start Program right away but combine it with Advantage for the first month at least. That will kill the fleas faster and bring your dog relief much sooner. Then you can comfortably use Program throughout the summer flea season.

Dr. Dondi's Concise Guide to Detecting and Wiping Out Fleas

Detection

- To look for fleas, have the dog lie down. Then, with your hand, a brush, or a comb, push back the fur at the base of the tail, on the tummy, and around the dog's neck and ears.
- Keep a sharp eye out for the fast-moving critters: they are dark brown in color, oval and flat in shape, and less than an eighth of an inch long. They can be very difficult to spot; don't celebrate if you do not see them right away live and in blazing color.
- Look for "flea dirt," the more easily seen residue of what fleas leave behind: black or brown flecks of dried blood and flea excrement. If you do spot flecks, pick them out and smear them on a wet paper towel. If you see a reddish-brown color, lucky you: your dog has fleas.
- And here's the really bad news: if you do find a few fleas or flea dirt, you can safely assume that there are *scores* of fleas and probably flea larvae too in your environment. Yuck!

- And here is more bad news: if you have a cat, you can safely assume that it, too, has fleas. Treat your cat in the exact same way, but using Advantage, Frontline, or Program for cats.
- There is another detection technique I like: put your dog on a white towel or in a dry bathtub and then use a blow dryer to ruffle his fur. If there are fleas, you might spot them jumping off the dog onto the white surface, or you may find those telltale flecks of flea dirt. Either way, keep your dog in the tub: that's where the shock and awe counterattack will begin.

Wiping Them Out

- There are three main ways to go here: a flea collar, which I do not recommend; topical treatments like Advantage and Frontline; or Program, an internal, once-a-month pill. I prefer Program, but take your pick. (See the main text for a full explanation why.)
- No matter which treatment you choose, start by giving your dog a thorough bath. Use a regular dog shampoo, a baby shampoo, or an anti-flea formula available from the pet store. Work the shampoo into a generous lather and then leave it on your suffering dog for several minutes. That will help relieve his itching from the flea bites, and it will drown a good number of the fleas still buried in his coat. (Fleas are notoriously poor swimmers.)
- If you plan to use Advantage or Frontline, read the instructions very carefully before applying. Open the single-use tubes and apply the liquid in three or four locations on the upper back, where the dog can't get at it. Pick up your trumpet and get ready to play taps.
- Now the house. To end a flea infestation, machine-wash the dog's bedding (and yours, too, if the dog sleeps there)

in hot water. Ditto for any blankets the dog uses and the towels you use to bathe the dog. If you're using a crate for dog training, hose that out, too. With soap. Vacuum all carpets carefully and, if your dog rides there, the car or truck, too. (Be sure to empty the vacuum bag into a plastic bag and seal it before you throw it away: fleas, too, seem to have nine lives.)

* The yard. Check with your local gardening center—there are safe, nontoxic methods for making your lawn and yard inhospitable to fleas. These include friendly little insects that love to eat flea larvae.

How To Treat A Severe Infestation

* Bathe the dog thoroughly. (See above.)
* Apply one month's dose of Advantage or Frontline. This will provide quick relief for the dog, kill the fleas, and provide interim protection for the next thirty days.
* Begin Program at the same time and keep the dog on it throughout the flea season. This combination should solve the problem, but you can repeat the Advantage or Frontline monthly if you are worried.
* Pray for an early winter. The only total relief from fleas comes from freezing temperatures.
* If all else fails, move to Alaska, Iceland, or the North Pole.

Ticks

Fleas are a pain in the neck, but ticks are worse. Much worse: they can transmit diseases that can cause severe illness and even death—in dogs and in humans. Ticks are also difficult to prevent. Ticks come in several different sizes and varieties, but all ticks have this in common: they suck blood. Big time. In spring, they hatch in large numbers, and then the young ticks spread out into the grass, trees, and underbrush. There they lurk—waiting. Waiting for deer, foxes, wolves, or mice to pass by—or, of course, you and your pooch. Then, aided by their sticky shells, the ticks latch onto their victim and search for a cozy spot of flesh. Then they burrow in and suck their victim's blood. In the process, they pass to their host whatever microorganisms they have on their mouths or in their system. And those microorganisms can lead to a variety of nasty diseases. Here are the main tick-borne diseases and what you need to know about them:

Lyme disease. This is the notorious bad boy of tick-borne diseases. It was first recognized in humans in 1975 in Lyme, Connecticut, hence its name, and it was found in dogs a decade later. The most common carrier of Lyme disease is the deer tick, a critter so tiny that it can be very difficult to find, especially in thick animal fur. Lyme disease is sometimes carried by larger ticks, as well. The real culprit here is the Lyme bacterium, *Borrelia burgdorferi,* a microorganism that in humans triggers fever, joint pain, lethargy, meningitis, and chronic arthritis. If you do get bitten by a tick, keep a sharp eye out for those symptoms, and if they do appear, get to a doctor pronto.

In dogs, it is a little different story. Many dogs become infected with the Lyme bacterium, but only a few actually develop the disease. Still, here are the symptoms to watch out for in your dog: fever, loss of appetite, lethargy, swollen joints, and muscle pain. In some cases, a dog will develop irreversible and deadly damage to the kidneys called Lyme nephritis. If your dog shows any of these symptoms, get him to the vet right away—especially if you have found any ticks on him in the days or weeks prior. A blood test will detect the presence of the Lyme bacterium. In both dogs and humans, the usual treatment for all tick-borne diseases is an extended course of antibiotics. But early detection is vital.

Vaccination is possible. There is a vaccine for dogs against Lyme disease, but my own experience with it has not been encouraging. I've had dogs come down with Lyme nephritis even though they had been vaccinated. I've had other dogs, though, that have come down with it without being vaccinated. Maybe it's the luck of the draw, but it's more likely related to the genetic predisposition of the dog. Either way, veterinary science does not yet understand why some dogs are affected and others are not.

Other tick-borne diseases. There are two other tick-borne microorganisms that attack dogs and humans. One is *Ehrlichia*, which causes Ehrlichiosis, a disease characterized by anemia, weight loss, arthritis, and hemorrhaging in dogs and humans. The other is *Rickettsia rickettsii*, a bug that causes Rocky Mountain spotted fever, a malady most prevalent in the southeast United States. (Yes, the name is misleading.) The typical symptoms, in both dogs and humans, are fever, rashes, and joint and muscle pain. *Rickettsia rickettsii* is transmitted by the American wood tick, the Lone Star tick, and the American dog tick. The treatment for both tick-borne maladies is the same: antibiotics for six to eight weeks.

Prevention. The best choice in preventing all tick-borne diseases is to avoid infested areas, especially in tick season. It may vary a bit where you live, but the tick season generally runs from April through September. During that period, be especially careful: do not let your dog venture into dense woods or underbrush, which are likely to be tick-infested. If she does go into those areas, search her immediately afterward and regularly each day throughout the summer season. Pay special attention to the areas around the ears and neck—these are favorite burrowing spots for ticks. Remove any ticks immediately. (See page 214.)

Anti-tick products. There is no magic solution here. Advantage does not kill ticks, and does not claim to. The same manufacturer, Bayer, has a new product out called Advantix, and it does look promising. Capstar is another new product designed to kill fleas, ticks, and all sorts of other critters. To date, though, the best tick preventive I've found is Frontline. Its manufacturer says that Frontline is 100 percent effective against both fleas and ticks, but in my experience Frontline has not been quite that effective against ticks. It is definitely better than nothing and almost everything else out there. You can find a number of collars that claim to ward off ticks, but the only one that I have seen any type of results with is the Preventic collar. Also, as with flea collars, tick collars are laden with chemicals that I do not want on my hands or body. The bottom line? Ticks are nasty and so are the diseases they carry. Therefore, if you live in a tick-ridden environment, I recommend using Frontline and keeping your dog out of infested areas and under close supervision.

Tick removal. If you or your dog does have an embedded tick, it can be very tricky to remove. I've heard of all sorts of ways to get them off, but I think the most reliable is with a pair of tweezers. Here's how you do it. First, put on a pair of surgical or other gloves to avoid potential contact with those disease-inducing microorganisms. Second, you might want to use bifocals or reading glasses to help facilitate a precise removal. Third, take the tweezers and try to grasp the head of the tick at the precise point where it attaches to the dog's skin. Then gently pull. Don't yank it: that will probably leave the head of the tick embedded in the skin. Finally, immediately apply a good disinfectant (I like Bactine) on the bite wound and the surrounding area. And now here comes the really fun part:

Try to save the tick intact. To do that, kill it by placing it in alcohol. Then save the corpse in a plastic bag. Label the bag with the precise date and, if you can figure it out, the locale from where the tick came. No, I'm not kidding. If you or your dog later comes down with a mysterious disease, take that bag with you to the doctor or vet: it might provide valuable information as to the cause of your or your dog's illness and the best possible cure. As I said, most tick-borne diseases can be treated, but the earlier the detection the better.

Caution: Never use your bare fingers to pull off a tick—and never crush the tick with your bare fingers. In both cases, you do not want any of those nefarious microorganisms touching your skin. After any tick removal, wash your hands and any affected areas thoroughly with soap and water.

Heartworm

Heartworm is another nasty parasite you want to take aggressive steps to prevent. Heartworm is found across most of the United States and Canada. In northern states, freezing temperatures in winter reduce the risk, but you still have to be careful in the summer months. Heartworm disease is transmitted by mosquitoes. A mosquito bites an infected dog and then transplants the infection to the next dog it bites. And before you know it, there is an epidemic. And it isn't pretty: the larvae incubate into adults in the dog's body, then collect in the heart and wreak havoc. The result can be life-threatening. But there is good news:

Prevention is easy. There are simple, chewable, once-a-month tablets that will prevent heartworm disease. Some even kill intestinal parasites, as well. There are many brands of heartworm preventive that can be purchased through your veterinarian. Before giving the tablet, you must have your dog's blood tested for the presence of heartworms. If the test comes out positive, the vet will begin treatment for the disease before beginning prevention. If the test is negative, the vet will put your dog on a course of prevention that is appropriate to the weight of your dog. Generally, most vets recommend starting puppies on preventive between four and six months of age. Be careful to watch the weight of your puppy monthly as it grows, because heartworm preventive dosing is dependent upon weight.

Fungus

I think of this as athlete's paw. If you have an active, athletic dog—especially one that likes to hunt and dig—you have to keep a sharp eye out for fungal infections; they come from Mother Nature's locker-room floor. Soils across America are rich in different fungal organisms, and all dogs get at least some exposure to them. The good news is that your dog's immune system is probably strong enough to ward off fungal infections. But dogs who dig a lot—especially around nests of birds and bats or around the holes of burrowing animals like moles and gophers—face increased exposure to fungal organisms. Veterinary medicine has not yet developed a protective vaccine. Fungal infections can cause hair loss, fever, loss of appetite, malaise, arthritis, and pneumonia. If you see symptoms of this nature, consult your vet immediately.

Spaying and neutering

This is a serious subject and one that you should discuss thoroughly with your vet. As I mentioned in the introduction to this book, millions of unwanted dogs wind up in shelters each year, and many millions wind up being put to sleep. It breaks my heart. The best way to curb this problem is for all dog owners to be well informed and to make responsible decisions about their pets. To be blunt about it, the best way to avoid unwanted pregnancies is for owners to have their female dogs spayed and their males dogs neutered. (Sounds obvious, doesn't it?) I know that many owners hesitate to do that. They imagine it will be fun—and instructive for their children—for their dog to have a litter of puppies. Some owners even imagine that they will be able to sell those puppies and make a profit. Well, let me tell you: those owners are wrong on several counts. Breeding is a very complicated process, it can be a major headache, and it can be very costly, as well. I said it before, but let me say it again: **Leave dog breeding to the professionals**.

Neutering. This is the surgical removal of a male dog's testicles. It is a relatively simple procedure, and usually does not require an overnight stay in the hospital. Many humane and rescue organizations offer special clinics where vets will perform this service, in an effort to cut down the number of unwanted dogs. I recommend neutering your male for population control and to make dog ownership a little more hassle-free. If you have a male dog who is not neutered, he'll be able to detect a female dog in heat many miles away, and he will move heaven and earth to get to her. Lucky you; you have to cope with keeping your dog constantly supervised—or cope with the irate owner of the female dog if he gets away. While I recommend neutering to stop unwanted breeding, I never recommend neutering as an answer to behavioral problems. In some cases it may help decrease aggressive tendencies, but in my experience you cannot count on it. Some people imagine it will calm the dog down and make it easier to train, but you cannot count on that, either. That said, in some cases neutering will discourage males from roaming and lifting their leg in the house; neutering seems to decrease their urge to mark their territory.

The best reason to neuter a male dog: it increases his chances of living a long, healthy life. Neutering removes the possibility of testicular cancer. It does not totally prevent all prostate cancers, but it does prevent some. It also helps prevent prostate infections and abscesses, which can be life-threatening. It may also decrease a dog's inclination to fight with other dogs.

Caution: it is important to neuter a male dog at an appropriate age. Most vets recommend neutering a dog at six months of age. For many dog owners the issue is aesthetic: they want to make sure their dog's masculine look and attributes are fully developed. Therefore, they want to wait until the dog is older to have him neutered. I do agree that a male dog will develop more muscle mass if left intact for a year or more. For that reason, I have no problems with my clients waiting until the dog is a year old to neuter him. My one caveat: that the dog is properly supervised and not allowed to freely roam the neighborhood. That is trouble in the making. As always, consult your vet about what's best for your particular animal.

Spaying. This is the surgical removal of a female dog's uterus and ovaries. It is somewhat more complicated than male neutering, as it involves cutting open the abdomen. Let me be blunt here: a female dog who is not spayed is much more trouble to own. Depending on the size and breed of the dog, she will go through a heat cycle anywhere from every three to six months. These heat cycles, or *estrus*, can last up to four weeks. That means that your dog will be making a bloody mess of your house for four weeks every quarter or so. For that reason, many owners of females opt for spaying early on.

Spaying is also good for the long-term health of the dog. If you spay before the dog's first heat cycle, which usually occurs between six and nine months of age, it will significantly decrease her chances of developing breast cancer, to less than one percent. Also, spaying at any age eliminates infections of the uterus, which can be very serious. Spaying will also make her safer: she won't have to fend off all those un-neutered males—

and you won't have to contend with throngs of lusty male dogs barking at your door.

Who does the neutering surgeries? Most general practitioners do this type of surgery. They are done under a general anesthetic, and normally require an overnight stay in the clinic. The recovery routine and time for spaying and neutering are about the same: several days of limited activity indoors, then limited on-leash walking outdoors. The vet will check on the dog about ten days later and remove any non-dissolving sutures. One caution here: neither procedure is reversible.

Alternative and Complementary Medicine

As in human medicine, there is a growing interest in veterinary medicine in alternative healing methods such as acupuncture, herbal medicine, homeopathy, and therapeutic massage. Twenty years ago, I suspect that most vets in the U.S. would have dismissed these methods as so much quackery, but now there is a growing body of evidence supporting the validity of these treatments, and there are many traditionally trained vets who are now specializing in alternative and complementary treatments. In our own clinic, we now have such a specialist on staff, and our team of doctors frequently turns to him for advice and counsel.

Are alternative treatments effective? My best answer is that some are and some are not. Our specialist says that alternative medicine shows the best results when it is used in treating aging dogs and chronic conditions such as arthritis. It is also proving effective in helping dogs recover more quickly from surgery and serious trauma, and in treating kidney and liver disease. As in human medicine, one area of great interest is treating cancer. Here, alternative medicine is often used in conjunction with aggressive chemotherapy and/or radiation treatments, to help the dog's body handle the resulting stress and debilitation.

The guiding philosophy. For the sake of simplicity, let me generalize with a broad brush: in Western medicine, we see a virus or a germ, and we try to kill it with chemical compounds. Most domains of alternative and complementary medicine take a different approach: by and large they use natural, nonchemical derivatives and holistic treatments to enhance the body's immune system and to mobilize the body's natural powers to fight disease. That is an overly simplistic explanation, but you get the point. There are three basic categories of alternative treatment:

Acupuncture. Acupuncture is an ancient science developed in China that is based on the body's internal "meridians," a network of energy pathways that are spread throughout the body and that nourish all the vital organs. Along those meridians there are scores of "acupoints" that can be stimulated by several different means: the insertion of special needles, the application of manual pressure (a practice called *acupressure*), or the application of electrical or ultrasound stimulation. When it is done expertly, the stimulation of these acupoints can help rebalance the body's energy flows, energize vital organs, and marshal the body's own healing powers to fight an array of diseases and chronic conditions. Over the past twenty-five years or so, acupuncture has become widely accepted and practiced in human medicine in the U.S., and it is now gaining a tentative foothold in veterinary medicine, as well. According to the experts, acupuncture in dogs can be especially helpful in speeding recovery from surgery, and in reducing pain associated with arthritis and other chronic conditions. It has also been helpful in treating dogs suffering from hypothyroidism. In some cases, acupuncture treatments have decreased a dog's need for thyroid supplements.

How does acupuncture work? I don't administer acupuncture, but I do recommend it. Here is what the experts tell me: acupuncture works on the body's natural energy pathways. With arthritis, for instance, the body's energy, what the Chinese call "Chi" or "Qi," becomes blocked or trapped in the affected joint, and certain vital organs are also out of balance. Using a pattern of needle placement that has been evolved specifically to relieve the swelling and pain associated with arthritis, the acupuncture treatment does several things simultaneously. It increases blood flow to the affected area, decreases inflammation, improves general neurologic function, and normalizes endocrine influences. The aim is to "unblock" trapped Chi, return the dog's body to a healthy energy balance, and restore proper function of his vital organs.

Homeopathy. While acupuncture is gaining wide acceptance, homeopathy remains a controversial form of alternative treatment. It is a system of medical practice based on a premise that many traditional doctors find difficult to accept: that you can treat disease by administering minute doses of agents that, in a healthy person, would provoke symptoms of that same disease. Homeopathy uses heavily diluted preparations of various minerals, salts, and plants. In fact, the preparations are so diluted that they provoke no pharmacologic action. Their action is designed to stimulate the body itself to fix the problem and speed the healing. For more information, ask your vet, or consult the Web site of the Academy of Veterinary Homeopathy at www.theavh.org.

Herbs. As you probably know, many native cultures around the world have long used a wide variety of herbs and other plants to fight disease and strengthen the body's natural immune system. In human medicine, herbs such as echinacea, Ginkgo biloba, saw palmetto, and St. John's Wort have now become mainstream; you can find them at your local drugstore and even in the big warehouse stores. And here's the interesting part: doctors are now using these same herbs to treat the same ailments in dogs, though of course in different doses. For instance, veterinarians are prescribing saw palmetto for treatment of dogs with enlarged prostate glands, just as it is prescribed for men with enlarged prostates. Likewise, if your dog appears to be suffering from depression, a veterinarian with expertise in herbal remedies might prescribe St. John's Wort, now an alternative treatment for depression in humans. According to the expert in our clinic, Western herb formulas tend to be simple and have few components in their formulations. Chinese formulas, by contrast, tend to be more complex, and contain many more herbs. As with most of the alternative remedies, herbs are used mainly to treat chronic conditions, especially in aging animals, and to help the body mobilize its own disease-fighting powers. Our expert is also beginning to integrate herbs and other alternative practices into a much broader wellness program.

There are several other forms of alternative and complementary medicine that dog owners can explore, among them massage, chiropractic treatment, magnetic therapy, and a field called "nutraceuticals." Nutraceuticals are derived from naturally occurring substances (as opposed to "pharmaceuticals," which are derived from chemical compounds), and the most popular ones I've seen are derived from shark cartilage, and are designed to help relieve arthritis and chronic joint pain. In my realm of emergency and urgent care, I am particularly interested in how these alternative treatments can be used to help dogs better recover from surgery and trauma. If the recent past is any indication, more of these alternative treatments will be further developed and will soon enter mainstream veterinary medicine. So if you are interested, don't hesitate to ask your vet or to do some serious research.

Dental Care

Clean teeth and gums are not just cosmetic issues: they are vital to the health and well-being of your dog. In fact, taking good care of your dog's teeth and gums make your pet's DogAge significantly younger. Dental problems are a more common occurrence than you might think. Many dogs suffer from tartar buildup, loose teeth, and calcium deposits at the gumline. Gum disease is also a common problem: by the age of three, some eighty percent of all dogs have some gum inflammation, called gingivitis, and even periodontal disease: gum inflammation combined with tooth loosening. These can be serious problems. I have seen dogs with such significant dental tartar and gum disease that they had a difficult time eating. Some dental disease can also lead to serious infections. The culprits here are the same as with humans: oral bacteria, tartar, and plaque.

Excessive wear and tear on the teeth is another serious problem. The worst I see is with dogs who like to chew on rocks or other hard surfaces, like the feet of your furniture. Separation anxiety can also result in extensive wear and tear on the teeth. However, there is good news here: regular dog food and rawhide chews do not cause significant flattening of the teeth. When it comes to all dental problems, the best remedy is prevention.

Brushing. Many veterinarians recommend that every owner brush his or her dog's teeth on a regular basis. I do not go that far. To me it depends on the individual dog. Most dogs do develop some degree of dental tartar, but many large-breed dogs are not prone to much. Georgia, my boxer mix, is ten, and she doesn't have an ounce of tartar on her teeth. Hannah, my rottweiler, tends to accumulate a little tartar on her canine teeth, but her back teeth are fine. Neither of them has ever required a professional dental cleaning. Many small breeds, such as Yorkshire terriers, poodles, shelties, and dachshunds, tend to develop significant dental tartar and gum disease. So I agree: owners of these breeds should brush their dogs' teeth on a regular basis. At your pet store or veterinarian's office, you will find special brushes and toothpaste that smells delectably like meat. (Imagine that, meat-flavored toothpaste. Yum!)

How to brush. If your dog has a predisposition to tartar buildup, I recommend that you brush his teeth three times a week or more. Use the dog toothbrush and toothpaste, or use a gauze square and warm water and actually rub the teeth to remove debris and soft tarter. But do not expect miracles. The health of a dog's teeth depends to a large degree on the pH of his mouth and the oral bacteria that live there. So, if your dog has a genetic predisposition to developing dental tartar and plaque, even with regular brushing you are probably not going to avoid a professional cleaning. But you may be able to decrease the frequency with which he needs them. And that is significant. So don't get discouraged.

Chew toys and bones. There are specially designed toys, bones, and chews that may be effective in removing plaque. Many of them have grated surfaces that scrape the dog's teeth clean as he chews. These are fine, but I still recommend that you have your vet check your dog's teeth on a regular basis; he or she may recommend a professional cleaning. Also, any time you see significant tartar buildup, make a special visit to the vet.

What will the vet do? The vet will have to scale off the tartar, just as your own dentist does. This is not a simple procedure. Most dogs will just not tolerate having their teeth scaled when they're awake. For this reason, most veterinarians will have to anesthetize the dog for any dental scaling or polishing. The same is true if the vet needs to remove an abscessed tooth or broken tooth. To remove heavy tartar buildup and those hard calculus deposits, veterinarians use sophisticated ultrasonic and high-pressure water tools.

Do all vets do dental work? Most general practitioners do some dental work as part of their daily practice. It is a skill that most vets develop once they're in practice. Many group practices have a licensed technician who handles the dental cleaning. There are certified veterinary dentists as well; I send my patients to one of those. He takes X-rays, just like my dentist. In fact, he did the dental cleaning on my twenty-six-year-old cat, and with X-rays he found that she had three abscessed teeth. She also had neck lesions, which are exposures of the root at the gumline. He temporarily filled the lesions using a fluoride treatment followed by UV light so that she didn't have to have all of her teeth pulled. You can send your dog to see a certified veterinary dentist, but your own vet might be perfectly qualified to handle your dog's routine dental care needs. If it is not routine, you might want to ask your vet to recommend a specialist.

Grooming

Right now I can hear some of my readers moaning, "Come on, Dr. Dondi, grooming? What's that got to do with wellness and helping my dog lead a longer, healthier life?" Well, relax. I'm not going to tell you how to take out the scissors and give your poodle a pompadour or how to trim the beard of your schnauzer. The fact is, like dental care, proper grooming is not just a cosmetic issue. It is absolutely essential to the health and well-being of your animal. Grooming is also an essential pillar of Dr. Dondi's DogAge Wellness Program. So in this section I am going to tell you how to take care of your dog's nails, coat, ears and more, and how, when you do the regular grooming, to spot any trouble in the making.

Bathing. A clean dog is less likely to develop skin infections than a dog who is dirty. Dogs who have a lot of oil and dirt buildup are just asking for trouble. Depending on the climate and environment where you live, most short-haired dogs probably don't need to be bathed more than once a month—unless they're an oily-coated breed. Long-haired dogs, like huskies, malamutes, and chows, tend to have less oil on their skin and coats, and so regular bathing isn't as necessary. However, those breeds do need regular combing and brushing to prevent matting. The same is true for the breeds that grow long, wavy hair: golden retrievers, Irish setters, Afghan hounds, and the like. They definitely need to have regular brushing and combing to decrease matting and keep their coats clean. Many dogs from those breeds can also benefit from regular trimming of their hair. A lot of people don't want to keep up with the brushing and combing, so they choose to shave their dogs. Note: when bathing any dog, be careful not to get soap in the eyes—it can cause burning and corneal ulcers. You can use lubricating eye ointment in the eyes prior to the bath to help protect against this problem, but the safest thing is to not get shampoo or dip in the eyes. If you happen to do this, make sure that you flush the eyes with copious amounts of water. Have your dog examined immediately if he is continuously rubbing or squinting his eyes after a bath.

Grooming Products. There are plenty of good over-the-counter shampoos and conditioners you can use to bathe your dog. If your dog has drier skin or hair that tangles, he may benefit from a conditioner, as well. Medicated shampoos and dips are also available to treat fleas and ticks. For more serious problems, there are medicated products sold only through veterinary hospitals to treat skin infections, yeast infections in the skin, and parasites like sarcoptic mange.

Professional grooming. There are, of course, a number of breeds whose grooming is done primarily for aesthetic reasons, such as when the owner wants them to look like the photos in the dog books: the poodles, cocker spaniels, Yorkshire terriers, schnauzers, and the like. For this, you may need a professional groomer. Start bringing your dog to a professional groomer when he is a puppy (after he has been fully vaccinated); this makes future visits less stressful. To find one, ask your friends or your vet, or consult the yellow pages. There is, though, a licensing procedure for groomers, and I would urge you to choose a groomer who has been certified. The issue here is more than cosmetic. A professional groomer will be trained to spot changes in your dog's hair, coat, and skin, which could signal an underlying problem. Your groomer can also check the ears for discharge and that type of thing. Moreover, cutting a dog's hair makes their skin and underlying structure more visible, so you or your groomer might be better able to spot new lumps and bumps.

Caution: Not all groomers are as concerned as they should be about health and safety issues. Today, groomers rarely use old-fashioned, hand-held dryers. Instead, they use cage dryers. These are hair dryers specially outfitted to sit on the door of the cage facing in. Most of them have timers that shut them off automatically after a specified amount of time. This is very convenient for the groomer: he or she has his or her hands free to begin grooming another dog. But guess what? I have had cases where the timer failed to shut the dryer off, or where the groomer got distracted and failed to pay attention to the dog in the cage. The result? The poor animals were virtually cooked in their cage. The result was very serious heatstroke and burns. I had a little Maltese patient who actually perished from a cage-drying accident.

There are other potential health issues to confront when your dog is at the groomer's: she may well be exposed to illnesses like kennel cough, parvovirus, and the like. So I urge my clients to be very careful when selecting a groomer. Pay a visit first and see if the shop is clean, ask how many dogs visit the salon each day, and how they're housed while they're waiting to be groomed. I also prefer groomers who ask owners for proof of a dog's vaccinations.

Ears. Keeping your dog's ears clean can help reduce the chance of ear infections. I recommend a regular inspection and swabbing, but don't use a Q-tip; it can puncture the dog's eardrum if you get it in there too far. Use a cotton ball or gauze pad moistened with water and a gentle soap. Swab the ear carefully and be sure not to stick your finger deep inside the ear. Watch for any discharge; it could be a sign of infection. If you do see a discharge or redness or smell a bad odor, or if your dog shakes his head a lot or acts as if his ears are painful, get him to the vet right away. Ear infections can be very painful, and they can also lead to loss of balance and even deafness.

How often should you clean your dog's ears? I have no hard-and-fast rule; it depends on the individual dog. Dogs with a genetic predisposition to ear issues can benefit from weekly cleanings. A lot of the spaniel breeds, too, have long earflaps that can trap moisture and bacteria, making them breeding grounds for infection. For them, too, I recommend a weekly ear cleaning. Also, if your dog tends to produce a lot of earwax, cleaning his ears once a week will help ward off secondary infections. It really depends on the dog. I don't think I've ever cleaned Georgia's ears in her life; she just doesn't make much earwax. If your dog has fur on the inside of his ears, it is not a good idea to pull or yank this out yourself. Let a groomer take care of that.

Nails. Vets and groomers will trim your dog's nails if you ask them to. But many dog owners like to keep their dog's nails neatly trimmed, both for aesthetic reasons and to avoid unnecessary scratching of people, floors, and furniture. So they buy their own nail trimmer and do it themselves. But it does take a certain degree of patience and skill. Long nails rarely present a health problem—except when they're so long they grow back into the paw pad or when they are not cut properly. Then watch out: you will have a very unhappy dog on your hands. All nails can be treated the same, including dewclaws. So, what do you need to know about nails and trimming them correctly?

Dogs essentially have one of two types of nails: pigmented or non-pigmented. Dog nails that are clear or white are easier to trim because you can visualize the vascular portion of the nail, which you don't want to cut: it will bleed, and be very painful for your dog. That's called "quicking" the nail. How to avoid that? Inspect your dog's nails carefully before you trim them. Their nails are like ours: we both have a nail bed that is vascular and pink, and a nail that hangs over the edge. Pigmented nails, meaning black or brown nails, are opaque, so you can't clearly see the vascular portion of the nail. It's much easier to quick them and cause bleeding and discomfort. What I try to do is look at the nail from the side to determine where it's the thickest—you do *not* want to cut there. Also, if you look at the underside of the nail you can sometimes discern where it starts to look more meaty and "busier." Again, you don't want to cut there. It's very difficult to be certain, so I tend to take little tiny snips, until I get back to a portion where I can start to see the quick visible at the end of the nail. Then I stop. My advice: go slowly and keep a styptic pencil or a bar of soap close to hand. If you do quick a nail, use them to stop the bleeding.

Is there a particular angle at which you should make the cut?

Yes, the nail clipper should be held vertically to make a vertical cut. This is not always easy to do. The best way to learn is when your dog is a puppy. At that time, his nails are soft and most of the time the nails are not yet pigmented, so it's much easier to see the point of the nail and stay away from the sensitive vascular portion. If you start clipping the dog's nails on a weekly basis, he will get used to it and you will make fewer mistakes.

What is that foul odor? As we all know, there are some dogs who simply cannot resist a chance to roll around in dirt, mud, or—heaven forbid—animal poop or something dead. Fortunately, a strong bath with a good shampoo will take care of most of these problems. But that brings us to two more delicate issues. The first is skunks. If your dog roots around in some wonderful-looking underbrush, he may find himself a skunk hole, and then watch out: he is almost certain to get sprayed. Lucky you. If you live in the country, you might consider this a ritual baptism in the joys of dog ownership, but that first big skunk stink is, nevertheless, never a picnic. What to do?

Tomato juice. For many experienced dog owners, this is the remedy of choice. Yes, you have to sponge the dog with it or, better yet, *bathe* him in tomato juice. Several times! There are, however, other ways to go, and some of them are very effective. At your pet store, you will find a few shampoos that specifically claim to work against skunk odor. I've had success with several of them—sort of. (When it comes to getting rid of skunk odor, all success is relative.) Actually, even with the special shampoos it has taken several baths to get rid of most of the smell, and it has taken many, many days for all hints of it to disappear. Keep this in mind, though: getting sprayed is no picnic for your dog, either. I have friends who swear that their dog was embarrassed for weeks after the spraying.

And now, dear friends, we come to a second odiferous problem: overfilled anal glands. This is a problem that affects many dogs, but small dogs in particular—papillons, Chihuahuas, and the like. Dogs have two small sacs on either side of the anus, located at the four o'clock and seven o'clock positions. These are scent glands that empty naturally during defecation in most dogs. A dog will often express the material that accumulates in these sacs when she is frightened. The secretion is gray or brown in color, and the odor is, shall we say, distinctive. Some people consider it worse than skunk stink!

How do you detect a problem with the anal sacs? Don't worry: either the odor will tell you or you will see the dog scooting his bottom across the carpet or floor, trying to empty the sacs and find some relief. Excessive licking back there is another telltale sign. Sometimes the anal glands can become infected and actually rupture. This is called an anal-gland abscess.

What to do? You basically have two choices: go to the vet, or go to the groomer. If your dog is having a problem with his rear end, it is better to have him seen by a veterinarian in case something besides a problem with his anal glands is causing his distress. If you know that your dog has a history of anal gland problems, you may want to make regularly scheduled appointments with your vet or groomer to have them expressed. This may ward off unnecessary infections. Some people even have their veterinarians teach them how to express their dog's anal glands themselves. I don't recommend that owners do this themselves. It's very unpleasant, and improperly expressing anal glands can cause problems. For example, if the anal sac is infected, too much pressure can cause it to rupture. If your dog is having trouble with his anal glands, he should see the vet.

CHAPTER TWELVE

A Concise First-Aid Manual

I HAD a client who was out for a walk in the woods with his pal Stevie, a handsome whippet. It was a lovely day and both were enjoying the time outdoors—until Stevie tumbled from a ledge and broke one of his front legs. This was a dicey situation: they were deep in the woods. The man knew that he needed help but wanted to immobilize the leg to keep Stevie more comfortable on the trek back. But how?

Looking through his backpack, my client came up with an ingenious idea. From the pack he took out a section of newspaper he had planned to read and he also found a roll of strong tape. He wrapped the newspaper tightly around Stevie's leg and secured it with the tape, forming an improvised splint. He then wrapped more tape from the splint up to and around the shoulder, effectively immobilizing the entire leg. With the dog's leg now secure, he carried Stevie to his car and rushed him to me. Thanks to that resourceful splint, he was able to minimize Stevie's discomfort, and we were able to successfully repair the break.

This story highlights three things that every dog owner must keep in mind:

Number One: Accidents will happen. Whether it is at home, in the yard, in the dog park, in the car, on the boat, or in the woods, accidents can happen to your dog—and you need to have a well-informed understanding of how best to respond. That is the entire purpose of this chapter. Of course, Stevie's situation was extreme—how often are you deep in the woods? For most cases, I don't recommend such doctoring as splinting your dog's leg; just gently and carefully get him to the vet! But I do recommend that you be prepared for accidents wherever you go.

Number Two: Be prepared. Keep a well-stocked first-aid kit at home within easy reach and another first-aid kit in your car, luggage, or backpack for when you travel with your dog. I'll tell you in a moment how to stock both kits.

Number Three: Know what to do. How you care for your dog following an accident can save him further injury—and it may well save his life.

Now, let's get down to specifics. As an emergency-care vet I've seen every conceivable sort of accident and trauma come into our clinic. I've treated dogs who have been brought in from auto accidents, house fires, dog fights, cat fights, heatstroke, accidental poisonings, and machinery mishaps. I even treated a dog who had been hit by the propeller of a prop plane! In this concise manual on first aid, I will tell you how to treat the common everyday injuries that you can handle at home, such as insect bites and scrapes.

First-Aid Kits

The essentials are simple enough, for both a home first-aid kit and a smaller first-aid kit for travel: a bottle of hydrogen peroxide, cotton balls, gauze squares, scissors, adhesive tape, an ACE bandage, Q-tips, Bactine, Neosporin, a syringe, a bar of soap, latex gloves, a thermometer, and a pair of tweezers. Here, step by step, is how to create a well-stocked first-aid kit for your home:

1. Buy a water-resistant plastic toolbox or fishing-tackle box, so that you can have everything handy and in one place in case of an emergency.

2. Assemble all of your dog's vital information and put it on one sheet of paper: name, address, phone number, breed, date of birth, any known medical conditions or allergies, medications that he takes (including doses), plus the name, phone number, and address of his regular veterinarian and the emergency clinic that you use. Put on the same piece of paper the emergency phone number for the ASPCA Animal Poison Control Center: 1-888-426-4435. It operates 24/7.

3. Make photocopies of your dog's rabies vaccination certificate, his other shot records and, if your dog has a microchip, a copy of his electronic number. All of these may come in handy in an emergency. Put all of these essential papers in a plastic, sealable bag and store them in the first-aid box.

4. Now, equip the box with the items I listed in the first paragraph of this section, along with a few others: a styptic pencil, a small flashlight, a small bottle of liquid soap, several individually wrapped alcohol wipes, and several small, sealable plastic bags. (Remember my advice about trying to save ticks *intact* in a small plastic bag? See Chapter Eleven.)

5. For travel, create a smaller, easily portable first-aid kit for your car, luggage, or backpack. Use a smaller, watertight plastic box and fill it with the essentials I listed above. Always carry plenty of bottled water for your dog, and I recommend that you also keep a blanket in the trunk of your car. As I will explain in the following pages, a blanket can be very useful in the event of a serious accident.

Now, before I begin listing common accidents and how to respond to them, let me offer a small apology to my sharp-eyed readers. In this section I repeat several of the remedies I set out in earlier chapters, such as how to treat heatstroke and diarrhea, and how to make your dog vomit in the event of poisoning. No, these repetitions are not proof that I am already getting senile. I just want to collect all relevant information here in Dr. Dondi's Concise First-Aid Manual, to make it easier for readers to find in an emergency. Also, to make the manual easier to follow, I start with the most common injuries, the ones you can easily treat at home, and then move to the really serious accidents, the ones that will definitely require an immediate trip to the vet or an emergency clinic.

Bleeding nails

If you clip your dog's nails too short and cut into the quick, the nail might bleed for a considerable period of time. Your dog will let you know that you have done this by giving out a yelp before she proceeds to dance around the living room carpet with her bloody paw. To halt the bleeding, use your styptic pencil to cauterize the nail. You can also pack cornstarch into the end of the nail to stop the bleeding. Another trick is to rub the end of the nail back and forth over a bar of soap, but in my experience, the styptic pencil works the best. It will sting a little for a second but it definitely stops the bleeding faster and more reliably. The carpets I'll leave to you.

Ear cleaning

Take a gauze pad, wet it, then wring it out. You don't want to leave any water behind in the ear canal. Next, gently swab the inside of the ear. If you find discharge or heavy wax, you might want to add a tiny drop of liquid soap to the gauze pad. Do

NOT use a Q-tip! You might puncture the dog's eardrum. I have heard of people using vinegar and water to clean their dog's ears. I've tried it, and it made my dog smell like a salad.

Allergies

For mild skin allergies, there are a number of over-the-counter remedies that you might try. If your dog seems really itchy, and you determine that he does not have fleas or ticks, you can rinse him with Aveeno colloidal oatmeal bath to help relieve itching. Put the dog in the tub, pour the soothing liquid over him, and let him shake it off. Don't rinse it off. You can do this several times a week if it helps. If your dog has severe itchiness or discomfort, or if his skin looks red or bumpy, take him to the vet.

Lacerations

Active dogs will get the occasional nick or laceration. To stop any bleeding, apply constant pressure with a cotton ball, gauze pad, or cloth for five minutes. When it stops, apply Neosporin to guard against infection. If the pressure fails to stop the bleeding, get the dog to the vet right away. With any deep cut, or a cut that will not stop bleeding, I advise seeing a vet within twenty-four hours because of the risk of infection.

Ticks and other insect bites

Find the swollen area and try to ascertain the precise cause. If it's a bee or wasp bite, use your tweezers to remove the stinger. Then apply a disinfectant like Bactine. If your dog's face begins to swell or if he develops hives after an insect sting, have him seen by a veterinarian ASAP. Allergic reactions can lead to serious complications if not treated properly. If it's a tick, follow the procedure I set forth in Chapter Eleven:

- First, put on a pair of latex or other gloves to avoid potential contact with potentially disease-inducing microorganisms.
- Second, use bifocals or reading glasses, if necessary, to help facilitate a precise removal.
- Third, take the tweezers and try to grasp the head of the tick at the precise point where it attaches to the skin.
- Fourth, gently pull until the tick releases its hold. Don't yank it: that will probably leave the head of the tick embedded in the skin. If your efforts happen to leave the head of the tick in your dog's skin, it will probably cause a red lump as the body reacts to it and breaks it down. Apply Neosporin or other topical antibiotic ointment until the lump goes away. Your dog's body will take care of the rest. If by chance, the area should begin to look angry, have it inspected by your veterinarian.
- Fifth, apply a disinfectant such as Bactine to the bite wound and surrounding area.
- Sixth, try to save the tick *intact*. To do that, kill it by placing it in alcohol. Then save the corpse in a plastic bag.
- Seventh, label the bag with the precise date and, if you can figure it out, the locale from where the tick came.
- Eighth, if you or your dog gets sick soon thereafter, take that bag to the doctor or vet: it might provide valuable clues as to the cause of your or your dog's illness and the best possible cure. Remember: most tick-borne diseases can be treated, but the earlier the detection the better.

Caution: Never use your bare fingers to pull off a tick— and never crush the tick with your bare fingers. After tick

removal, wash your hands and any affected areas thoroughly with soap and water.

Vomiting

If your dog vomits a time or two, but is acting normally, it may just be a minor tummy upset. If you feel comfortable watching him at home, withhold food and water for the next six to eight hours. If no more vomiting occurs, you can begin to reintroduce small amounts of clear liquids for the next four to six hours. If your dog keeps this down, begin feeding small amounts of food every few hours for the next twelve to twenty-four hours. Then go back to your regular schedule. If the vomiting persists or if your dog begins to act lethargic, see the vet.

Diarrhea

During his lifetime, your dog will have occasional bouts of diarrhea. He may eat something that didn't agree with him, have a bout of nerves, or change foods too abruptly. If your dog is acting normally, you can try to treat the problem yourself. Here's how:

- First, withhold solid food for twelve hours, but provide clear liquids. Water, chicken broth, and Pedialyte are fine if the dog will drink it.
- Second, after twelve hours of providing clear liquids, return the dog to solid food with a bland diet. Here are some suggestions:
- Try boiled white chicken meat (no bones!) and cooked rice, or boiled hamburger, with the fat strained off, and cooked rice. If you have a small dog, chicken baby food and rice

works nicely. Cooked pasta can be substituted for the rice. Continue the bland diet for three to four days, then gradually switch back to your regular dog food by slowly mixing it in over a three- to four-day period. If the diarrhea persists longer than two days, or if your dog begins to vomit or becomes lethargic, see the vet.

Burns

Whatever the cause of the burn—fire, spattered cooking oil, strong acids, cleaning solutions, even sunburn—do *not* try to treat it yourself. Go to the vet. Almost all burns require professional treatment.

Lameness

Sometimes a dog will be out for a walk or a run and suddenly pull up lame. This may be serious. If the dog yelps in pain and does not stop, get her to the vet as soon as possible. If the lameness is mild, and your dog is able to eat, drink, and rest comfortably, you can treat it as you would a sports injury. Restrict your dog's activity to short leash walks only for the next three to five days. If the lameness persists, or if your dog stops eating or begins to act sick, see the vet.

Broken bones

Some broken bones are obvious, because the limb will actually dangle and appear broken. Others are not so obvious. I do not recommend you splint the injured limb. In either case, the break will be very painful for your dog, so treat him very, very gently and get him to the vet as quickly as possible.

Head injury

If your dog runs hard into a wall or falls hard or gets hit on her head, even if she's not bleeding, and you're concerned about the incident, I'd suggest you take her to the vet. You don't want to wait to see if she starts acting strangely . . . if it's a concussion, every minute counts.

Eye injury

No matter what happens—a scratch, an allergic reaction, or something lodged in the eye—I don't recommend that you do anything but get to the vet if your dog has an eye problem. Eyes are very sensitive, and any tampering could make things worse.

Breathing problems and heatstroke

Too much exercise on a hot or even warm day can cause heatstroke in your dog. (See Chapter Seven.) So can leaving your dog in a warm or hot car. (Never do it!) Remember, too, that bulldogs, Boston terriers, and pugs are especially susceptible to overheating, breathing problems, and heatstroke. So are black Labradors, rottweillers, and other dark-coated dogs, especially if they are overweight. Now, how do you spot trouble and how do you respond? First of all, watch for these *symptoms of heatstroke:*

- While walking or playing in hot weather, your dog starts panting heavily or simply gives up on the walk or play activity and lies down. Don't force him to continue! He could be suffering from heatstroke. If he can't stop panting, becomes extremely lethargic or wobbly, or cannot get comfortable, you have need to worry. So what should you do if you see these signs?

• *In all of the above cases, get your dog to a vet or emergency clinic as fast as you can.*

• Before you go, or even en route to the clinic, pour cool or lukewarm water over the dog to cool him down. (Never pour ice water; it will be too much of a shock to his system.) Also, give him plenty of drinking water before and during the trip to the clinic.

• Let the vet take it from there: your dog needs urgent treatment.

Hypothermia

Many hunters and fishermen love to take their dogs with them on their trips, even in very cold weather. And some hunting dogs wind up spending loads of time swimming and fetching in cold water. Luckily, most hunting breeds have thick fur, and can stand the cold. Sometimes, though, these dogs do come down with hypothermia, and so can little dogs with thin coats. In the short term, they will shiver intensely and later become listless. What to do?

First, get the dog into a warm car or house and cover it with a blanket. Dry the dog off, if necessary, and rub the dog's body to improve circulation. If you have your first-aid kit with you, use the thermometer to begin monitoring the dog's temperature. If your dog's temperature is below 99 degrees, she should see a vet. Make warm (not hot) chicken soup. I'm not kidding! It can help to warm your dog up from the inside. I have a friend whose English springer spaniel adores his homemade chicken soup, especially when he comes in from a long winter hike!

Choking

I've seen it all: dogs choking on squash balls, golf balls, rawhide bones, dog toys, children's toys, and acorns. Obviously, this can be dangerous. If your dog has something stuck in his throat and can still breathe well, try to remove it with your fingers. Be careful to sweep with your fingers—do not push, because you could push the object farther into the throat. If you fail, get the dog to the vet. If, on the other hand, your dog is choking and cannot breathe, and you cannot dislodge the object in his throat, you should quickly perform the canine Heimlich maneuver, which is suitable for all types of dogs. Here's how:

From behind, wrap your arms around the dog. Make a fist with one hand and place the thumb in that fist up under the dog's sternum (where the chest joins the abdomen). Then, close your arms tight around the dog and, with a sharp, strong jerk, pull your hands up toward the dog's shoulders, to expel the oxygen from his lungs and, hopefully, to expel whatever is lodged in the dog's throat. Do this repeatedly if necessary. With a small dog, hold the dog against your own chest, facing out, and perform the same maneuver. If this does not work, you can try turning a small dog upside down and repeating the chest pulls.

Drowning

Most dogs instinctively know how to swim, or they'll learn real fast in an emergency. If a dog does go under, though, get the dog onshore as quickly as possible. If the dog is conscious, use cupped hands to pound on the sides of his chest until he begins to cough. If he is unconscious you will have to proceed to the next step.

CPR

Yes, there are special CPR techniques to use on dogs. In fact, I unfortunately do CPR all the time at our clinic. The techniques I use include special equipment and are a lot different from what someone can do at home. However, if your dog has stopped breathing or has no pulse, the basic technique you can try is this:

* Lay the dog down on his or her side.
* With your finger, clear the mouth of any obstructions by sweeping the finger around.
* Use your hands to close the muzzle and lips (so air does not escape).
* Now, place your mouth over the nose and mouth of the dog and blow air in regularly.
* Do this once every four or five seconds, about fifteen times a minute.
* *Begin chest compressions.* With small dogs, lay the dog on its side, place the heel of one hand on top of the chest wall and the other under the same area to provide support. Then, with the "up" hand begin doing firm downward compressions. Continue to do this rhythmically, about sixty times a minute, meaning one per second.
* With tiny dogs, use one hand to cup the chest behind the forearms and compress firmly between your thumb and fingers. If your dog dies of natural causes or is not breathing and has no pulse, you will likely do no harm in doing CPR. Unfortunately, the chances that you will bring your dog back are sadly minimal.

Poisoning

This is a very dangerous problem. As I explained in Chapter Eight, there is a wide range of substances that are toxic and potentially lethal for dogs. These include rat poison, antifreeze, fertilizers and pesticides, snail and slug bait, cleaning materials, cans of paint or varnish, and many human medications. (For the complete list, see Chapter Eight.) Also, there are many foods that are potentially toxic to your dog. These include chocolate, cocoa, coffee, coffee beans, tea, onions, grapes, raisins, macadamia nuts, any alcoholic beverage, and decomposing foods. **If you suspect that your dog has consumed any of these toxic substances, get your dog to the vet or emergency clinic as fast as you can. On the spot or en route to the vet, try to make your dog vomit.** Here's how:

Take your syringe (or, in a pinch, a turkey baster) and fill it with hydrogen peroxide. For a small dog, inject three to five ccs (about a teaspoon) into his mouth every five or ten minutes, until he begins to vomit. For a big dog, inject fifteen ccs (about two tablespoons) at similar intervals. Do not administer more than three doses of hydrogen peroxide. Tell the vet how much you gave the dog when you get to the hospital.

I almost had to use this procedure recently with Chili. My dad was visiting, and as we sat down to breakfast he went to take his blood-pressure medicine and dropped the pill on the floor. Before we could get it, Chili had the pill in her mouth. Now you can only imagine what an adult dose of blood-pressure medicine can do to a three-pound Chihuahua. Luckily, we were able to retrieve the pill before she swallowed it, but if she had, you can bet that I would have been reaching for the hydrogen peroxide. Please take this lesson to heart: keep that hydrogen peroxide and syringe close at hand in your first-aid kit.

Bloat

If your dog's abdomen appears bloated and he is uncomfortable and retching unproductively, it could mean that he is "bloated." This a common term referring to gastric dilatation-volvulus, a condition in which the stomach twists on its axis and fills with air. This is a surgical emergency that requires immediate medical attention, so get your dog to the veterinarian ASAP! It can mean life or death.

Heart failure

How do you diagnose canine heart failure? We veterinarians diagnose it by taking X-rays. At home, heart failure usually (but not always) occurs in dogs with a history of heart murmur, and it comes in a slow progression. In dogs you know to be at risk, watch for coughing, exercise intolerance, decreased appetite, and labored breathing. More dangerous signs to watch for are gray gums and tongue, violent heaving, a rapid cough, and unusual posturing (a dog will sit awkwardly with its head and neck extended). If you see these symptoms, there is nothing you can do at home. Get the dog to the vet ASAP. Minimize stress, and keep the dog in a cool environment on the way.

Dog fights

Let's say that you and your dog are out at the dog park and your dog suddenly gets into a fight with another dog or is attacked. What do you do? I wish I had a magic answer for you, but I don't: there isn't a good way to break up a dog fight, and whatever you do it's very dangerous. People frequently get bitten trying to break up dog fights. My best advice is this:

Don't ever go near the other dog; that is asking for even more trouble. If you can do so safely, grab hold of your own dog by the collar and pull him away. But you have to be careful: your dog may be enraged or confused and bite you himself. A better strategy is to combine voice commands and distraction. A few weeks ago I was at the dog park with Georgia and she was attacked. Luckily, she's a good dog and she was trying to get herself out of the situation, but the other dog kept coming at her. So I kept commanding her to sit, and at the same time the other owner managed to distract his dog with a ball. He threw the ball and he and his dog ran after it, and that resulted in the dog forgetting all about my Georgia. Phew!

Now, if you're bitten trying to break up a fight, make sure that you get the owner's name and phone number, for health and insurance reasons. You'll also want to make sure that the dog has been vaccinated for rabies. Then go to a facility where you can wash the wound with soap (antibacterial if possible). Then contact your doctor for further advice. If your *dog* gets bitten, again get all the necessary information you need from the owner, and take care of the wound. Because of the risk of infection with even the smallest of bite wounds, I recommend that your dog see a veterinarian as soon as possible, but definitely within twenty-four hours of being bitten. Apply direct pressure to the wound to stop the bleeding. If you apply a bandage and blood seeps through, simply add another bandage on top, because blood clots in the bandage. Leave it to the vet to remove bandages. If your dog has been bitten by a wild animal, you should go to an emergency clinic immediately.

Snake bites

As a first preventive step, I urge you to ask your vet or the local humane society what kinds of snakes are indigenous to your area. Via the Internet or the library, you can learn to recognize those snakes on sight, and learn about the kinds of places or situations in which you're likely to encounter them. Then stay away from those places! That's the best way to keep your dog safe. If you think that your dog will instinctively know to avoid snakes, forget it; your dog is much more likely to go in for a closer inspection. Now, what do you do if your dog is bitten by a poisonous snake?

- Do *not* apply a tourniquet. Do *not* try to suck out the venom.
- Restrain and calm the dog as best you can and get to the closest emergency clinic (veterinary, of course).

Approaching a major accident scene

This scene is always disturbing: a dog has been hit by a car and lies helpless in the road. Your immediate reaction might be to rush in and help. But be careful: this is a *very* dangerous situation. And here is what you need to know *before* you do anything:

If it is not your dog. Any dog who has been hit by a car or burned in a house fire will most probably be in shock and terrible pain. It is therefore very dangerous for anyone other than a trained professional to approach a wounded dog. *Don't!* And don't let anyone else approach it, either. Instead, call 911 and/or animal control and await professional help.

If it is your dog. My advice here is basically the same: don't approach the wounded animal yourself; wait for professional help. Even if it's your dog, he may not react normally if he is in pain, and he could bite you. I've seen it happen over and over.

Still, if it's your dog and no immediate help is available, take the blanket from the trunk of your car and use it to protect yourself as your approach your dog. If you don't have a blanket, you can use a sweatshirt or a heavy coat. If you choose to rush your dog to the vet on your own, wrap the blanket around the animal and immobilize him, always keeping the thick part of the blanket between you and the dog. Then lift him into the backseat of your car. Better still, if you can find a board or a big piece of cardboard, use it as a stretcher to brace the dog and keep him flat as you put him into the car. If you call animal control, they have special tools for transporting injured animals. So that is the safest way to go—for you and your dog.

Nonemergencies

Many times what may seem like an emergency may not really be. If your dog experiences car sickness, for example, it can be very alarming. But many dogs have car sickness when traveling, and it's usually more inconvenient than harmful. There are medications to help avoid car sickness; ask your vet about your options.

A limping dog can also be alarming, but often it's just a splinter or a pebble in the paw. Try to gently extract the object yourself. If the area is inflamed or swollen, or your dog won't let you get near the splinter, take her to the vet.

If your dog gets salt or a deice chemical on his paws, or runs through any other chemicals, rinse the paws thoroughly with water.

Teething puppies will most likely swallow their lost teeth—this is perfectly normal.

Remember, a safe dog is a younger dog! Accidents will happen, but learning how to handle them is the best way to help your dog live younger.

CHAPTER THIRTEEN

The Aging Dog

AMBER HAD A crushed skull. She was a little golden retriever puppy who had been rushed to the clinic, and as soon as I saw her I thought, "What in the heck happened to this poor little pup?"

As I assessed the extent of the damage, her owner told me the harrowing story. As he explained it, the family had a sweet, elderly dog, a fourteen-year-old Labrador mix, and the family knew he was reaching the end of his days. So they decided to get a puppy and begin the transition to a new family dog. Amber came into the family circle and seemed to get along pretty well with the older dog. Then one day, while the dogs were playing together with a rawhide bone, the owner gave them a cheerful call: "Okay, let's go for a walk!" The older dog snatched up the bone and headed for the front door. Then Amber made an innocent but very serious mistake: she leapt up playfully after the big Lab and raced him for the door. Running through a narrow doorway, the two dogs were squeezed together and there it happened. Now, I don't know if the older dog was protecting his bone, or protecting his dominant status in the hierarchy, or maybe he was just in a crotchety mood, but he turned around and bit the pup, crushing her skull. The result, I can tell you, was a frightening sight.

It took a lot of work and a lot of aftercare, but we were able to save the puppy's life and finally put her on the road to a full recovery. And I'm happy to report that today Amber is doing just fine. That said, her story carries many cautionary lessons about aging dogs.

- Aging dogs present special challenges, and many need special care.
- Many of them become quite feeble, physically and emotionally.
- Even very sweet dogs can become dangerous late in life, especially to small children, other dogs, and even to themselves.
- Your best protection is prior knowledge and full understanding.
- You should read this chapter carefully and also talk with your vet about how to give your aging dog the special care he or she needs.
- Share with everyone in the family, especially small children, the need to treat aging dogs with special understanding and respect.
- Finally, you need to know what to do if your dog descends into irreversible decline and suffering.

The Telltale Signs of Aging

One of my friends has an aging dog, and the first thing he noticed was that she just didn't show the stamina she used to in their daily hikes. After a brisk forty-five minutes on the trail, she'd be pooped. In the summer heat, even that was too much for her. Then he spotted a distinct graying around her muzzle and her eyes: now his little lady was definitely showing her age. There are other signs you may see, as well: a fading or lackluster quality in the coat, a bluish tint to the eyes, hearing loss, and some stiffness in the morning. Later on, when the dog is elderly, you may see some loss of bladder and bowel control, and you may also see signs of senility and significant changes in your dog's mood and temperament.

All that said, I want to make this point loud and clear: old age itself is *not* a disease. And just because a dog is getting old and showing some infirmity, it's not a reason to give up. As I will explain, even dogs who suffer serious illnesses late in life can recover and have many more years of happy, pain-free existence—and you and your dog can have many more years of happy companionship together. So let's look at some of the specific health problems that aging dogs are prone to, and let me explain how you can best respond. My aim here is to show you everything you need to know to help your senior dog live the rest of his or her life in a safe, healthy, happy, and dignified manner.

Weight problems

One of the most common problems afflicting the aging dog is unhealthy weight gain or loss. This is only natural: as with humans, the metabolism of the aging dog slows down, and that is often accompanied by a decline in the dog's overall energy level. The result is a nasty cycle: the overweight dog is less inclined to enjoy exercise and strenuous activity, and that sluggishness leads him to put on even more weight. If your aging dog does start putting on weight, I suggest that you first put him on a restricted-calorie dog food and radically cut back on the treats. To start out, try a good over-the-counter dog food with fewer calories and higher protein content. (More on that in a moment.) If the commercial dog food fails, ask your vet for a more restrictive prescription food. If you are rigorous about enforcement (no treats!), a prescription food should take off the pounds—and it may well extend the life of your dog. If it fails, though, go back to your vet: the dog may have a thyroid problem or some other underlying health issue.

UNDERFED   **IDEAL**   **OVERFED**

Diagram provided by Nestlé Purina PetCare, © Nestlé

Now, cutting calories is not enough: you should feed your aging dog more protein, as well. Veterinary scientists have done some excellent research in this regard. They found that by increasing your dog's protein intake by 24 percent starting at age seven, you can help him maintain lean body mass and a strong immune system. A lean physique helps minimize stress and strain on your dog's skeletal and cardiovascular systems. It also helps protect your pet against the joint pain that often afflicts overweight dogs. So I and the DogAge team have come to a firm conclusion here: by simply giving your older dog a food that is richer in protein, you can improve his health and help him live a longer, more comfortable life.

Now, what about aging dogs who are too thin? Well, they too are prone to problems—specifically, bed sores and other injuries associated with decreased muscle mass. To avoid these, provide surfaces with traction for your dog to walk on. And give him or her a soft orthopedic bed to sleep on.

Joint pain

In this respect, too, dogs are very much like us: as they get older, they tend to suffer from swollen joints, arthritis, morning stiffness, and increasing problems with mobility. Some larger breeds, such as Labradors, are especially prone to degenerative joint disease. (See Chapter Nine for a detailed list of breeds and their predispositions.) The best way to avoid these problems is to keep your dog slender and give him a well-balanced diet. If your dog is experiencing joint problems, ask your vet about giving him supplements of glucosamine and chondroitin, or a dog food enriched with those supplements. If your dog is suffering more severe joint problems, ask about other medications that can be prescribed. In many cases, they can be very effective and make your dog much more comfortable. Acupuncture and herbal treatments may also be effective in treating arthritis and joint pain.

Osteoarthritis

What are the telltale signs of canine osteoarthritis? You may see that your dog is having difficulty getting in and out of the car, going up stairs, and maybe navigating slippery surfaces. These may be signs of osteoarthritis. Another common cause of osteoarthritis is canine hip dysplasia (CHD). The larger breeds are the most predisposed to hip dysplasia, but it affects some smaller breeds, too. There are several ways to treat osteoarthritis, including medication, acupuncture and herbs, and even surgery. But the best strategy is to work hard to avoid the onset of osteoarthritis in the first place, and here I have good news.

In a fourteen-year study sponsored by the Nestlé Purina Pet-Care Company and published in the *Journal of the American Veterinary Medical Association*, a team of researchers studied the root causes of osteoarthritis and their impact on the health and longevity of Labrador retrievers. The results were stark: keeping the dog at an ideal weight and size decreased the incidence, prevalence, and severity of osteoarthritis in the Labradors they studied. The lesson here rings loud and clear: weight management is the best strategy to prevent serious joint disease. Learn the lesson and act accordingly; your dog will thank you for years to come.

Eyesight

Just like humans, aging dogs tend to lose acuity in their eyesight, both in terms of sharpness of vision and in depth perception. As a result, you may see your aging dog having difficulty negotiating stairs and curbs. Or you may see him bumping into walls or furniture. It can be very sad. In response, you should be proactive on several fronts.

First, don't move the furniture around. Keep the dog in a familiar setting, so that he can navigate the house with little chance of accident. Second, if your dog is losing his sight, don't just chalk it up to old age and do nothing about it: check with your vet. There are certain illnesses that can cause eye problems, and these include high blood pressure and glaucoma. Your vet can make sure there is no underlying health issue. Third, pay close attention to your aging dog's eyes when you do the monthly owner's exam. (See Chapter Three.) If your dog's eyes start to have a cloudy look, consult your vet right away: it could be the onset of cataracts. As your vet will explain, cataract surgery is available for dogs, and it is performed by veterinary ophthalmologists. The surgery is expensive, but the results are often excellent.

Hearing

Many aging dogs slowly lose their hearing. As you may witness for yourself, your dog won't hear you when you call, or he might not even hear when you come into the room. In this case, you and your family have to be very careful: dogs with hearing problems are much more easily startled when they're sleeping, and they might snap if awakened unexpectedly. So make sure you explain the dangers to your children. Now, what can you do to respond to your dog's hearing loss?

Not much, I'm sorry to say. Some of this is just genetics. With any dog who is losing his hearing, there is just not much we can do to slow the decline, beyond keeping the ears clean and free of infection. Check with your vet and make sure there is no medical cause for the hearing loss. Also, be very careful when you are outside with the dog: in the event of trouble, he may not be able to hear your voice commands. For that reason, I recommend keeping most aging dogs securely on the leash.

Cognition problems

Many of us have grandparents or parents whose minds wander. They frequently repeat themselves or constantly misplace their car keys or eyeglasses. Well, it happens with aging dogs, too. If you see any behavior that suggests your dog is getting a bit dotty, consult your vet: there may be a metabolic or other physical reason for the behavior. If those things are ruled out, you might be left with a very sad diagnosis: senility. This condition can affect aging dogs, but I don't think it's as common as it's diagnosed. Caring for a senile pet can be a serious and very trying responsibility at times, as I have experienced with my twenty-six-year-old cat. It can also be a very difficult condition to treat because there are not a lot of medical options. Homeopathic remedies may be helpful, and there are some newer medications that have recently become available. Even sedatives can provide some relief.

Gum disease and tooth loss

Grandpa, put your dentures in! Yes, aging dogs have similar problems in this domain. Gum disease, known as gingivitis, is common in aging dogs, and so is tooth loss. As usual, the best strategy is good prevention, meaning regular brushing of the dog's teeth and professional cleaning when necessary. (See Chapter Eleven for details.) If your dog does develop serious gum disease or tooth loss, of course see your vet. But you should also be very careful about diet: hard foods can be very difficult for an aging dog to chew, and may cause gum bleeding and considerable pain for your dog—and we surely don't want that.

Incontinence

At younger ages, this is a problem that most commonly affects spayed female dogs. It can arrive between the ages of three and five years, due to a lack of estrogen in the female system. Some aging dogs, though—both male and female—also develop problems with urinary incontinence. There can be several causes—neurologic dysfunction, infection, or kidney degeneration—so consult your vet right away. He or she may ask you to collect and bring in a urine sample, preferably from the first walk of the morning. There are medications that may be helpful in controlling the problem.

Some aging dogs also lose control of their bowels. If that happens, see your vet. And get to the pet store: you can find diapers for aging or ailing dogs, and those can help you cope with the problem. Let me add one last thought here: this can be a very embarrassing problem for your dog. Of course he wants to please you and not make a mess in the house, but the problem is beyond his control. So please treat your senior citizen with dignity and respect; he's earned it!

Cancer

This is the number-one killer of dogs in America. Thanks to numerous advances in veterinary medicine, our beloved pals are leading longer, healthier lives. But the inevitable consequence of that is an increase in the occurrence of diseases that afflict aging dogs, and the most common and most insidious of those is cancer. I covered the many issues related to cancer in Chapter Four, and I also discussed the wide variety of treatments now available. Here, though, let me add a few tips on my favorite theme: prevention. If you want to do your utmost to protect your dog against cancer, please follow these guidelines:

- Don't smoke. Your pet is susceptible to secondhand smoke.
- Spay or neuter your dog. Female dogs who have been spayed are much less likely to develop breast cancer. And male dogs who have had their testicles removed are not susceptible to testicular cancer, and are less likely to contract prostate cancer.
- Feed your dog a well-balanced diet, using a high-quality dog food. Supplements of vitamins C and E may be helpful, as well. Dosage depends on your dog's weight; ask your veterinarian to prescribe the right dose.
- Keep your dog away from herbicides, pesticides, and lawns that have been treated with weed-killing fertilizers or other chemicals.

- If you have a white or light-colored dog, apply baby sun-screen to the hairless portions of his skin that receive sun exposure.

Don't Give Up Too Early!

Choo Choo had the heart of a lion. I first saw him six years ago, when he came in with cancer at the age of ten. He was a cute, fluffy little shih tzu, and his general health up to that point had been good. His owners wanted to do everything they could to save the little guy. They are not extraordinarily wealthy people, but they have no children, no college educations to plan for, and they were happy to pour all their love and loads of re-sources into treating Choo Choo. Well, that dog had surgery and chemotherapy and he came through his first bout with can-cer quite well. Several months later, though, he was back with another malignancy. We treated that one, too, and over the next four years we treated him for a total of five different cancers. Each time he came in, we all thought that Choo Choo would never make it through another round of surgery, chemotherapy, and more.

But with each cancer, his owners carefully weighed the risks and merits of trying to keep their dog alive. His quality of life remained good, he was still happy and able to get around, and Choo Choo certainly had an indomitable spirit. So his owners decided each time to help the little dog fight his battles. And each time the gamble paid off. Then, however, when Choo Choo was almost fifteen years old, they brought him in with a severely infected gall bladder. I feared it had ruptured. This time Chooch was really, really sick. On top of the gall bladder problem, he was having kidney problems, too, and we found a tumor in his lungs. The tumor was not causing his illness, but it made the overall picture very dark, indeed.

I got on the phone with Mary, his mom, and said, "Look, he's got to have surgery for his gall bladder, he has weak kidneys he has a tumor in his lung, and he'll obviously be at great risk if we give him anesthesia. On the other hand, if we don't operate, Choo Choo is going to die." His parents talked it over, and again they decided to keep fighting. "He's beaten the odds and gotten through everything else," she told me. "If he's going to die, we'd like to have him die trying."

So we took Choo Choo into surgery and this time everyone feared the worst. The odds were stacked sky-high against us. But that little Choo Choo once again proved all of us wrong. He was back and eating within three or four days, and he kept trucking on. He lived another two years past his gall bladder surgery. And those were great years. Recently I had cause to see Choo Choo again, this time on a much sadder note. His kidneys had given out, he refused to eat, and he had become too weak to get up. I had no remedies left for his condition, and his owners knew that his quality of life was not one that he would choose. There was no battle left to fight. So they made the difficult decision to say good-bye. We were all present when Choo Choo peacefully passed in his parents' arms. He will always live in my heart and serve as a lesson and inspiration for me and my elderly patients.

Now, whenever an elderly dog is brought into the clinic with cancer or some other serious disease, I always say to the owners, "If you're not ready, don't give up too soon! With proper care and a strong will, your dog just may surprise you and live happily for several more years. Just like Choo Choo!"

Quality of Life

Modern veterinary medicine can perform miracles. In my own practice, I have seen how new technology and medications are helping us provide better care to injured and sick animals, and I have seen how our understanding of aging and disease has expanded and deepened in recent years. But there comes a time in every dog's life when there is little or nothing more that we can do. When that time comes, our primary concern shifts to making the dog as comfortable as possible and trying to make sure that the animal does not unduly suffer. This can be a time of difficult and very painful decisions, and I urge my clients to weigh those decisions the way Choo Choo's parents did: in terms of the dog's quality of life. I ask the dog owners to consider these kinds of questions:

◆ You, the owner, know what your dog loves the most. A good meal. A good walk. Playing with a particular toy, or just a good long session of ear or neck scratching. Is he still able to enjoy those activities? Or is he in too much discomfort or pain to enjoy much of anything?

◆ Does your dog still have any appetite at all? Sometimes when a dog is very sick or uncomfortable, he will simply lose the will to live, and not eating is his way of communicating that to you.

◆ I've seen old dogs who have become withered and bony, lose control of their bowels and bladder, and face each morning not as a joy but as a new ordeal. Watch carefully: sometimes you can look into their eyes and they'll actually tell you that it's time.

♦ When that time comes, some owners simply cannot make the final decision. I understand: it is not just the dog's life that is coming to an end, it is an entire phase of your life as well. But I urge you to think first and foremost of the dog: what would your dog vote for in this situation? This is difficult to do. After all, we are the ones who have to stick around and miss them when they are gone.

How We Do It

Often, when it's time, my clients come to me for consolation and say, "Tell us, Dr. Dondi, will our decision cause the dog any pain? What does the procedure of euthanasia entail?" I explain that we give the dog an IV injection of an anesthetic called pentobarbital. It's just a super-concentrated form that first anesthetizes the dog and then stops the heart. My dentist used a similar substance on me when he took out my wisdom teeth. He and his nurse asked me to count back from one hundred, and I only got to ninety-seven. I had a kind of euphoric feeling, and I saw what looked like clouds as I fell asleep. Sometimes I think my patients see something similar, because they often look up and around, and sometimes they lick their nose. Some dogs close their eyes and some dogs don't. Sometimes afterwards, there are muscular contractions that resemble deep breaths. These are just a release of electrical activity and are not conscious on any level.

Most veterinarians will allow owners to be present with their pet until the end if they so choose. This is a deeply personal decision. In any case, after the dog is euthanized, owners do have a few different options regarding what to do with the body. If they have a place to bury their dog, they can take the body with them. If they want to have their dog's body privately cremated and get their ashes back, their vet can provide them with the name and telephone number of a service that does that. There are also pet cemeteries, where you can have your dog buried privately. If the vet handles the cremation, it is usually a cremation with other pets, and they are buried at the pet cemetery together.

The end of a dog's life is tough for everybody, including the owners and their vet. I know it is always tough for me. By that time, I have usually gotten to know the animal and his owners well, and the death can be very emotionally wrenching. At the same time, I know that each of us has done everything we possibly can to save the dog and make him as comfortable as possible. I will never euthanize a healthy pet, and most of the patients that I do euthanize are very, very ill. So there's a certain amount of relief that you feel for them as their pain and suffering are finally at an end.

For me, the saddest part is understanding what their owners are going through. I know all the love they feel for their dog, because I feel that same love for my own dogs, and I know all the warmth and love and devotion that every dog brings to his owners and families. We grieve for our dogs the way we grieve for a very special member of our family, and we grieve for our own loss, as well. We are losing a true friend and soul mate, and we are experiencing the end of years—years of the deepest kind of companionship and love. But here's the good news, the best news I can bring:

With the dogs who we love, the memories and the affection never die; they just grow richer and deeper, as you will see from the last stories that I have to tell.

CHAPTER FOURTEEN

Celebrating Our Dogs

IN JAPAN THERE IS a legendary story about a dog named Hachiko, a big white Akita stout in heart and soul. Each morning Hachiko would accompany his master to Tokyo's Shibuya train station, to see him off to work. And each night Hachiko would be back in front of the station, waiting to greet his friend and to share the walk home. For years and years, their routine was the same, and Hachiko and his master became a treasured sight in the heart of Tokyo.

A day came, though, when Hachiko's beloved master fell sick and died. But that did not stop Hachiko. Such was his devotion that every night for years to come, he still went to the station to look for his friend and accompany him home from work. Today there is a bronze statue of Hachiko in front of the Shibuya train station, commemorating his loyalty, fidelity, and love. And it commemorates something more: the deep, immutable bonds that connect all of us to our dogs.

That's why I find it so important to have dogs in my life and to help my dogs and the dogs I treat at the clinic live a long and healthy life. DogAge is one great way to ensure that you and your best friend share as much quality time together as possible. I encourage you to take the DogAge Test and seriously consider each aspect of Dr. Dondi's DogAge Wellness Program in this book. So many dogs leave this world prematurely, and in many cases it's certainly preventable. DogAge is one of the best ways I know to help your dog live a longer and healthier life.

At some point, though, the time is right for a dog to pass on, and it's one of the most painful experiences in life. I have had dogs all my life, and each one of them still holds a special place in my heart and memories. I still love Patch, the Dalmatian we had when I was a tiny girl, and today I'm crazy about each of my three dogs, Hannah, Georgia, and Chili Beyoncé. I have also developed deep bonds with many of the dogs I've treated over the years, and when they have died each has been most difficult for me. I have discovered, though, that it helps to find creative ways to keep honoring them long after they are gone.

When I work with grieving families, I urge them to collect any photos they have of the dog and make them into a special album, to be cherished for years to come. Many families love to take videos of their dogs, especially when they are doing silly things or getting into mischief, and after the dog is gone they enjoy editing the videos into a full life story. My clients tell me this can be a very healing process. I understand: through those loving photos and videos your dog can live forever, just as he always will in your heart and memories.

Wrigley's story shows another way to handle the grieving and healing process. Wrigley was a yellow Labrador who had spent her entire life as a proud member of the Williams family. Everyone in the family adored her. I first met Wrigley when she was twelve years old and had developed a tumor in her chest. We did preliminary tests and they gave us a measure of hope that the tumor was benign. We then performed surgery, removed the tumor, and sent it to the lab for a detailed evaluation. Unfortunately, the results were not what we had hoped for: the tumor was malignant.

At that juncture, I began working closely with Bridgett, the mother of the family, to decide whether to treat Wrigley or not. It was a bad malignancy, and with chemotherapy we figured we could extend Wrigley's life by only about three or four months. It was a difficult decision: the treatment was expensive and would not extend his life by very much. On the other hand, we felt confident that the treatment would not cause Wrigley any further illness or pain. In the end, the Williamses decided to treat Wrigley, and they wound up getting another six months of companionship with their dog. Wrigley had a very good quality of life right until the end. In the final days, though, Wrigley lost her appetite, and Bridgett knew that was her way of saying it was time to let go. Wrigley also had a special "wag" when she got excited, and she would do this when she went for a walk or when it was time to chase a ball. When Wrigley failed to respond in this manner to anything, her family knew it was time to say good-bye.

The grieving period was rough. Wrigley had been a very special part of the family—she had been there before the two daughters were born, and had helped raise them both. Their bonds were very tight. Some time later, though, I had a Lab puppy in the hospital that was up for adoption. I gave Bridgett a call to see if they were ready to take on another dog. She informed me that they just weren't ready yet; they were still busy remembering Wrigley.

A few months after that, an organization that trains dogs for the military and other professional services brought in a new patient: a yellow Lab who was nine or ten months old. His name was Moscow. He had injured his knee while training to be a service dog for the blind. His training had been promising, but Moscow's injuries had spelled the end of his service career. After Moscow underwent surgery to repair his knee, he would be up for adoption. The Williams family immediately came to mind.

Again, I called Bridgett. There was something about

Moscow that reminded me of Wrigley, and it ran deeper than the fact that they were both yellow Labs. "I have a dog here who needs a home and he really reminds me of Wrigley. Are you guys interested?" It was then that she told me about the golden retriever puppy who they had adopted several weeks before. They had named her Maggie, and though she was a bit of a handful, everyone was thrilled to have another dog in the house. Bridgett immediately said no to Moscow. Maggie was delightful but very lively, and a second dog would be too much to handle. I said fine, but I still gave her the name and phone number of the training organization, in case she changed her mind.

I hung up the phone and thought, well, that was that. But then something strange happened. Bridgett got off the phone and had a sudden, unexpected feeling, as if the spirit of Wrigley was giving her a nudge. She picked up the phone and called Moscow's training organization, just to find out a little more about the dog. Moscow sounded like a lovable animal, and Bridgett did feel a pang of interest. But it was not to be: the organization told her there was a long waiting list of people eager for their dogs. The wait, they said, could be up to two years. Okay, Bridgett said, but she put her name on the list just the same.

Two days later, she got an unexpected call. Was she still interested in adopting Moscow? If so, they would move her to the head of the line. Now that is strange, Bridgett thought; what the heck is going on? Well, I had mentioned the Williamses to Moscow's trainer, and he had put in a word on their behalf. In any case, a week later the Williams family came to meet Moscow, and Moscow met them. It was love at first sight, and the adoption was settled right on the spot. This was a match that was simply meant to be: in a single stroke, Moscow had a new home, the Williamses had a new member of the family, and Maggie had a new pal.

"Oh, Dr. Dondi, Moscow's perfect for us," Bridgett called to tell me, "and we just adore him. I think it was destiny that brought us together."

I agree with her: it was destiny at work. Time and again, I see instances where the right dog and the right owner magically find each other, and then they each transform and enhance the life of the other. Throughout the course of *DogAge*, I've told you many stories that highlight the uplifting, enduring love that develops between a person and a dog. Remember Annie, the golden retriever who ate the rat poison, and how her owner moved heaven and earth to find her a cure? Remember Max, the poodle who refused to behave? And remember how his owners put themselves into training, to make the relationship work? Remember Cinnamon, the churlish chow who had bitten two of the family children? And do you remember how hard that family worked, so that Cinnamon wouldn't be sent back to the shelter? And then, of course, there was Choo Choo, whose family stood by his side through five different cancers, never once flinching in their devotion and support.

Yes, my friends, the story of Hachiko is not an isolated tale. Behind almost every dog is a wondrous story of fidelity and devotion. I have spent my entire life working with these pets and their owners, and I often feel as though I'm working in a mystical realm: treating these animals in circumstances of life and death, and working with families whose love for their dogs breaks all earthly bounds. And with *DogAge*, I have tried to communicate to you a wealth of information and advice to help your dog live a long and happy life. If, along the way, I have inspired you as these dogs' stories inspire me, then I can close the book happily and know in my heart that my job is complete.

Index

abandonment, fear of, 190
abdomen, 54, 61, 62, 98
Academy of Veterinary
  Homeopathy, 221
accidents and injuries, 28,
  77, 232–33, 247–48
accidents (elimination),
  171
  See also housebreaking
accreditation of veterinary
  hospitals, 75
acetone, 116
ACL (anterior cruciate
  ligament) tears, 58
acupuncture
  for arthritis, 58, 220
  benefits of, 220–21
  for joint pain, 253
  in veterinary science,
  219
Addison's disease, 52–53,
  55
additives in food, 90–91
adrenal glands, 52
adult dogs, 163–64, 181
Advantage, 207–8, 210,
  211
Advantix, 214
Advil, 116
Afghan hounds, 226
age of dogs, 7–13, 29–30
  See also DogAge Test
aggression
  in breeds, 129–30
  and neutering, 217
  and professional
    trainers, 178
  in puppies, 169
  and socialization, 28,
    174–76
aging dogs, 249–62
  alternative medicine
    for, 219, 222

exercise for, 110–11
issues for, 251–58
nutrition for, 88
signs of aging, 250–51
airplanes, safety in,
  123–24, 127
alcohol, 80, 244
allergies
  and ear conditions, 46
  first aid for, 234, 236
  and flea treatments,
    208–9
  and hives, 46
  and smoking cigarettes,
    51
  and vaccines, 204
alternative medicine,
  219–22
American Animal
  Hospital Association
  (AAHA), 75, 201
American dog tick, 213
American Kennel Club,
  178
American wood tick, 213
amino acids, 90
ammonia, 116
anal glands, 231
anatomy, *38*
anemia, 44, 204
anesthesia, 75
Animal Poison Control
  Center, 234
antifreeze, 116, 119,
  120–21, 244
anti-inflammatory drugs,
  59
antioxidants, 90–91
ant traps, 119
aortic stenosis
  in boxers, 145
  in English bulldogs,
    149

  in German short-haired
    pointers, 151
  in golden retrievers,
    152
  in Great Danes, 153
apartment living, 130
appetite
  and Addison's disease,
    53
  and cancer, 54
  changes in, 32, 41
  and diabetes, 53
  and heart problems,
    49, 245
  and inflammatory
    bowel disease, 54
  and kidney failure, 62
  and kidney infections,
    61
  and Lyme disease, 212
  and parvovirus, 53
  and quality of life, 260
  See also food
arrhythmia, 49
arthritis
  in aging dogs, 253–54
  alternative medicine
    for, 219, 220, 221,
    222
  and Ehrlichiosis, 213
  and fungal infections,
    216
  and obesity, 27, 57
  treatment, 58
  and ulcers, 55
ASPCA Animal Poison
  Control Center,
  234
asthma, 51
atopy, 152, 154, 157
atrial septal defect, 145
Australian cattle dogs,
  101, 102

Index

Index

Fischer, Julia, 166–67
fish oil, 88
flavoring agents, 91
flea collars, 207, 210
fleas, 26, 36, 47, 206–11
fly strike, 34
food
  for aging dogs, 251–52
  and boarding dogs, 127
  chicken soup, 241
  and children, 139
  decomposing food, 244
  and diarrhea, 238–39
  and DogAge test, 29
  food allergies, 46
  food labels, 89–95
  and health issues, 27
  ingredients, 91–94
  people food, 82–84, 98, 170, 179
  quality of food, 84–85
  raw food, 88
  refusal of, 32
  as reward, 170, 185, 186
  selecting a dog, 139
  switching dog food, 95–96
  toxic foods, 80
  wet vs. dry dog food, 84–85
  while traveling, 123, 126
  See also appetite; nutrition
French bulldogs, 108
Frisbee ®, 28, 100, 104–5
Frontline, 207, 208, 210, 211, 214
fuel oil, 116
fungus, 216
furniture polish, 116

gasoline, 116
gastric dilatation-volvulus (GDV), 54, 153, 245
gastrointestinal (GI) system, 53–56, 95–96
generic dog food, 84
genitals, 38
German shepherds, 132, 150–51
German short-haired pointers, 101, 151

giardia, 56
gingivitis, 223, 256
Ginkgo biloba, 221
glaucoma, 46
  in aging dogs, 254
  in basset hounds, 141
  in beagles, 142
  in Boston terriers, 144
  in Chihuahuas, 146
  in cocker spaniels, 147
  in toy poodles, 157
globe proptosis, 45
glucosamine, 88, 253
golden retrievers, 129, 152, 226
grapes, 80, 244
grass, 98
Great Danes, 153
greyhounds, 101–2, 191
grieving process, 264–65
groomers, professional, 227–28
grooming, 225–31
group practices vs. sole practitioners, 69–71
growth rates, 87
growths, 37
gums
  of aging dogs, 256
  caring for, 223–25
  color of, 41, 44
  and emergency vet visits, 41, 42
  gum disease, 26
  and heart failure, 245
  in monthly physical exam, 35

habits of dogs, 32
Hachiko, 263
hair. See coat
head injuries, 240
head shaking, 35
health certificates, 126
hearing loss, 251, 254
heart problems, 49–50, 52, 245
heart rate, 39–40
heartworms, 215–16
  and breeders, 134
  prevention of, 4, 26
  reminders from vet offices, 205
  and wellness plans, 77
heat, safety issues, 122

heat cycles of female dogs, 218
heatstroke, 28, 105, 108–9, 119, 240–41
heaving, 245
"heel" command, 188–89
Heimlich maneuver, 242
hemolytic anemia, 204
hemophilia, 143, 151
hemorrhagic gastroenteritis (HGE), 56
hemorrhaging, 213
hepatitis, 147, 148, 201
herbal medicine, 219, 221–22, 253
herbicides, 257
herding dogs, 102
hide-and-seek, 109
hiding, 28
hierarchy in dog training, 162–63, 164–65, 172, 183–84
high blood pressure, 254
hiking, 111
hip problems, 133–34
  in boxers, 145
  in English bulldogs, 149
  and exercise, 105
  in German shepherds, 150
  in German short-haired pointers, 151
  in golden retrievers, 152
  in Great Danes, 153
  injuries, 105
  in Labrador retrievers, 154
  in Rottweilers, 158
  in Siberian huskies, 159
  in Weimaraners, 160
hitting dogs as punishment, 184
hives, 46
homeopathy, 219, 221, 256
home security, 132
hookworms, 56
hospital stays, 75
housebreaking, 115, 167–73
household safety, 114–17
humane societies, 137, 196, 202

Index